SURPRISED BY KINDNESS

Nelda Vaughter McGraw

Combray House

Cover by Emi MacLeod.

Further information: Combray House Books LLC, P.O. Box 783, Amherst MA 01004

ISBN 978-1-958659-12-0

Preface

With Jim, my life partner and husband of 62 years, I became aware that our three daughters remembered very little of their early childhood. We joined the Agency for International Development in 1962 and spent the next six years living in developing countries in the Middle East. Jim and I talked about writing the stories of our adventures, but it was only after his death that I put pen to paper. Jim's spirit is evident throughout the book. His commitment to his family and his work, his intelligent, ethical contribution to everything he did, is woven into our journey. I am hopeful these stories about our family adventures will fill some spaces in the lives of our three daughters. They were three and five years old when we went abroad and one was born in Cyprus. They are women now, mothers with children and grandchildren and living their own adventures forward. They are compassionate, courageous, curious, and creative women. It is my joy to see them passing along their wisdom to our grand and great grandchildren.

I was asked, recently, if given the chance what advice I would give to my 30-year-old self; at the age of 50, I would have likely given a list of do's and don'ts but at my 90 years of age, I would not change that 30-year-old, so full of adventure and curiosity about life and people and cultures, so eager to love and learn and contribute to make the world a better place. I am grateful to Jim for taking me on this journey and to Jenna, Nyna, and Melinda for being with us always.

~

This book takes place during the years 1962-1966, in places where the word servant was not only still in use but also was a signification of a respected career choice. I have therefore chosen to use the word here.

ONE
A Great Adventure

The month of May was full of color in the District of Columbia in 1962. The Japanese cherry trees planted around the Washington Monument's reflecting pool were in full bloom. Yellow forsythia blossoms decorated green lawns and snuggled close to white, red, and purple Rhododendron. A hint of the hot humid summer soon to come poked holes through the warm days.

When Jim came home from his job on the Taiwan desk at the Agency of International Development that spring evening, there was still some daylight outside. As usual, four-year-old Jenna and two-year-old Nyna vied for their dad's attention while I put supper on the table. After dinner Jim and I stuffed wiggling girls into pjs and Jim took his turn reading the bedtime story they had chosen for the evening.

After putting the children to sleep, we flopped in front of the TV and caught up with our day. I looked forward to our evening ritual of 'adult time.' That evening I perked up even more than usual when Jim said, "I have something to ask you." The solemn tone of his voice grabbed my full attention. He took a deep breath, then presented me with an unexpected and exciting proposal that would shape the remainder of our lives. "I have been offered a job overseas."

"Yes!" I couldn't get the word out fast enough.

Jim smiled at my enthusiastic response then in a less enthusiastic voice he continued, "Though," he took a breath, "I don't suppose this would be a good time for us to consider it." He paused.

For a second, I was stunned. What was he saying? He had trained in graduate school for just this moment. I thought, surely, it was not possible that he would turn down this job. In his usual rational tone of voice, he went on to explain the reasons for his hesitation. "The girls are so young," he continued, "and we have just bought our first house and..."

I was upset. I didn't want to hear more of his 'rational reasoning.'

I jumped in. "Of course you must take the job. This is the reason you joined USAID. Tell me about the offer."

As for me, I was intrigued by the possibility of an overseas tour, no matter where it was. I had stopped working as a Medical Technologist at Children's Hospital in Washington, D.C. and I missed the work. I loved being a mom and a homemaker, but I also missed using my professional training. I searched his face to see how he had responded to my outburst. I was hoping for some hint as to what he might be feeling. I knew of his propensity to think the worst, in order to shield himself from disappointment. I was practically holding my breath hoping this was not one of those times he would stop himself from following his true feelings.

In a moment Jim's face relaxed, and I could see that he was pleased at my response to his news. It was evident that he wanted very much to take this job. We grinned at each other like a couple of nuts and he leaned in and hugged me. After planting a big sloppy kiss on my lips, he began to fill in the details. His boss at USAID, Joe Toner, had accepted the director position to open a USAID mission on the Island of Cyprus. He asked Jim to join him as his second in charge.

I listened intently, then reached for my notebook and pen and began to make a 'To Do' list. Not that I was so organized, but I had learned that list making was a step in the right direction. The practice had served me well throughout the years. I learned about list making as a teenager. I would begin a task and get distracted and turn to something else, finishing nothing. My mother, in desperation, demanded I make a list and check off my chores one by one. Well, here it was now, still coming in handy.

The thought of moving to a totally different culture did not intimidate me. I had survived a move from West Texas to the East Coast. On our honeymoon, driving from Texas to Washington, D.C., I crossed the Mason Dixon Line for the first time in my life. I had expected the move from West to East would be a piece of cake. Boy, was I wrong. The move was an enormous cultural shock. Oh, there were some trying times. I had assumed that since I would be living in the same country. I'd be with people who spoke the same language and ate the same kinds of food.

That turned out not necessarily to be the case.

People I met on the East coast had accents I struggled to understand. Even years after the move, I had to call someone to translate a message from a railroad worker who was telling me a 'paula caw' (parlor car) was available. My Texas ear didn't understand the word when the r's were missing. And, I had to adjust to different foods. I was profoundly disappointed the first time I was served a hamburger. Hamburgers were not quarter pounders cuddled in lettuce, tomatoes and mayo but a thin meat patty stuffed between two pieces of bread. I was definitely not in Texas anymore.

Language and food were not the only adjustments I faced. Instead of straight, clearly labeled thoroughfares, the roads in Washington D.C. were curvy and frequently unmarked. An occasional traffic rotary would appear unexpectedly, making a drive through the city a maze of contradictions. I imagined that the move from Washington D.C. to another country could not be any more challenging. There was no more discussion that night. The decision was made.

The next day we sat with the girls and talked to them about going on an adventure. We told them we would have a new home in a different country. We talked about swimming in the ocean and seeing interesting people and visiting places we'd never seen before. That they would go to school and meet new friends. And best of all, we would have a long ride with dinner on a big airplane. They listened, eyes wide, then Jenna asked if she could take her toys. I told her yes, but only her favorites. I said I would need both of them to help pack up their rooms. That seemed to satisfy them for the moment, but I knew to expect many more questions before the trip was finished.

I had read the stats. "Cyprus is the third largest Island in the Mediterranean with an area of 3, 572 sq. miles. It is 38 miles from the Southern coast of Turkey, 56 miles from west of Syria, and 225 miles to the nearest part of Greece. It has two mountain ranges. Along the coast is the Kyrenia Mountains and to the North are the Troodos Mountains which reached its peak in Mount Olympus, 1,953 m above sea level. Because of its location, Cyprus lies on an axis of movement, a crossroads of three continents, Europe, Asia, and Africa. From June to September the weather is hot and dry. November to March it is mild and can be wet. Snow often falls on the Troodos Mountains in the wintertime." I was thankful for this information. Not a lot of detail, but it helped me begin to plan for our three-year tour.

For the next four months after Jim accepted the assignment, I had very little time to fantasize about what Cyprus would be like. I focused on doing what was necessary to prepare for life on the Island. From the moment when Jim had presented me with the possibility of joining John F. Kennedy's overseas AID project, my days were filled with preparations for the move. There was so much to be done and little time to prepare. We had to be packed and ready to leave by the end of August. The red brick house on Finch Street in Silver Springs, Maryland had to be put on the market, furniture sold or given to Goodwill, passports for the girls had to be ordered, vaccine requirements fulfilled.

The girls had been vaccinated as infants and toddlers according to US practice: chicken pox, diphtheria, measles and polio. But in addition we were required to receive additional vaccinations, cholera, hepatitis A and B, yellow fever, and typhoid. My sweet little ones endured red and feverish arms with very little complaint. We all dreaded the shots, but a trip to the soft ice cream stand helped soothe the pain. I thought making a game of choosing new clothes for the trip might help, but the ice cream was much more successful. Choosing clothing to cover all four seasons was too complicated to be much fun. Too much planning involved. After all, the children were young. They had a lot of growing to do in the next three years.

The day I bought the black metal trunks with brass fittings, the Cyprus dream became real. I prepared the trunks to be shipped with us on the plane so that we would have a smattering of familiar belongings in our new home. I thought a few recognizable objects would help us feel less strange and more comfortable in our new surroundings. Something old and something new.

One trunk was for the girls. Along with her clothes, each child got to choose a few favorite toys to pack in her trunk, some special books, and a favorite stuffed animal. One trunk for Jim and me contained our clothes, warm jackets and swimsuits for the family. I packed a third trunk with the household items: towels, a set of sheets each for the girls, one set for Jim and me and our favorite pillows. I tucked in some decorative items as well. Included were the three brass candlesticks we had purchased for our first house. Our everyday placemats and cloth napkins for the table, a salt and pepper shaker, and a set of four Merrimac dishes. They would travel well. The set of silverplate knives, forks and spoons Jim's parents had given us for a wedding present were a welcome addition to the trunk.

Larger household effects such as records and pillows and blankets were boxed into a crate for the government to ship to the Island. The ship would dock in Famagusta a couple months later. Tables, chairs, beds and couches were to be provided by the State Department.

KINDNESS

TWO
Arrival in Nicosia

The way we make choices in life varies. Some choices require a great deal of thought and research. Some are spontaneous and are a result of a gut feeling or attention to a strong intuition.

We may believe we know the consequences of our decisions when we make them, but life tricks and surprises us at times. Jim attended State Department briefings in preparation for his job in Cyprus. His presence was required in Washington, D.C.. The State Department included briefings for wives as well. I chose to forgo the spouse briefings and travel to Texas instead. My parents were apprehensive about our decision to take the children so far away. I understood their concerns and wanted them to have a chance to dote on their grandchildren as much as possible. All the doting Jenna and Nyna could store up would have to last for the entire three years of our assignment abroad. I would, however, come to learn that missing the briefings might not have been the sharpest decision I'd ever made.

We celebrated Nyna's birthday in Lubbock on August 20th in my parents' backyard. Big girl Jenna's June birthday was held in Maryland but with little fanfare. We promised to celebrate the next one with a big bash. Jim was required to remain in Washington, so his gift to Nyna was a Happy Birthday serenade over the phone.

My mother invited some of her young teacher friends with small children for cake and punch. The pecan trees were in full leaf and a brightly colored birthday cake was placed in front of the three-year-old happy Nyna. The party and the last-minute packing served as a distraction from our looming departure so that we were able to say our goodbyes without too much drama. A few days after the party, we made our teary goodbyes and boarded the plane to join Jim.

One early morning in the last week of August, we boarded a plane and waved out the windows as we left the mainland, heading to Rome,

Italy.

We had a layover in a hotel close to the airport. By the time we landed the girls were starving and couldn't wait for lunch. We made our way to the restaurant without pausing to settle into our rooms. A thin middle-aged man with an ample shock of dark hair and a kind smile approached our table. Neither Jim nor I spoke Italian and were unsure what to order, but the waiter seemed to glom onto the urgent requests coming from the hungry girls.

The waiter held up a finger and said, "Excuse." He left and moments later, bowls of steaming pasta magically appeared. There were shrieks of surprise and joy from the girls as the aroma of herbal tomato sauce tickled our noses. Oh bliss, oh happiness. The waiter had hit the jackpot. I was happy for the girls, but I was not as thrilled for myself as I rarely ate pasta. I should have known that pasta would be the dish of the day. We were in Italy after all. My lunch choice didn't matter. I was too tired to be very hungry.

I was surprised when the waiter approached our table once more. This time he brought plates of veal cooked in a delicious lemon sauce with green beans on the side. I could see Jim was as surprised as I.

I raised my eyebrows in an unspoken question as to how this new dish had come about. I was thinking maybe Jim knew more Italian than I'd thought. Maybe he had ordered the perfect dish after all. Jim answered my question with a grin and a shrug. We had obviously not understood that the pasta dish (each one enough to feed an entire family of eight) was just a 'starter.' Whatever Jim had ordered for us, we had lucked out. The waiter refilled our glasses with a fruity red wine and as soon as he left our table Jim and I broke into a quiet laughter. I tried to keep my voice low and said, "I think we are a bit naive." Jim answered. "I guess we have a lot to learn." That thought was disturbing, but delicious to us both.

After the girls had filled their little tummies with as much pasta as they could possibly eat, we said goodbye to our perceptive waiter and went to the concierge for information about activities children might enjoy.

It was still early afternoon in Rome, and we wanted to keep Jenna and Nyna awake as long as possible so that their nights and days would not become mixed up. The concierge told us about a puppet show that was held every afternoon on one of the hills surrounding Rome. Jim hired a driver, and we took the girls up to the park. There was, indeed, a Punch and Judy show that afternoon. We made ourselves comfortable on the hillside. There was green grass for us to sit upon and tall trees that provided shade enough to stave off sunburn.

I couldn't take my eyes off the beautiful view at the bottom of the hill. The city of Rome sprawled below forming a red and white mosaic with polka dots of green sprinkled here and there. The scene was more like a painting in a museum than a real live bustling city. Especially since the cacophony of honking horns and din of motorcycles did not reach up the hill. We could survey the city below us in silence. I leaned back onto the lawn soaking up the view as the mosaic blended with the songs of hillside birds.

The girls didn't understand a word the puppets were saying, so we were surprised when they laughed at the right places. I was reminded that humor is universal. Jim and I hoped the pasta and the fresh air on the hill would help relax the girls. While it was still light outside, the girls were beginning to fade and we needed them to get some sleep.

We assumed they would object to being tucked into bed while it was still sunny outside but the time change was catching up with all of us. Back at the hotel Jenna chose a book from her suitcase and looked at the pictures. Nyna was holding her toothbrush in her hand, struggling to stay upright in a chair. Jenna's eyes began to close and Jim and I told them it was siesta time in Rome. There was no fuss when we tucked them into bed, clothes and all. We pulled the shades, closed the door to their room, and joined them for a nap.

Very early the next morning we roused the sleepy-eyed girls, dressed them, brushed their hair, took them down to the dining room for pancakes, then boarded a Pan Am plane to Nicosia, Cyprus.

The plane leveled in flight, and I cracked open the shade next to my seat. I stopped breathing for a moment. What I saw outside the window was totally unexpected. The color of the Mediterranean Sea below shook me through and through, as though a bolt of lightning had struck me. It was as if there was a blue path shining up from the sunlit depths of the sea transporting us to another world. I had no idea how to describe it. Azure blue? Turquoise? The image I saw below the plane sparked a fantasy of an emerald Island filled with exotic architecture and rare flora. I swallowed a sob that was trying to escape from my chest.

I looked over at our children. Not for the first time I wondered how our decision to travel would affect their lives. Jim and I had talked it over and had convinced ourselves that taking them to live in other cultures would make them better people. We thought they would become educated in a way they could not receive from books. That the experience could deepen their understanding of people and their world. They were such beautiful, happy, curious children. My eyes misted with love. Five-year-old Jenna was sitting contentedly in the seat next to me, reading a book. Nyna was in the seat next to Jim on the aisle across from us. She wiggled and fidgeted, always moving. She loved to skip down the aisles. Everyone on the plane knew Nyna's name by the time we landed. Both children had been real troopers. I prayed our decision to join USAID would turn out to be the right one. I looked up when the buckle up lights began to flash and caught Jim's attention. It was time. We strapped the girls into their seats and gathered their belongings as the plane began to descend. After months of preparation, we were arriving in Nicosia.

We landed around noon. An embassy representative ushered us through customs with no delay. As we stepped out into the bright Mediterranean sunlight I looked right and left taking in the vista before me. Nothing but a dry sandy terrain in sight. Talk about disappointment! The flowers in the beds next to the stucco terminal building were filled with the same mundane flowers I'd left in Lubbock, Texas. My fantasy of a beautiful emerald Island filled with mysterious plants and exotic architecture went 'poof' as I took in the reality of my surroundings.

A car from the embassy awaited us and took us to the Coronado Hotel. The hotel was a small three-story building sitting alone on a sandy dry lot on the outskirts of Nicosia. The facade was made of yellow stucco, the roof was red tile. Very New Mexico-ish in style but more angular. There was little or no greenery around just a few patches of dried field grass. Hardly lush and exotic. In fact, it was fairly ugly. We checked in and Jim was immediately whisked away in the waiting car to the AID offices to meet with Joe Toner, the director. I set about getting the girls settled in their room, oblivious to the fact that I was about to learn the first of many consequences of my choice to skip the State Department training sessions.

I had just begun unpacking the girl's suitcases when I received a call from the front desk informing me that a car was waiting to take me to meet the Ambassador's wife. I couldn't believe what I was hearing. I told the person on the phone that I needed a moment and hung up. I slumped onto the bed and held my head in my hands. I didn't know what to do. My first inclination was to tell the driver to come back tomorrow. I was not about to leave my two little girls in a hotel room in a country where English was not the first language.

I was irritated when I heard a knock on the door. I assumed it was hotel staff and I was prepared to tell them I was not going down to the car. Instead, I was face to face with a pleasant looking woman with two young girls standing behind her. Jeanine, another foreign service wife, had come to welcome us. She hesitated a moment before speaking and I realized I didn't have a welcoming look on my face. I apologized and invited our visitors into the cluttered room. Bags were spread around the room, and I moved my purse off the most comfortable chair. The girls peeked out from the bedroom, curious as to what was happening.

I wasted no time explaining my dilemma. Jeanine nodded and appeared to understand. "That's very unfortunate," she said. "You have hardly gotten into your room before you are being asked to leave." I was relieved that she understood and felt my stomach calm to almost normal.

"On the other hand," she went on, "as you are no doubt aware, failing to appear at the appointment would not be a good idea. It is a dilemma for sure." There was no way she could have known that I had skipped the protocol session back in the States and missed that little detail. She recited the protocol pertaining to newcomers: "The first task of a diplomat's spouse on her arrival to the Island is to present herself to the sitting ambassador's wife."

Oh dear. I sat on the edge of a couch and took deep breaths. I didn't want to admit to my newfound friend that I was ignorant of the rules. I was in a bind for sure. Jeanine saw I had become agitated again and after a moment's thought, she offered to watch the girls while I fulfilled my obligation. I relaxed my shoulders. Words of gratitude and appreciation tumbled out of my mouth. Jeanine seemed like a sincere, trustworthy woman. I accepted her offer with relief.

I later learned that Jeanine was born in France and had met and married an American officer working at the US Embassy in Paris and recently transferred to Cyprus. She and her daughters were living in the hotel waiting to be settled into their new house. Coco, her twelve-year-old daughter was a beautiful young girl, tall for her age, with skin like coffee and cream. Her younger sister looked to be around nine or ten. I looked over at my girls. Nyna and Jenna were excited to meet new children. Jeanine's girls, on the other hand, were a little shy at first but it was not long before all four girls were gathered around the books Jenna had brought out to show them. I sighed and took a minute to compose myself. I had no time to shower. The best I could do was to freshen my travel clothes. I smoothed my black pants with the palms of my hands and checked my green silk blouse for any stray Cheerios, then rushed to the waiting car.

I don't remember much about that first trip to Nicosia. I do remember the driver delivering what I took to be a welcome speech to me. He spoke English with a thick Greek accent. I believe he was called John. He was dressed in black jacket and trousers with a white shirt and light blue pullover underneath. The uniform for all USAID drivers. I remember we were chauffeured by him many times while in Cyprus. That first day I was flustered and a bit trepidatious on the ride to the Ambassador's home. I looked out the window of the fast-moving car without truly seeing much. Jet lag, maybe, or fatigue.

I was greeted at the door of the Ambassador's home and ushered into a large living room. The greeter indicated I should take a seat. It was a relief to be out of the searing afternoon sun. The room inside was much cooler. Heavy ecru colored drapes were drawn to shut out the fierce heat. It was decorated with well polished American antiques. A large floral brocade covered the comfortable couches, which were flanked by chairs sporting a pale green, moiré silk. Walnut antique chests served as side tables, each topped with a white ceramic lamp. If this was the standard State Department issue, I was very impressed. Not my taste but quite lovely for traditional decor. A book of matches from the airport lounge in Washington D.C. lay in an ashtray on one of the side tables.

I sat on the couch, squirmed a bit right and left to center my bottom into the soft cushion and looked at the lovely art covering the walls. I stifled a yawn. I didn't want to become too comfortable. I was dangerously tired and yearning for a nap.

A slim, well-coiffed woman dressed in a pale blue suit entered the room and sat in one of the chairs next to the couch. She was so 'put together' that she scared me. I stood as she introduced herself and motioned for me to sit. She opened the conversation, asking about home, my family, and the reason we had come to Cyprus. Our discussion cen-

tered around the children and Jim's role in USAID. The usual 'get acquainted' conversation. She was very good at putting me at ease. I don't
remember that she shared anything about her life. In spite of being a bit
numb with jet lag and enthralled with being on the ground in a foreign
country, I could see that I was in the presence of a pro. The interview
didn't last long. It was business-like and informative. I was eager to get
back to the girls and when Mrs. Ambassador rose, signaling it was time
for me to leave, I smiled to myself. "One last word," she said. I hesitated.
Her tone was neither scolding nor encouraging. Simply and matter of
fact. "It will do you well to remember that you are *never* to sit on the
right side of an ambassador's wife."

I thanked her and left the room as quickly and politely as I could.
I felt a hot flush creeping across my cheeks. The realization that I'd been
sitting in the wrong place the whole visit was enough to make me want
to melt into the carpet. I was close to a full-blown panic when I realized
this might just be a prelude to future embarrassing moments to come.
How many more times might I be confronted with information I would
have learned had I not made the choice to go to Texas? Had I not ignored
the State Department briefing? Gloom and a hint of despair filled the car
on my way back to the hotel. All I could think of at that moment was that
I had ruined Jim's diplomatic career before it had even begun.

At the end of the day, I confessed my embarrassment and fears
to Jim but only after he told me about his first day at work. Jim listened
quietly to my tearful apology then pulled me into a bear hug and assured
me that I needn't worry. He promised all he cared about was for me to
be myself. I was to leave his career to him. I took a deep breath. Tears
dripped down my cheeks. I could not have been more thankful for his
understanding and reassurance than I was at that moment. As grateful as
I was, I couldn't stop myself from falling asleep as Jim continued to talk
about his day. Fatigue had won.

The next day I was assigned an embassy wife to take me house
hunting. I can't remember her name nor what she looked like. My attention was focused on what was outside the car. We drove across town into
the residential neighborhoods. The streets were lined with clusters of
white stucco homes. Blue doors and window frames appeared to be the
fashion. The streets were narrow, some paved, some dirt. An occasional
small green shrub stood close to a family home. I was pleased to have a
tour of the capital city of Cyprus. I was eager to find a place to live and

get my family settled in a home.

The streets and houses I was shown that first morning eventually became a blur and impatient as I was, I realized the house hunting process would take more than one day. We would be living in the hotel longer than I'd hoped. Not that the hotel stay was unpleasant. The children had playmates there and I enjoyed the work of the talented French chef employed by the hotel. His version of Steak Diane was on the menu almost every week we lived at the hotel. The aroma of that special dish wafting into the dining area created an unforgettable culinary memory of our first weeks in Nicosia.

The hotel stay was uneventful until the day watermelon was on the menu. The girls and I went down to lunch that day. I was sitting at a table alone. Jenna and Nyna were feeling very grown-up having been allowed to lunch at a separate table with the manager's six-year-old daughter. I ordered my meal and kept my eyes on them looking over, occasionally, to check on how things were going. I hoped they were having a good time. This was their first contact with a Cypriot child, and I was curious as to how they would handle the meeting.

Their lunch seemed to be going smoothly until suddenly, I was startled by a loud wail. Diners around the room stopped eating, their food halfway to their mouths. Everyone looked around, searching for the source of the blood curdling scream. I was up and quickly crossed the short distance to my girl's table.

"What happened?" I asked. "Are you ok?"

Both girls nodded. We turned our attention to the manager's six-year-old daughter as she ran across the room to her mother. I wondered what our girls could have possibly done to that poor child? Jenna and Nyna sat, frozen in their chairs, seemingly as shocked as I at what was happening. I looked across at the mother and the screaming girl. I strained to see if there was a sign of blood on the child or a hand pressing on her tummy. Something that would explain her distress. There was no outward sign of a problem, but the wailing didn't stop. The child was obviously upset. Something was seriously wrong. Between sobs, she was explaining something to her mother in a language I couldn't understand.

I turned my attention back to the girls. Both had concerned expressions on their faces. It wasn't clear if their concern was for the child or if they thought they were in trouble with me. I could see nothing to indicate they had a clue about what had gone wrong. I looked them both in the eyes.

"Okay. What happened?" I managed to speak in a moderate tone though I felt like screaming at them, as if that would squeeze the truth out of them. I looked first at Jenna. She just shrugged her shoulders. She was obviously as much in the dark as I.

I looked at Nyna. She glanced at her sister and after a moment said, "Don't know what happened. Jenna started to put salt on her watermelon and the little girl hit Jenna's hand and started saying 'oh, oh'. Or something like that." I was thankful, as usual, for Nyna's propensity for 'telling it like it is.'

I tried to envision what had taken place. It sounded as if the manager's daughter had become upset when Jenna sprinkled salt on her watermelon. I imagined she had tried to tell Jenna that salt does not go on watermelon, but Jenna had ignored her warning. Our family always added salt to watermelon. Jenna wouldn't have known what was going wrong. The child had become frustrated when she couldn't stop Jenna from making, what seemed to her, a terrible mistake. Language misunderstandings had worked both ways. Jenna didn't understand why the girl was objecting to the salt and the little girl was brought to tears when Jenna didn't obey her command to stop. She must have thought Jenna did not know she was about to put salt on her melon.

I left my girl's table and stepped over to where the mother was comforting her child. I asked if her daughter was ok. The mother was quick to apologize for the interruption to our lunch and assured me that there was nothing wrong.

I went back to my girl's table. "I'm sorry her outburst frightened you," I said. "The poor little girl thought she'd failed to save Jenna from making a terrible mistake. You did nothing wrong. It's just a reminder that not everyone here speaks English." I gave Jenna a quick hug, and Jenna resolved to teach her new friend how to speak English.

THREE
Making a Home

I intuitively knew that we needed to leave the hotel and find a house in order to create a life for ourselves. The dining room kerfuffle only underlined my convictions. We needed privacy. We also needed to settle the children into school and begin to make a home. Jim purchased a small green British car, a Vauxhall, and everyday after work we practiced driving on the left side of the road as we looked at the houses I'd had been shown that day. It felt weird driving on the left side of the street. More than once Jim and I started down the wrong side only to check ourselves quickly to avoid an accident.

We had been living in the hotel for about two weeks when I found it. The house was in a quiet neighborhood called the Acropolis. Duh. The name was no surprise as the house sat on the highest hill overlooking the city. "I think you will like it," I told Jim and I hurried to describe the layout.

"The driveway is extended under an overhang, and it creates a perfect parking space for our small car." I rushed to tell him the rest. "There is a very tiny backyard with a lemon tree!" I was thrilled. There is something so earthy and organic about growing fruit in our own yard. "And there is enough space for us to place a small swing set for the girls. I'm told they have them at the PX."

Jim agreed to see the house and he liked it! YAY! The deal was done.

One beautiful sunny day in early September, we rose at dawn, too excited to sleep. Eager to move into our new home. Jim took the day off to help pack. He checked the drawers and closets and hidden spaces around the hotel rooms, collecting anything we'd left behind. He recovered a small pink sock, several hair clips, a red crayon and a paperback copy of *Good Night Moon*. We'd been looking for that. The girls were happy to have it back.

We packed into the car, our laps piled with bags and stuffed animals. An embassy van followed, carrying our suitcases and trunks. We looked out the car windows and waved goodbye to the hotel. We made our way through the curving streets and up the hill to the Acropolis. Jenna and Nyna began to pepper us with questions, "Will there be any children to play with us? Will I have my own room? What color will my room be?"

I laughed at their excitement, "I know you are curious. Just wait. You are about to see for yourselves."

The government furniture had been delivered to our house the day before. As expected, the furniture was nothing like the furniture that so artfully graced the Ambassador's home. Our furniture was mundane but served the purpose. The couch, easy chairs, beds, chests, and dining room furniture were the same couches, easy chairs, beds, chests, and dining room furniture placed in the home of every embassy employee on the Island.

We received a small allowance with which to decorate. Inadequate, but I was thankful for small favors. I imagined what it would feel like to be sitting on the same fabric in all the American homes we might visit during our stay on the Island. I chuckled to myself thinking how funny it would be if someone at a party had too much to drink and, mistaking the familiar looking couch as their own, lay down to take a nap. Quite a shock for the hostess I would think.

As soon as we arrived at the new house and were out of the car, I called the girls to come to the backyard. Jenna followed and Nyna skipped ahead to explore the new space. I called their attention to the small tree in the corner of the yard and pointed to the branches. There were several slightly yellow lemons adorning the limbs. Lemon trees didn't grow in Washington, D.C.. It sounded like so much fun to have fruit from our own tree on the table. Or in a drink. Jenna reached out to touch one and I stopped her hand. These lemons were smaller and slightly greener than I was accustomed to.

"It's curious," I explained later to Jim, "Remember I read a book about Cyprus entitled *Bitter Lemons*. I wonder if our lemons are the bitter kind or the sweet kind." I was as eager as Jenna to taste the pale-yellow fruit.

Inside the house, a tile staircase curved gently up one floor to a large landing. The living room, dining room and kitchen completed the first floor. In the kitchen, sunshine flooded through a large window making the room bright and inviting. I could see myself preparing meals there. A second staircase led to bedrooms on the top floor. The master bedroom was large with windows on the side and back of the house. The girls' rooms were large as well. There was a smaller room that could be a guest room if necessary.

We entered the house and Jenna and Nyna began to explore. We could hear Jenna and Nyna 'discussing' the layout of the rooms. Jenna claimed the largest room with two windows was hers. Nyna was objecting for a minute, but not for long. Her attention quickly turned to another room. Hers was smaller but had a balcony over it. A special perk for our Leo girl.

On Monday I settled the children into the car and drove to enroll them into the British School. I walked with the headmaster, or headmistress in this case, as she escorted the girls to their proper classrooms. I watched as each of my darling little ones was greeted by their teacher. I had worked at Children's Hospital in D.C. during Jenna's first three years, but I'd never been away from Nyna so many days in one week. I'll admit I struggled to hold back tears as I watched them walking bravely down the hallway. I raised my arm to wave goodbye but neither Jenna nor Nyna paid any attention. Their attention was already focused on the children in their classrooms.

I returned to the office where the very efficient secretary provided me with a packet of necessary information about the school. Included in the packet were the annual school calendar of events and instructions for purchasing the obligatory school uniforms. I saw from the brochure that the uniforms were simple navy-blue pleated skirts and navy sweaters. I didn't know what Jenna and Nyna would think about the uniform requirement, but they were resilient little beings and eager to begin school. I was fairly confident they wouldn't complain too much.

The school was attended by English, Greek, and Turkish students. Quite a diverse population. Jenna and Nyna had no problem fitting in. There were other 'new girls' in class that September. Children of diplomats were often moved from place to place, and the school accepted the turnover with typical British decorum.

Teachers in the elementary school had been well trained in England and both girls were happy with their teachers. Their classes were excellent and challenging enough to capture Jenna's attention. Whew.

What a relief. We'd had to scramble in the past to provide her with enough mental stimulation to stave off boredom. Under the British system, Jenna was allowed to learn at her own pace. Boredom was never a problem. Nyna was thrilled to be learning to read like her big sister and surprised no one when she soon became everyone's 'best friend'.

It was a joy to attend teacher's conferences. The teachers confirmed what we already knew; both girls were quick learners, listened well, and participated in classroom discussions. Their teachers spoke of their charm and ease of adjusting to their new surroundings. The girls were excited to join all the extracurricular activities offered by their school. They were particularly thrilled about performing. Concerts or plays. Whatever was offered.

That first year Jenna was a bit miffed when the teacher chose her to be the narrator for her class play. I was asked to have a costume of blue satin made for her. Jenna liked her costume, but not the role she had been assigned. The day she came home with the news that she was assigned the role of narrator, I felt sad for her. "I don't know why I have to be the narrator," she complained, almost in tears. "I already know all of Cinderella's lines." I had no doubt she could say the lines verbatim. "I don't want to be the reader."

She pouted all through dinner. I tucked her in that night still unsure of what to say. I decided to try and impress upon her how important the role of narrator was to the play. "Without the narrator, the play wouldn't make sense," I explained. "It is the glue," I told her, "that holds the story together." Jenna listened and stared at me with her big blue eyes. I couldn't tell if she was convinced or not, but I could see that she relaxed and was beginning to fall asleep.

Nyna played a little piggy in her class skit that first year. Her costume was easy, pink tights, pink ballet attire, and a pink cap with ears. She only had two lines but delivered them perfectly. Her little pixie face captured the attention of the audience, and I could hear some parents sitting behind me at the performance commenting on her cuteness several times during the play.

With the girls happily involved with school, and Jim very excited to be in a job that required his diplomatic skills side by side with his superb organizing skills, I was on my own to find a way to make an Island life for myself. I fell into a daily routine of making breakfast and packing lunches and dropping the girls off at school. I returned home to plan menus and made certain I had the required ingredients. I made 'To Do' lists, checked the completed items off the list, and added new ones.

Only then was I free to explore the crooked, mysterious streets in the old part of Nicosia. It was with excitement and joy that I made my way into the old town and began the important search for fabric to cover the living room furniture.

This freedom to explore the town intensified my curiosity about Cypriot culture. The town was a labyrinth of cobblestone streets, ancient churches, shops and cafes. Women and men dressed in Europeans style clothes shopped the narrow streets and alleyways. On occasion I encountered a man dressed in an old style blousy black pantaloons and with a white a shirt with full sleeves. I was most curious about the people I encountered on the streets and in the shops. Most had dark black or brown hair and beautiful tanned complexions. The Turkish residents were sometimes recognizable for their darker toned skin and almond shaped eyes. I could make out some of the languages being spoken: Greek and English and some unusual sounding words that I took to be Turkish. I wondered what kind of exotic items they had on their shopping lists.

For the most part, the streets were narrow and crowded with small cars and bicycles. Old Nicosia town was not just called old, but in truth was centuries old. Small shops abutted each other and I was surprised and fascinated at the array of merchandise displayed. The embassy wives had directed me to the best places in which to search for upholstery fabrics. Most of the recommended shops were owned by English speaking merchants and carried designs recently popular in Europe. The fabrics were beautiful but not suited to my more modern taste. For weeks I searched through bolts of fabric on display until I found a less Victorian pattern.

Tucked between the tidy European style shops there were small shops filled with Greek or Turkish delectables. Those shops were the most intriguing. They had displays of carpets from the Orient, and brass and copper trays and pitchers engraved with beautiful designs. In one of my favorite shops, shelves were filled with vases and dishes designed by Cypriot artists. I was particularly attracted to an artist who displayed white glazed ceramic pitchers decorated with patterns of bright yellow lemons. Another shop featured shelves piled high with shiny brass cooking utensils. I had all the cooking utensils necessary for my cooking, but I convinced myself that I needed a small brass mortar and pestle. It made me happy to look at its shape and gleaming brass color.

The stores that lined the cobblestone streets were not very different from those we had seen lining the streets in Rome, with a few exceptions. Some had awnings over their entrances to protect goods and customers from the fierce Mediterranean sun. Most had signs announcing their wares in English, Greek, and Turkish.

Small European cars honked and rushed along the road showing little patience for the slow bicycle rickshaws weaving in and out of the traffic. I realized with a shock how embarrassed I felt when a large American car plowed its way through the crowded street, pushing everyone and everything to the side. Ugly American I thought, as if I knew the driver personally.

I began to feel comfortable with shopping along the main streets even though I was acutely aware of having a language problem. I was relieved that body language was an amazingly effective substitute for verbal language. When asked if I needed assistance, I pointed, and gestured to an item of interest or I tipped my head back and clicked my tongue, the Cypriot way of saying no.

There were British merchants with brightly lit cases of well-organized goods next door to Greek and Turkish shops with their goods arranged in less organized shelves interspersed with baskets and boxes of bright colors. Those shops tended to be more dimly lit and were crammed with local goods. There was no discernable difference between businesses at the end of the day when metal security gates were pulled tightly across all shop doors.

I became more adventurous and explored some of the less expensive shops along narrow side alleys. There were places along these alleyways that had bins of open spices on display. Others carried mundane items such as spades, rakes and sewing materials. It seemed there was nothing ever made that could not be found in that maze of alleyways. Most but not all the shops were welcoming. Time to time my cautious peek into a darkened shop was met with a silent stare from a person sitting in the back of the room. I didn't hesitate but retraced my steps to stand in the sunshine and moved on.

It was on one of those days that I was overtaken by curiosity. I was poking around the fascinating shops when I lost track of time. I hadn't been paying attention to the turns I'd made down a narrow alley when I felt a stab of anxiety. The lane I had followed became a dead end.

KINDNESS

I stopped in the middle of the street and looked around. I didn't recognize anything. Not a sign nor a shop front. Not one familiar thing.

"I'm not afraid," I mumbled to myself. "Can't let a little matter of losing my way deter me. I am on a mission, after all. I have work to do." That's what I told myself. I was feeling a bit guilty and needed to rationalize the time I'd spent searching through the fun shops. I had yet to find the fabric to decorate our couch. I knew I wouldn't find the fabric in these small shops, but my curiosity had gotten the best of me. My anxiety eased somewhat when I took a deep breath and caught a familiar scent of herbs and spices. I remembered passing a small grocery shop a few turns back. I put my nose in the air and followed the smell of rosemary back to the main road.

Island aromas became so ingrained into my mind that, to this day, the smell of roasted lamb with rosemary conjures images of those ancient streets. The fragrance of fresh rosemary, thyme and mustard followed us from open stalls in towns and villages all over Cyprus. We were grateful when the pungent earthy smells masked the stink of the occasional donkey pile. Vats of green fresh olives standing next to buckets filled with exotic varieties of olives reeked of strong flavored olive oil and savory herbs. Special stores sported barrels filled with the milky brine, home to creamy chunks of halloumi cheese and white caterpillar-like worms.

We never tired of catching a glimpse of a bicycle messenger carrying long sticks of freshly baked bread under his arms. Trips into certain parts of town were always mouthwatering experiences.

The day I got lost awakened me to the fact that if I were to continue exploring the Island alone, it was imperative that I read and speak Greek. I consulted a friend at the embassy and was directed to a retired Greek professor who would come to our house every week and teach Jim and me the alphabet and vocabulary. The professor was a distinguished looking man who appeared to be around seventy years old. Every Wednesday he arrived at precisely 4:00 pm. He was an immaculate dresser. A starched white dress shirt and a blue tie completed his black suit business attire. His gray hair was thick and wavy, and I never saw a strand of hair out of place. He had a gold watch attached to a chain and tucked into a vest pocket under his jacket.

I was grateful for the professor's patience. He taught methodically and slowly, repeating letters and words and teaching phrases we could use in everyday life. I never became as fluent as I wanted to be, but I was happy when I could converse with village women about their children or say something about a special dish they had prepared for our visit. Most often my attempts at the language seemed to be appreciated, but there were situations in which I wondered if their smiles were smiles of approval or mirth. I chose to believe the 'approval' interpretation whenever they occurred.

For sure, using a newly acquired language in the country of origin can be a rocky road. There is always the chance of making a mistake. A bad one. To my great humiliation, my biggest language faux pas occurred right in our own neighborhood.

For weeks I had practiced using words for grocery shopping so that I could go to the neighborhood kiosk alone. One beautiful, sunny morning I was feeling a bit cocky and decided I was ready to shop on my own. I went into the kitchen where our house cleaner, Ellen, was washing dishes. Ellen was a tall, robust, well-tanned Cypriot woman with black hair and brown eyes. She served as a babysitter anytime we needed. I asked her to listen as I read my list out loud. Ellen gave me her approval and I walked a block down the dusty road to the neighborhood kiosk.

The usual four or five neighborhood men were sitting outside the door of the shop smoking pipes and staying cool under the shade of the grape arbor. I had seen them many times before when I shopped with Ellen. I nodded and a couple of them nodded back.

I entered and stood for a minute while my eyes adjusted to the small, dimly lit shop. There were a couple of young boys putting cans of Cypriot fruits and vegetables, English jellies and tins of soup onto the wooden shelves that lined the walls. After stopping and staring at me for a few minutes, the boys turned back to stocking the shelves.

I looked around, checking my list for the items I needed. I easily found everything on my list, except I was missing one item. I hesitated and looked around the store. The man behind the counter asked in Greek what I was looking for. I responded in Greek that I wanted some bread. The man's eyebrows went up and his upper lip mustache twitched a bit. "Hmm" he said. Just then my eyes landed on the item I needed, and I pointed to a large basket behind the counter full of long sticks of freshly baked bread.

The shopkeeper turned his back and slowly chose a piece of the crusty bread for me. I noticed his shoulders shake slightly but didn't think much of it. He returned to the counter and wrapped the bread in brown paper. We both turned to glance at the door of the shop when the men outside at the store began laughing uproariously.

I wondered what was going on. It seemed strange. The men had always been quiet when I'd shopped there before. Something must have been extremely funny. Who knew what the men talked about every morning under the arbor. I paid the clerk and glanced over at the men as I left the shop. The joke must have been a little shady because every one of the men looked away.

I arrived back home proudly carrying my groceries with the crusty stick of Greek bread poking out of the bag. I was particularly proud of the fresh balls of halloumi I had fished out of a vat at the store. I was careful not to spill the milky liquid as I placed the plastic container of halloumi into the fridge. I'd had to gather my courage to dish the cheese from the worm-infested fluids keeping the cheese fresh.

Ellen asked me how my shopping went. I turned to put away more items in the fridge and told her everything was easy. "I had no trouble finding everything on my list," I answered. Once again, I felt proud of myself. I hesitated a second. "But, there was one strange thing." I said. "I heard the men outside the kiosk laughing loudly about some-thing. I'd never heard them do that before."

She asked for a second time what I had said in the shop. I told her, "I found my groceries without any trouble, but I did have to ask for the 'psylie.' It was in a different place than usual."

"What did you say?" Ellen put her hand over her mouth and struggled to choke back a chuckle until she could contain herself no longer. She doubled over with laughter. I thought that was rude but be-fore I could say anything she wiped tears from her eyes. "You, you asked for what?"

"For psylie," I replied.

Ellen spoke through spurts of laughter, "No wonder the men were laughing. You asked the merchant for a man's penis."

I couldn't believe what she was saying. I must have looked per-plexed for Ellen went on to explain, "The word for bread is 'pysomi,'" and she laughed again. "The men outside must have heard what you asked for." She wiped her eyes and turned to put away the dishes. I was mortified. I knew then and there that Ellen would be doing the neighbor-hood shopping for me from that day on.

Ellen was Egyptian by birth and almost six feet tall. She had unruly black curly hair and an evenly tanned skin. She was overly talkative at times, but she was kind and enjoyed the children.

She was efficient and friendly. She served as house cleaner, babysitter and party server. I was happy to have her assist when we hosted a party. One evening we were hosting a particularly large group of diplomats and Ellen was serving canapes and drinks. About an hour into the party, I pulled Jim aside and asked if he had noticed something different about Ellen's behavior. I had become suspicious that Ellen had sampled a cocktail. Or two. Jim agreed that he may have heard a subtle slur in her speech, but we were busy visiting with our guests and became distracted and I didn't pursue the issue right away. That turned out to be a bad move.

Jim was engrossed in a conversation with some colleagues when Ellen sidled up to him, pushed a tray of martinis at him, and said in a loud voice, "Hey, Jimmy, you want another drink?"

Our guests looked as shocked as Jim and I thought I heard a snicker or two. Jim looked over at me, nodded his head toward Ellen and I got the message. I moved in quickly, took Ellen by the arm and guided her into the kitchen. I closed the door and told her to go home. She began to object, pointing out that I would need her to clean up after the party ended. I assured her that I was tired, and we could clean up the party dishes the next morning. That was the end of Ellen's waitressing work at the McGraw home.

The 'Ellen incident' prompted me to abandon my usual fastidious practice of cleaning up after a party. Often tired after a long day and evening, I began leaving empty party glasses until the next morning. I was surprised to discover the change in routine was serving more than one purpose.

One morning I went downstairs earlier than usual and found Nyna and Jenna had gotten down before me. They were feasting on leftover olives and cocktail onions from the empty cocktail glasses cluttering the room. They looked at me with sheepish grins on their faces and I tried not to laugh as I sternly ordered them not to do that again. They said ok but we both knew this was not the last of their foraging for those delicious tidbits.

Ellen was an unusual character. She had migrated from Egypt to become a Cypriot citizen. She spoke multiple languages and though she had little formal education, she was an intelligent woman. She enjoyed teaching me about life in Cyprus. By and large she was an asset to our family with one exception. She chain-smoked cigarettes. At the time her frequent 'cig breaks' did not bother me too much. I was not a smoker, but Jim smoked, and it was common practice among Europeans and Middle Easterners. It was not unusual for a party room to be hazy with cigarette smoke when we attended social gatherings. I thought nothing of it. I was more conscious of people smoking in our home and very aware of Ellen's constant habit, in particular, her carelessness with her cigarettes. On one occasion she was staying with the children when Jim and I had to be out for the evening. Ellen accidentally dropped a lighted ash on Jenna's arm. My poor grown up girl still carries the scar. A painful memory of our Cypriot maid.

The evening of our first official embassy gathering was a memorable occasion. I had spent days planning an appropriate wardrobe. Embassy personnel from all nations were represented. Jim and I were excited to attend our first formal diplomatic affair. Jim and I were mixing and mingling when suddenly a man stepped in front of us and stuck out his hand. "Greetings," he said. "I'm Alexander Popoff. From Moscow."

Mr. Popoff was a short, stocky man with a round face, small blue eyes, and thinning blond hair. He spoke with a thick Slavic accent. He didn't mention a title so that it was unclear exactly what position Mr. Popoff held in the Russian embassy. He pointed his crystal vodka glass at us and grinned like a Cheshire cat. "I know you," he grinned more broadly and pointed a finger at Jim's chest. "You graduated from Columbia University in New York City, but you were born in Oklahoma."

Mr. Popoff turned and looked at me, "And your wife is from Texas."

I was surprised and looked over at Jim, hoping to catch his response to this man's pronouncements. Jim only smiled and I turned back to Mr. Popoff. He wasn't exactly leering at me but his expression made it clear he was pleased to see my reaction. "You have two children, I believe."

I took another quick glance at Jim. How could this man know so much about us? Jim saw the confused look on my face and murmured under his breath, "I'll tell you later. Spy."

I cringed when Mr. Popoff's voice grew louder as he railed on and on recounting intimate details about our families. It was astounding how much he knew about us. He had obviously done his homework and he and his vodka could not help popping off to show his expertise. I became more uncomfortable by the minute as his voice grew louder and louder. And it seemed to me that every time his voice rose in volume, his nose became redder.

I struggled to keep my emotions under control but I couldn't help showing my displeasure at being an open book to everyone present at the gathering. I couldn't help wondering if there were a multitude of Popoffs around the world with special access to our personal information. The thought of being so exposed made my skin crawl. It was scary to contemplate.

He kept going on and on revealing even more details about our lives and it looked as if he would go on for the remainder of the evening. Jim and I looked at each other and silently agreed that it was time to escape creepy Mr. Popoff. We made our excuses as diplomatically as possible and moved to introduce ourselves to a group of British folk. standing close by. I took a deep breath, relieved to be away from Popoff's intrusive presence.

Later that evening Jim explained Popoff's behavior to me. It seems it was common knowledge throughout the spy world, at that time, that Columbia University was a premier training ground for American Intelligence. From that evening on, I found myself scanning social gatherings, eager to spot the man again in case we wanted to avoid him. Fortunately, we never saw Mr. Popoff again. Our speculation was that he and his bottle of Russian vodka had been recalled.

The encounter with Mr. Popoff planted a question in my mind that had never occurred to me before. Was it possible that Jim was indeed trained to be a spy? I believed Jim's firm denial, but the possibility of his indulging in clandestine activities continued to haunt us throughout our overseas work. And provided fertile ground for speculation for years to come.

Social life in the foreign service was, for the most part, much more exciting than our social life in Washington, D.C. We seldom had the time or money to go out when we started our lives together in D.C. Like most young people Jim and I were both working, parenting children and keeping a house. Living overseas, on the other hand, meant access to a babysitter and it was easy to rationalize our many evenings away.

Social obligations were an integral part of our work with USAID.

Attendance at official events was a requirement for all officers in senior positions. It was made clear to Jim and me, in case we had any doubt, that our presence was mandatory on those occasions. Night after night we were expected to show up at a dinner or more frequently, a cocktail party. Aside from feeling guilty at times for leaving the children with babysitters so often, I looked forward to the opportunity to become acquainted with AID people and representatives from other embassies.

Jim and I particularly enjoyed the parties when Australians were included. It was easy to bond with people from Australia. It was not unusual for us to close down a party together, drinking and singing songs around a piano. One evening we were standing with a group of Australians when one of the Aussie officers threw his arm around my shoulders and announced in a loud, slightly drunk voice, "Texans are like us. We are a friendly and open group of people. Not stiff-assed like the Brits."

I laughed and agreed, then, in a moment of panic, glanced quickly at the other guests standing around the room. I held my breath for a moment, hoping our British friends had not heard the comment. I glanced behind me at the closest group and was relieved to note that no one was looking over at us with disapproval. I breathed again.

After we became settled into a routine, the constant cocktail parties could be a real drag at times. I was never good at small talk and the nightly rounds of AID cocktail parties were a challenge. Making conversation with the same folks night after night became a chore. When we first arrived, I was eager to meet people. Overexposure dulled my enthusiasm.

The routine went like this; at first introduction you asked, or were asked, "Where are you from?" That question was good for weeks of gatherings. The next level of questions moved the conversation to another level. A broader, more personal discussion. "Do you have children? Is this your first time on the Island?" All of those questions opened doors for getting to know more about one another. I came to realize that people liked to tell me their stories and I relaxed into simply listening. No need for small talk.

The next level of questions began to make me slightly uncomfortable, however. "What is your job here?" That question was a logical next step and seemed innocent enough, but our encounter with Popoff had left its mark. The possibility that CIA- type officers from my country and other countries were secreted among us served to make me aware that I could inadvertently put someone on the spot when I asked that question. Perhaps not the first chink in my 'puppy-dog happy to meet you, open' Texas persona, but definitely one of the most profound.

Months later, I realized that I was not the only person in the room struggling to keep conversation going. It depended on the party. If there were seasoned senior officers present, I could never hear enough of their stories. The experiences of those who had been stationed in foreign countries around the world fascinated me. Listening to firsthand accounts of the different cultures was an education in world history, not from the perspective of national events, but stories of real people. I had so much to learn about the world. I soaked up all the Foreign Officers' tales of diplomatic adventures and unusual cultures available to me.

It wasn't long before I spoke to Jim about my dilemma. I was bored with the endless cocktail and dinner parties with the same people, night after night. We discussed the options available to us. I searched my mind for something with a little pizzazz. Jim and I settled on a Come-as-You-Are Pajama Party. I made a list of friends we thought might be up for an out-of-the-ordinary kind of party. Our list included invitations to UK friends, the Aussies, and selected AID folk. We were happy to receive so many enthusiastic responses. Almost everyone replied yes to the invitation. Some told us later they had accepted the invitation because they were curious to find out what a Pajama Party would be. Others expressed sentiment similar to mine. The parties in such a small post had become tedious. They looked forward to something different.

I prepared a buffet of fresh fruit, salted nuts, and every kind of melon I could find. I made deviled eggs and a pan of cheese enchiladas. I'd been able to find a tin of tortillas and canned enchilada sauce at the PX one week. I couldn't think of a better time to break open those rare treats. A tray of goat cheeses with bowls of olives and fresh bread completed the brunch. Jim made pitchers of mimosas and Bloody Mary's.

I donned my silk bathrobe over a white gown and my pink house shoes. I combed my hair and admit to having cheated and applied a bit of lipstick to my lips. Otherwise, I was dressed for bed. Jim looked in the drawer under his casual shirts and pulled out a pair of pajamas. I didn't know he even had pajamas. He had bought them to wear only in case of emergencies, he said. We dressed Jenna and Nyna in their cutest gowns and put Jenna's hair into a ponytail. I smoothed Nyna's cowlick into place. The girls thought it great fun when we let them join us to greet our guests at the door dressed in our pajamas.

We were not certain if our guests would show up in night dress. We were pleased when some folks were brave enough to actually come dressed in gowns or pajamas and robes. Most of the British friends couldn't quite bring themselves to stoop to such indignities. House shoes were all they could manage. We applauded their effort. There were older AID folk who made no effort at donning bedtime attire and simply came to enjoy the food and camaraderie. The party was deemed a success.

The next morning, I went about my chores, pausing every once in a while, to reflect on the previous day. Our guests had left in good spirits, and I felt I had made some progress toward relieving party boredom. Around noon Jim phoned from his office. He just couldn't wait to tell me about his morning at the office. It seems he had hardly begun to work when a group of six Cypriot colleagues appeared at his door. The men crowded into his room for the express purpose of seeking information about the unusual American holiday that had taken place over the weekend. Jim explained there was no holiday involved, simply an early luncheon. He tried his best to bring the men back to the topic of work, but every time he made that attempt it seemed the men could only focus on one subject. What was the meaning of a 'Pajama Party'. More than once, Jim made an attempt to explain our strange behavior. More than once he tried to direct the focus of the men's attention to the work at hand. But to no avail.

At last, the men cleared his office and Jim began to wonder. How had the Cypriots even become aware of the party? It was, after all, held at our home, nowhere near the American Embassy. The answer remained a mystery for some time.

Then it dawned on us. The intense interest in our Pajama Party served to alert us to a part of Cypriot culture that was not mentioned in the post report. Like small towns everywhere, a gossip network served an important cultural element. Curiosity and gossip were a kind of entertainment. Cyprus was no exception. Intense interest in any American activities provided days or maybe even weeks of conversation for the Cypriot population. Gossip. We found that whatever we did or wherever we went, practically the whole Island would be talking about us the next day.

FOUR
Island Life

Having been alerted to the 'Gossip Line' on the Island, I vowed to conform to a more conventional social life. Our family settled into a normal routine. The girls went to school and Jim went to the office. I cooked meals, shopped at the Naval Station PX and organized dinner parties. On Sunday we attended St. Paul's, a small stone Anglican Church. The Church looked like every other Anglican Church we had ever seen, with the exception of Lichgate. The Priest was a middle-aged man, a large ruddy-faced Scotsman who was a former British soccer player in the UK. Archdeacon Farrar had a great sense of humor and he and his wife became our good friends.

I was unhappy to find there was no Sunday School for the children. After consultation with the priest, I was soon creating and teaching a Sunday school class. Jenna and Nyna attended every Sunday morning with four or five British children. I read Bible stories to them and provided crayons and paints to fill out the time. I can't say the girls were enamored with the Sunday School, but they preferred it to sitting through the adult service. Though Nyna rather liked the standing up and sitting down and kneeling. She learned that bit quite easily. I've often wondered if anyone kept the school going after we so abruptly left the Island.

My job was to be of help to the USAID director's wife. Becky Toner was a brilliant woman. She was mother to two college-aged boys back in the States. She had a career in journalism before coming to Cyprus. She was skilled at helping to organize the new AID mission. I respected her intelligence and looked up to her to coach me in the intricacies of a spouse's role in the organization. Our relationship was grounded in the purpose of providing aid to the Island population where needed. I was eager to participate in any way I could with the developing AID community, and I made myself available to help Becky whenever possible. The AID mission was growing rapidly and I assisted in helping AID families to settle.

Becky was not a demanding boss so I was surprised when she made a request that I never would have expected. Becky called one afternoon asking me to accompany her to visit the offices of the wealthiest and most powerful businessmen in Nicosia. She was chairperson of the Cypriot delegation to the UN Women's Charity Fund. I'd never solicited charity money, or any other kind for that matter. I wasn't convinced that I could be of any help but Becky had a plan. She would do the talking, and I would do the smiling. Becky thought that I'd help by sitting beside her and smiling a lot. "It sounds like I'm window dressing," I grumbled to Jim. I pictured myself sitting across from a businessman silent and with a smile on my face. It was embarrassing to contemplate and I didn't see what good it would do. It turned out that Becky was right on. For reasons I can't fathom to this day, the combination of Becky's erudite speech and my smile raised quite a lot of money for the charity that year. She did the talking, making a coherent and well rehearsed plea for the donations and I smiled.

Becky and I had little in common, except for our Democratic politics. I was fascinated with her ability to express herself. I envied her easy use of words. I loved how discerning she was. Most endearing, she won me over from the beginning when she commented on how classy and well-groomed Jim was. She never failed to mention how he was always clean shaven, his hair in place, and how he wore a crisp white shirt each day. She said Jim was the best-groomed man she had ever met. I had nothing to do with Jim's tidy good looks, but I burst with pride every time Becky mentioned it.

Many cities on the Island were well along the road to economic independence but some villages, primarily in the Turkish areas, were less developed. USAID brought new technology to outlying villages that relied on outdated water wells for their livelihood. Young Peace Corp men and women lived in the most undeveloped villages to bring their agriculture and community needs up to date.

USAID brought scientists to the Island who worked with the Cypriots to look into building desalination plants. AID personnel helped to educate and design up-to-date irrigation practices. There were times when available expertise was stalled or blocked progress. In spite of the frustrations that accompanied new projects, and given the time we had in Cyprus, the Toners and Jim were able to build a healthy, working AID mission. We were all disappointed when our mission and our relationships were abruptly terminated.

Winter in Nicosia was mild. Not too cold and not very warm. We needed sweaters and flannel pajamas but rarely winter coats. We were very aware when the weather changed into Spring. The hills around the Island were covered with wild anemones. Fresh light green leaves peeked through the tired yellow rimmed leaves on the lemon tree in the backyard. Easter arrived in early May that year. That Easter morning the 'Easter bunny' left each of the girls a surprise. A large white fluffy bunny with a pink bow around its neck for Nyna, and a large white soft goose for Jenna. Mother goose had a long, elegant neck and blue satin bow. The goose was carrying a small woven basket under her arm.

I was in Nyna's room laying out her Easter dress when the doorbell rang. I called Jim to answer the door but he was not dressed. I hurried down the stairs, wondering who in the world would be about on an early Sunday morning. I opened the door to find a neighbor holding a loaf of bread with a red colored egg baked in the middle. "Christos Aristos," she said. She presented me with the bread and turned to leave. "Thank you," I replied and stood for a moment, touched by the greeting, the offering, and the significance of the gesture. I paused a moment to think about the lovely gesture. Especially from a woman I hardly knew. I pulled myself back to the job at hand and went back upstairs to dress Jenna and Nyna in their new Sunday clothes.

The weather was still somewhat chilly, so they didn't complain when I put light coats and hats over their new Easter dresses. We stepped out of the front door and were greeted by another neighbor, "Christos Aristos." Christ has arisen. She smiled and held out the loaf of freshly baked Easter bread. The bread was the twin of the first gift. The same color of egg had been baked in the middle of the loaf of bread. I accepted the gift. "Christos Aristos," I replied. "Efharisto." I thanked her and waved as she said goodbye.

I turned to herd the girls into the car. Both had their Easter surprises snuggled against their chests. Nyna asked if they could take the stuffed toys to Church. I responded they could bring them into the car, but not into the Church. Nyna hugged her rabbit and said, "Thanks Mom." Jenna held her white Easter goose at arms length, eyed it top to bottom and threw it on the ground. "This is not an Easter bunny," she said. I realized at that moment that I had made a bad mistake thinking that Jenna would rather have a beautiful more 'grown up' gift. We had no time for me to explain my decision as we had to leave for church. I spent the remainder of the day wondering how I could explain my choice of the goose for her. By the end of the day. I was contrite and sorry I'd disappointed Jenna. I realized I was wrong to have underestimated the Archetypal Child who lives in us all forever.

One day not long after we had settled into our routines, Becky Toner called to warn me that I was going to receive an invitation to meet 'The General's Wife.' I'd heard about the General's Wife. Rumor was that she was a bully, prone to pull rank in the American community. I wasn't looking forward to receiving that particular invitation, but I assured Becky that I would attend if invited. I'd seen the woman across the room at large gatherings, and I remembered being struck by her dark hair and deep brown eyes. I couldn't remember ever seeing her smile. I was told she scared the hell out of the junior officers' wives.

When the invitation arrived, I responded as promised. I showed up at the appointed time. This wasn't a visit to the Ambassador's house, nevertheless, I reminded myself not to sit on the General's wife's right side. Just in case.

I was greeted by Mrs. General and comfortably ensconced on a sunny screened porch. Coffee and cake were sitting on the table in front of us. Conversation centered around our homes in the US and our families. Perfume from the lemon trees wafted in and out of the porch on the soft spring breeze. A flock of small birds was flitting through the branches.

The tension in my shoulders slowly subsided as I sank into the soft cushion of the chair. I was thinking this wasn't so bad after all. And then, Mrs. General asked if I played bridge. I'd thought I'd escaped the dreaded bridge game request. I told her Jim and I had weekly bridge nights with our friends in D.C.. I didn't have time to explain to her that our games were casual, friendly and fun before Mrs. General abruptly stood and motioned to the door, "Good. I'll expect you back here next Tuesday at 2:00."

I had been dismissed.

How hard could it be? It was, after all, just a game, I told myself. Wrong again. The General's wife had a different kind of bridge in mind from the kind I had ever played. Upon arrival on bridge day, I was greeted by two military wives whom I'd never seen before. The women were cordial enough but my attempts to get to know them were met with short responses and it didn't take me long to catch on to the situation. Mrs. General's bridge games were not intended to be social gatherings. The game in this house was business.

We'd played only a few hands when Mrs. General put her cards on the table and announced that we had to cut our bridge game short. She looked straight at me and explained that something had come up. I could tell by the look on my new friends' faces that they were not terribly surprised and one of them seemed a bit relieved. Mrs. General had made it clear that my game that day was not up to the standard to which Mrs. General was accustomed. I didn't need her to tell me that I was in way over my head. I was simultaneously embarrassed and relieved at being so curtly dismissed. Most of all, I was overjoyed at the thought I'd never be invited to visit the General's wife again.

We were fortunate that most of our new acquaintances were not as impressed with rank and power as the General's wife. Jim worked with a large array of international officers assigned to Cyprus. One of his favorite new acquaintances was Sir Ernest Vasey. He was the acting UN Representative to Cyprus. Sir Ernest was a distinguished, gray-haired man in his late seventies. Lady Vasey was his beautiful, elderly wife.

Jim arrived home one day carrying a written invitation to join the Vaseys for Sunday lunch. The invitation included the children. I enjoyed meeting the couple and was happy to hear stories of their grandchildren who lived back home in Nairobi, Kenya.

That first invitation was the beginning of a valued friendship. I was apprehensive when the idea of a bridge game arose, but I soon relaxed when the game with Sir Ernest and Lady Vasey became as much about sharing our lives as enjoying a few hands of bridge. I could never get enough of hearing Sir Ernest and Lady Vasey recount stories from their long and varied foreign service experiences. I loved the music of their British accents. Sir Ernest and Lady Vasey had served in exotic-to-me posts all over the world. India, Japan, Thailand, all of these countries sounded like fairy tale countries.

Lady Vasey was a gracious woman with beautifully coiffed gray hair and a fan of smile wrinkles around her eyes. Their home was comfortable and inviting and filled with rare and expensive artifacts from their many assignments. Carved furniture pieces made from exotic woods, and beautiful objects fashioned from gold and silver graced their home. We were particularly impressed by one extremely unique object. The Vaseys had adopted a mongoose. The shy, sneaky little animal was fascinating. Mongooses are kept on the island to keep snakes from building nests around the gardens.

I don't know if this is particular to all mongoose, but this one loved to explore bags and purses. On those days when Jenna and Nyna were invited to come to visit, the two of them peeked under and behind pieces of furniture trying to catch a glimpse of the shy creature as it slinked around the room. The sneaky animal loved to hide in unexpected places. Even forewarned, I let out a 'yikes' when I reached for something in my bag and came face to face with a pair of small ferret eyes. He slithered away and Jenna and Nyna tumbled onto the carpet, rolling with laughter.

The first June that we were in Nicosia, Lady Vasey asked me to bring the girls for afternoon tea. It was the week of Jenna's birthday. We had promised Jenna a special party this year to make up for the one she'd missed the past year, but I could never have planned a splendid surprise like the one we discovered when we were ushered into the Vasey house that day. We stopped at the living room entrance. Gob-smacked. The living room was filled with a maze of pink and yellow strings that wove a canopy across the room. The easy chairs had been pulled to the side and I spotted an olive pit on the floor. The colorful canopy was tacked to the walls just high enough for Jenna and Nyna to walk under it.

Lady Vasey proceeded to give each child an end of string. Jenna and Nyna looked at me as if to ask what was happening, but I was as baffled as they. Lady Vasey smiled to see the confused looks on our faces. She didn't hesitate, and quickly set about instructing the girls about the purpose of the extraordinary sight before us. She tied the end of a yellow string to Jenna's wrist and a pink string to Nyna's. I could see by Lady Vasey's face that she was excited about what was to come next. As she tied the strings around the girl's wrists she explained that they were to roll the string into a ball until they reached the other side of the room. At the end of each string they would discover a prize.

A momentary stab of guilt ran through me as I thought about how much my parents would have enjoyed watching the girls giggle and laugh as they tried to follow the strings across the room. I thought of how many of the children's special days their Grandparents at home in the U.S. were missing. I looked at Lady Vasey's kind face and was reminded of my mother. I hadn't realized I'd been missing my folks at home. I pushed the thought out of my mind but resolved to write home the next day to tell the Grandparents about Jenna's unusual birthday party.

I was greatly touched by Lady Vasey's thoughtfulness that day. I felt that the girls were getting a taste of what it might be like to have a grandparent nearby. They quickly caught on to the game and began to wind the string around their small wrists. They giggled and ducked their way across the room eager to capture a wrapped gift box at the end. The strings became a little tangled now and then. The girls shrieked with laughter as they struggled to become untangled from the strings. But with a little help from Lady Vasey and me, they each reached a beautifully wrapped package at the opposite end of the room. The day was not at all what Jenna had imagined when we'd promised a special birthday party but it was one of the most creative and unique.

FIVE
Exploring Our New World

The drive from Nicosia to Kyrenia on the sea was our favorite outing. The two-lane curvy highway took us past olive groves and fields of yellow mustard plants. The girls watched the unusual rock formations pass by as we sang songs together in our little Vauxhall car. Jim regaled us with Broadway songs from *My Fair Lady* and *The Sound of Music*. We joined in and sang at the top of our voices.

The road took us up a small mountain and down the other side to the coast. Jenna and Nyna vied to see which one would be the first to spot the blue waters of the Mediterranean. As we topped the hill they sat up straight, noses pressed to the car window, eager for a glimpse of the harbor and village below. "I see it, I see it," they would shout. Some days when the weather was just right, Jim would stop the car on the side of the road. We would sit for a moment and take in the beauty below.

We never tired of the stunning vista. It was like a movie set. The white stucco houses, the red tiled roofs, the fishing boats filled with shouting men mending their nets. St. Hilarion Castle sat on top of the hill guarding the village. We stopped at the ancient Crusader castle on the way from time to time. Jenna and Nyna ran up the steep incline ahead of us each one anxious to be the first to reach the Queen's rock seat. From the seat one could look out the window overlooking the village. Guidebooks called this open window perch the 'Queen's Chair'.

Jim held each girl up to the narrow slots carved into the rock walls. He wanted them to see where soldiers in ancient times would shoot arrows through the narrow slits. He told them about arrows being the only weapons they had to protect the castle from being taken over by enemies.

It was a short ride down the hill from Hillarian Castle to Kyrenia. The small fishing village was built around a beautiful horseshoe shaped harbor. Jim and I sat on a rock and relaxed, lulled by the rocking of small fishing boats in the harbor. The children took turns splashing in the warm water and building castles in the sand.

When the weather was cold, we skipped the harbor and beach and drove to the other side of the Kyrenia to Bellapais Abbey. Three weathered stone walls had survived the ages and stood roofless in the open air. The wall facing the ocean showed carved remains of a large arched window. We read from the guidebooks that a magnificent stained-glass window graced the wall in the 'olden days,' as the girls called ancient history. There was also mention in the guidebook that Richard the Lionhearted had stopped at the Abbey to rest on his way to fight in the Holy Land. Parts of the building had crumbled into huge chunks of rock and the girls happily climbed among the ruins.

We took advantage of free weekends to visit historical sites across the island. The girls roamed through ancient marble pillars of Salamis with its statues of Apollo, Herakles, Aphrodite, Artemis and Hygeia. I stood for a moment in awe at the sight of my children walking the same paths as the Greek Gods of old. We walked through the sacred site and recounted myths associated with each of the Gods and Goddesses. We had hoped to explore the whole Island and see all the beauty and ancient history Cyprus had to offer.

Events didn't allow us to complete our tour. I was disappointed when we couldn't manage a trip to the beach at Famagusta nor to the Rock of Romios in Paphos where legend has it that Aphrodite was born.

As we visited various areas around the Island, we didn't sense any signs of political unrest. After the British rule ended, Cyprus was declared an independent country. The majority of Cypriot residents were of Greek heritage. If Jim was aware of any conflicts between the two major Cypriot factions, he didn't bring up the topic with me. He spoke often of meeting with the president, Greek Bishop Markarios, and Vice President Turkish Dentash. Jim met more often with VP Dentash and considered him an honorable and intelligent man. Turkish villages were more likely to be in need of AID assistance. As a result, Jim's office had more frequent contact with Turkish representatives. Jim often voiced his respect for VP Dentash and felt the VP was doing a good job representing the Turkish Cypriots.

My experience was that Turkish women were more likely to be educated in the English language than their Greek counterparts. The Island culture was mired in the old attitudes regarding the value of women versus men. A similar division existed between the haves and the have-nots. The people living in the wealthiest communities were considered to be the more intelligent and desirable folk. Every economic success USAID was able to bring to the least wealthy villages was a step toward making everyday life for those people more comfortable.

When we arrived in Nicosia, late August 1960, Cypriot folk appeared to be working in harmony with each other. In Nicosia, Turkish enclaves were centered around the old town while most of the Greek population was clustered on the hills. Traffic flowed freely between the two parts of the city. Merchants delivering goods, electricians, and gardeners, and residents of all ethnic groups could be seen doing business throughout the city. The Island appeared to have a peaceful and thriving exchange between cultures.

As time passed, we became friends with people of all ethnicities. The more we became acquainted with people, the more open and trusting our conversations became. One evening we were dressing to attend a dinner party at the home of some Greek friends. Jim asked me if I would pay attention to one guest in particular. He asked me to use my 'spidey sense,' my intuition, and let him know what I thought about the person. Certain evenings, Jim would alert me to become acquainted with a particular person. I was always intrigued when those alerts came my way, and I felt a warm glow of pride that I could be helping Jim do his job. I asked for more information, but Jim always answered that he simply had an 'uneasy feeling.'

Jim's suspicions proved to be concrete. On the surface, life was going as usual, but underneath, something was astir in the political realm. I became aware of different ideas popping up in conversations at cocktail parties. Jim picked up similar ideas being whispered about at the office. Together, we began to form a different picture of the political situation in Cyprus. There was no doubt there were underground tensions between different factions, particularly within the Greek population. Some Greek Cypriots were eager to be annexed by Greece. Others wanted to stay totally independent of Greece and remain the independent nation of Cyprus. EOKA was the name of a group of fighters that fought to end British rule and campaigned for eventual union with Greece. They were strongly opposed to communism. The other Greek factions, along with the Turkish population, were devoted to Cypriot independence and wanted to stay an independent nation. I was surprised to learn that our neighborhood was a hotbed of EOKA fighters. I had no idea, when I chose the house, that any such organization existed.

~

We had lived in the neighborhood for two months when our shipping container arrived from the port in Limosol with the remainder of our household effects. Small groups of curious mothers, nannies, and children gathered in the neighboring yards to watch our items being off-loaded from the truck. I wondered what they were thinking as they saw the boxes taken from the truck to inside the house. I wondered what was going through their minds as they watched Jenna and Nyna run around the back yard, happy to stretch their legs. Were they wondering if we were friendly? Our neighborhood was quiet and friendly as far as I could tell. I was hoping their silent, distant presence was a sign we were welcome. I couldn't concern myself with that thought at that moment, so I focused on the job before me.

It was a day of great celebration for our little family. We enjoyed the candlesticks, photos of grandparents, and small objects scattered around the hotel room. They were our constant friends. But opening the recently arrived crates containing household items was most exciting.

We greeted each familiar item as if it were valuable art. Towels and bedspreads pulled from crates immediately spruced up our sparsely decorated bedrooms. Having a variety of clothes, after having lived out of suitcases for a month, made us feel like fashion models. Toys and books were greeted with squeals from the girls as we opened the packing boxes marked for their rooms. Flattened stuffed toys were pounded and fluffed to put them back into hugging shape. Books were smoothed and laid out on the floor, treated as if they were like old friends. And in a way, they were. Old toys felt new all over again. We felt as if we were having Christmas in the fall. Unpacking the crate and taking our belongings to their proper places in the house took no time at all. In the twinkle of an eye, we created our second home.

We made our house into a home and Jim and I turned our focus to activities that we felt would interest the girls. I suppose there was a bit of guilt involved, or maybe more than a bit, but both Jim and I were eager for the girls to have the kind of fun we imagined they would be having in the states. We searched for fun places to take the children.

We were directed to a small park in Larnaca. Calling the space a park was an overly optimistic description. The area was not large but flower beds and paths crisscrossed dry areas that served as green lawns in an attempt to beautify the grounds. The children's playground was located in the middle of the park. The playground consisted of two swings, one merry-go-round and a slide. The merry-go-round wobbled and the rusted metal swings squeaked. The slide was not slippery so the girls duck-walked up and down it for fun. They played happily on the equipment, delighted to have something to play on. After they had tired of the squeaking and wobbling, and of getting stuck on the slide, they skipped along the paths, oblivious to the stares and smiles they received from local families visiting the park.

SIX

Getting to Know You

Jim's primary work centered on numbers and financial matters, but once in awhile he was asked to evaluate a project on site. One spring day, he invited me to join him to visit an AID project. We were driven in an AID car to a village in the Troodos Mountains where cherry trees were the main source of income. The driver parked next to a medium sized structure with a large grape arbor attached to the front of the building. Jim and I were invited to sit in one of the chairs that were arranged in a rough circle. The thick growth of vines covered the roof of the arbor blocking out the hot sun and providing a cool place to rest. Eight or ten men dressed in white shirts and black pants were lounging in the chairs. Pipe smoke filled the air with a thick fruity aroma.

We were grateful that our seats were in the shade. There was little breeze and no clouds in the bright blue sky that day. Our driver proudly made a pronouncement that the men sitting with us under the arbor had agreed to grant me the rare privilege of being seated with them under the arbor. I was being granted this very special and unique privilege, he said, because I was Jim's wife. Women were automatically excluded from the men's gathering place.

Jim heard what the driver had said and for once it was Jim who seemed to be rattled by this pronouncement. I could see by the look on his face that he was about to challenge the tradition. I was not eager to cause a problem and decided this was not the time or place to object to the practice. I reached across and touched Jim's hand. He read my meaning and stayed quiet.

I asked the driver to convey my thanks and appreciation to the assembled men. I was thinking to myself that I'd learned a valuable lesson. I had experienced gender inequality in action that morning. I was eager for our girls to learn that men and women were equals and not to be excluded because of their gender. The exchange this morning had alerted me to be watchful as to what our children were absorbing from different cultural norms.

We were offered a lukewarm orange soda and I sipped and listened to our driver explain the local cherry-picking business to Jim. I kept looking around for the women of the village, but there were none in sight. No women came to shop at the kiosk behind the grape arbor. No women were sweeping the entryway to their houses or pushing baby carriages. I sat in the shade and watched as a green lizard slithered along the roots of the grape vines. Quietly twiddling my thumbs and wondering where all the women in the village had gone.

Our guide, proud of his ability to speak English, carried on a stream of information filling gaps of silence, as he described the life of the cherry growers. I wondered if the men sitting under the arbor with us were listening. One of the older men chimed in with a brief statement once or twice. In Greek, naturally. The driver would translate, then we would sit in silence once more.

An hour passed. The wait was becoming tiresome. A man came out of the kiosk. The air around us was filled with a pungent aroma. The man stopped in front of me and offered a tray of tiny white porcelain cups filled with Turkish coffee. I thanked the man and took a cautious sip of the black hot liquid, feeling the fine coffee grounds on the back of my tongue. This was not my first time with coffee served Cypriot style. Skerito, meaning without sugar or milk, was offered everywhere we traveled on the Island.

The guide was beginning to run out of something to say. My mind wandered and I mulled over how the men seated under all the grape arbors on the Island could sit, day after day, doing nothing. True to my young American attitude of 'get on with it,' I was thinking it was way past time for something to be happening.

I perked up when I spotted a woman coming up the path. The woman's face was wrinkled from life in the sun. She trudged into the shade and shrugged the large basket from her back and set it onto the floor of the kiosk. The basket was filled to the brim with deep red, ripe cherries.

One after another, the cherry-picking women began to arrive. Young, middle aged, and old women walked the path toward the grape arbor, their baskets filled with cherries picked that morning from the orchards above. Their backs were bent from years of carrying heavy loads.

KINDNESS

I marveled at the strength of those village women whose job it was to climb up and down the hills picking cherries for as long as the season lasted. I was disgusted that the women did all the work. I was having bad thoughts about the lazy men watching the women doing the hard work. I didn't have a name for my feelings about the division of roles in the country, but I was a feminist before the movement gathered momentum in the public consciousness.

The lolling men rose to their feet and began loading the contents of the baskets into crates affixed to the backs of donkeys standing outside the grape arbor. I could see that their part of the work had finally begun. Women's job was to pick. Men's job was to take the cherries down the mountain to sell in the villages below. We took this as a signal that our visit was over, and we thanked the villagers for their hospitality.

I was stiff from sitting still so long and gave my hips a small twist, hoping the men didn't notice. Jim and I turned to walk back to the car when one of the women pickers rushed toward us holding bags of cherries. We thanked her and she motioned for us to open the bags. We opened them, took out a sweet juicy cherry and plopped it into our mouths. The cherries were delicious! We 'yummed and oohed' and thanked her, again. This time with big sticky grins and red juice dribbling down our chins. Our reaction pleased her. She was smiling ear to ear as she bowed a quick goodbye.

Our road trip came to an end and that evening we presented the girls with gifts of ripe, red cherries for dessert. The visit to the village that day whetted my appetite for further excursions outside Nicosia.

My wish came true. A young man from a village south of Nicosia approached Jim at the office to ask for a favor. Kormakitis was one of four Maronite villages on the Island. We had never heard of Maronites. The young man told Jim the story of Maronite Cypriots. They originated in Lebanon and had immigrated to Cyprus in the 1800's. The Maronite religion, the young man said, was akin to their Roman Catholic brethren, except they were called Eastern Catholic Christians. Eastern Catholics differed from Roman Catholics in philosophy, but they shared the same Pope and rituals.

Jim showed an interest in learning more about the villagers. The young man presented Jim with an invitation to visit. He proceeded to make the well rehearsed case that Jim would learn about Maronites and that the villagers would learn more about Americans. He made the prospect of a visit more attractive by asking Jim to bring the whole family.

He then got to the core of his request. The mayor's daughter was about to be married and the village would regard it a great honor to have an American family attend.

Jim suspected the young man was trying to gain favor or hoping to find a sponsor for immigration to the US, but he also saw the invitation as an opportunity to learn more about a minority population on the Island. Jim agreed and said we would be honored to visit Kormakitis. I was particularly pleased to make the trip because I was seldom able to interact with Cypriot women. I packed pajamas, bathing suits, and a clean change of play clothes for Jenna and Nyna. I carefully folded their favorite party dresses into the bag, hoping they would not become too wrinkled. I was unsure as to the terrain in the village and decided not to take their little black Mary Janes. Their everyday sandals would have to do.

Given so little information about our trip to Kormakitis, I realized the girls too, would be encountering a weekend of unknowns. I always tried to inform them as to what they were about to see on our travels, and I felt bad that I had so little information to give them this time.

Going on the premise that a little information was better than none, I began by telling them what I did know. I supposed they would be meeting the Cypriot children living in the village. I wanted to prepare them for the possibility that the children might not know how to speak English. I wasn't clear what kind of activities would be available for the girls. I suggested they put on a friendly face and try to be patient. Best to wait to be invited to join any children's activities.

Jenna, or maybe it was Nyna, asked why we were going for a sleepover away from home. We had never spent the night in a village before. "We have been invited to take part in a wedding celebration. It is a special wedding," I said, "because it is the marriage of the mayor's daughter, and the mayor is a very important person in the village." I added that we considered it an honor to have been asked to attend.

"I don't know much about the celebrations there, but there is sure to be a special feast." I lowered my voice. "With special dishes." I almost whispered. "I want to warn you though. There could be some weird looking food on the table. Food that you and I have never seen before. You will be happy to know you do not have to eat something you do not like." Both girls did a little dance.

"But," I added. The girls stopped smiling and Jenna interrupted, "I don't like it when you say that word." She put on a pouty face. They watched my response to see if I was being serious. I continued, "I have a special favor to ask." Both girls shrugged. "Oh, it's not that bad." I said. "I'm just asking that you take at least one bite of everything you are offered." They began to object. I held up my index finger to stop their back talk. "If the food is hard to take, you only must take one bite. No more. But please, do take a small taste of everything." I waited for the objections to escape from their sweet mouths.

Their eyes widened and I could see more questions and complaints were about to come. Before that could happen I held my hand up once again. "One exception."

Jenna said, "Uh, oh."

"If you are offered the delicacy of sheep's eyes, you are both allowed to say no thank you." Jenna looked at me with disbelief and said, "Sheep's eyes? Ugh." Nyna's brown eyes grew larger than usual, and she gave a huge sigh of relief. I said, "Try to say no thank you in a very polite way, but in this one instance, you are allowed to just say no without tasting." Their expressions told me I conjured up an image more disgusting than they could ever have imagined. No more objections from either of them. The mention of sheep's eyes brought the discussion to a halt.

I needn't have been concerned about food offered at the wedding. Jenna and Nyna had already proven themselves great little culinary troopers! Jim and I had been surprised and delighted when they were offered their first bite of halloumi. Jenna watched as we had fished for cheese in a vat of milky liquid and wiggly caterpillar-like worms floating inside. She asked, "Did this cheese really come out of that barrel of worms?" Both girls had a 'you have to be kidding if you think I'll eat that' look on their faces.

Jim and I took a bite of the cheese and assured them we would not ask them to eat anything yucky. They paused, looked at each other and slowly took a small bite of the cheese. Surprised at the mild salty taste, they smacked their lips and asked for a second slice. Jim and I tried not to smile. It turned out halloumi fried in butter, brown and crisp on the outside, soft and gooey on the inside became one of their favorite Cypriot dishes. They were less hesitant to try grape leaves stuffed with rice and herbs when first offered. Those delicacies were funny looking but at least they were not surrounded by moving things.

We introduced exotic foods to the children very gradually. They ate a typically American diet for the most part. Access to an American PX made typical American fare available when necessary. Peanut butter and jelly, and macaroni and cheese from a box, were always on hand. I cooked with vegetables and meat from local markets and introduced new tastes into the girl's diet whenever possible.

We discovered our favorite Cypriot treat one day as we were walking through a park in downtown Nicosia. We came upon a middle-aged man dressed in immaculate white pants and shirt, standing by an umbrella-covered table. He was filling pockets of pita bread with juicy, savory smelling meat. Our mouth's began to water as soon as we were near enough to breathe in the aroma. A cocoon shaped mound of Medi-terranean-fed lamb was rotating over an open flame.

I watched as the man wielded a normal looking kitchen knife with amazing skill. I was impressed. With one quick downward motion he was able to slice the meat so thin it was practically transparent. We watched the man carve paper thin shavings of lamb releasing juice that oozed and dripped, making happy, quick, sizzling sounds as it landed in the flames. I couldn't take my eyes off the expertise with which the cook piled the slices of lamb onto the flat side of the knife and tucked them into a pita pocket without dropping a tidbit of meat into the fire. With a flick of his wrist, he plopped creamy yogurt mixed with bits of fresh mint on top of the meat. He smiled at us as he wrapped the warm sandwich into a square of brown paper and handed it to Jim.

The shawarma sandwich that we discovered in the park that day became one of our favorite Island dishes. The girls declared a dessert made from pine nuts layered between paper thin sheets of filo dough and soaked in honey was the best dish on the Island, but for Jim and me, Shawarma had no competition.

The topic of food didn't come up again as we passed through mustard fields and herds of sheep on our way to Kormakitis. We arrived early in the afternoon as instructed and were greeted with handshakes and smiles. Our young AID friend introduced us to the mayor, his family and friends, then escorted us to a visitor's cottage sitting just off the main road. We had a moment to settle into our room before our young host appeared at the door and invited us to take the girls for a swim. Jim thought that was a brilliant idea and he donned his bathing suit while I wasted no time helping Jenna and Nyna change into theirs.

I followed behind our host, Jim, and the girls as they made their way down a short path to a small sandy beach. I found a comfortable rock to sit on and watched them frolic together in the warm Mediterranean waters. I vowed I'd never forget that cinematic moment. With the warm sand covering my bare feet, the sound of gentle waves lapping against the shore was interrupted only by the squeals of joy the children made as Jim picked them up and threw them into the gentle waves over and over again. The sun, the water, and the car ride from Nicosia were powerful relaxants. We didn't have to suggest an afternoon nap more than once. Excited though the girls were, minutes after we returned to the cottage, we all enjoyed a satisfying nap.

I woke with a start, confused for a moment as to my surroundings, then jumped into action to rouse the family. It was almost time for the wedding ceremony. We did not want to call attention to ourselves by walking into the wedding hall late. Dressed in our Sunday-go-to-meeting clothes, we walked down the street to a small chapel where the marriage ceremony was to take place.

I was foolish to think we could avoid drawing attention to ourselves. It soon became obvious that our family was one of the main events. All eyes were on 'the Americans' as we were escorted down the aisle to front row seats. I didn't know whether to smile or to keep a solemn, reverent look on my face. I admit to having the impish urge to look right and left, waving my hand back and forth like I was the Queen of England. The girls were totally at ease looking around at the people and the place. They were oblivious to the stares.

We were seated in the front row next to the mayor's wife. I was happy to discover she knew a smidgen of English. She was a plump, pleasant looking middle-aged woman, elegantly dressed in pink from head to toe. I was appreciative when she whispered a brief translation of the wedding ritual to me.

Though the ceremony was officiated by a Christian clergyman, and though the words were foreign to us, the solemnity of the moment, the flowers and candles decorating the altar, the beautiful bride in her white dress and most of all in the love and joy that was being expressed, the service was familiar indeed. Not so dissimilar to our own religious wedding vows at home. Marriage vows taken, the bride and groom led the way out of the chapel to a large tent where tables and chairs had been erected.

Our family was ushered to a table close to the bride and groom and the feast began. There were trays of grape leaves filled with rice and herbs, trays of cheeses and pickled vegetables. Hummus and pita bread were some of the girls' favorite dishes. A platter of steaming vegetables and huge dishes of moussaka were served next to a savory lamb stew that was tender enough to cut with a fork. Conversation began to lull. Everyone became too busy eating and drinking to continue chatting. The girls were great. They tasted everything I put on their plates without a frown and told me later that the food wasn't 'that bad.' Both mentioned their relief that they didn't have to see platters containing sheep's eyeballs.

Wine from the hill region was served and we raised our glasses to toast the newlyweds. We were full of delicious food, the sun, and the ocean air and I could see the girls were tired and sleepy. Nyna was squirming in her seat and Jenna was beginning to look bored with the whole affair. I wanted to shout out a hearty 'thank you' when the newlyweds rose from their table and made their way out of the tent. The guests fell into a line behind them. I assumed we were free to return to our cottage but instead, the crowd formed a parade. It appeared we were to escort the couple down the road to their house.

Jim, the girls and I followed along, stretching our legs as we walked. We were unsure what was happening. I looked around for the bride's mother hoping to get an explanation for this strange turn of events. She was nowhere to be seen. We stood with the rest of the guests and watched as the couple went up the steps of the small white stucco cottage, turned to the crowd, smiled and waved. They turned to each other, kissed, and entered the house.

Once again, I assumed we were free to return to our cottage. I interpreted the couple's goodbye wave as an indication the wedding had come to an end. The wedding guests stayed in place. Unsure what was going on, I told Jim I'd put the children to bed. He nodded and said he would wait there for me to return or if the crowd broke, he'd come back to the cottage.

The girls set a record for the time it took to get out of their party clothes and into their pj's. They were almost asleep by the time I tucked them into bed. It had been a long day for our four-and six-year-old sweet ones. I hugged them and told them they had been wonderful guests. Neither child was awake enough to respond.

I was pleased and fascinated with the ease both girls had managed the unusual day. Only while playing in the sea were they not being stared at by large groups of people. They had endured long bouts of sitting, listening to speeches and conversations in a language they couldn't understand, surrounded by people they didn't know. There had been almost no bickering or complaining or rolling of the eyes. It was as if they had recognized the importance of this time and place. They had joined gracefully into the adventure. Their behavior had surpassed all expectations, and I got a hint into who our children were becoming.

I could feel my own body giving in to tiredness. The wine was making itself known and I thought about getting undressed and joining the girls. The thought soon evaporated. I was too curious to sleep. I had to solve the mystery as to why Jim and other people were still milling around the outside of the house. I had a sense that they were expecting something to happen. That seemed strange as I assumed the couple could be there all night. I took a last glance at the sleeping girls and made my way back to the prika house, meaning bride's house. I spotted Jim in the crowd talking with our young AID host. I pulled him aside and asked if he knew what was going on. He shrugged and said he was as puzzled as I. All he had been able to learn from our young office friend was that this was a part of the wedding ritual and it had always been done the same way. I mulled the situation over for a moment then decided to stand beside Jim and wait to see if something happened. Either the crowd would leave, or the couple would reappear, or something.

The mother of the bride suddenly appeared beside me. She could see that I was confused as to what was going on and began to explain. She said that I must be patient. We were about to witness a very important part of the wedding ceremony. She told me that the bride and groom had retired to the house the bride's father had provided. Fathers were required to provide the house and all household goods before their daughters could marry. She continued, " These houses are called 'prika' houses." We stood with the guests and waited. Jim and I were tired but fascinated by the suspense that had come over the crowd. A short time later, a strange lull came over the crowd and the crowd parted, making a path for an elderly woman. The mayor's wife whispered. "That is my mother," she pointed. "The grandmother."

The woman was slightly stooped and clad in black. She carried herself with dignity as she made her way to the door of the cottage. I noticed a petal of a yellow flower hanging on to the hem of her dress and squashed an urge to reach out and brush it off. The grandmother stopped at the door of the cottage, hesitated a moment, then entered. She closed the door and the wedding guests stood, waiting. All eyes on the door. It was as if the whole village was holding its breath.

The grandmother emerged after a few minutes. She was holding a folded white sheet with a small red stain on it. I sensed the crowd relax as she circled through the guests, holding the sheet for all to see. "It's the grandmother's job to show proof that her granddaughter was a virgin and that the marriage has been consummated," the mayor's wife said.

I was tempted to remind her that girls could lose their hymen in many ways before having marital relations. But before I could speak, my hostess hastened to add that this part of the ceremony was an old tradition. "It is not unheard of," she said, "that these modern brides sometimes prepare fake blood to prove their virginity." I nodded that I understood.

I was too tired to give any thought to the ritual we had witnessed that evening. But as rituals are meant to do, that unusual wedding ritual made a strong impression on me.

The next morning the image of a bloodied sheet kept coming to mind. I thought about a classmate in Texas who had given birth out of wedlock. The whispers, and the nuanced glances when she entered a room. The shaming looks aimed her way from supposedly Christian women. The ritual we had witnessed in the village may have been ancient, but the meaning behind the ritual wasn't any different from the West Texas Bible belt. High value was placed on virginity above all other assets. Just as both cultures put a higher value on boys over girls.

It became clearer, as I got to know more of the country, that Greek Cypriot women on the Island in the 60's were highly valued as mothers, house keepers, and workers in the fields. As domestics. They were not encouraged to pursue careers outside the home. I wanted to learn more about the lives of women on the Island. To learn if the women there felt the restraints put upon them, but I would never have a chance to ask.

SEVEN
Becoming a Home

Our first year in Nicosia was unfolding smoothly until the girls came home early from school one afternoon with sore throats. I felt their clammy foreheads and rushed to find a thermometer. I had to remind Nyna twice that she couldn't talk to me with the thermometer in her mouth. Both girls had around 101 degrees fever. I gave them Tylenol and some warm chicken soup and tucked them into bed. It wasn't unusual for children to catch colds and sore throats from other children at school. In fact, I'd been somewhat surprised and relieved that our family had been healthy since leaving the States.

Jenna read a book and Nyna told me about a new friend she had made at school. I surprised them by taking their supper to their beds that evening. Having supper in bed only occurred on special occasions. I checked their temps again and was disappointed to find their fever had not gone down but increased after the Tylenol and soup. I'd hoped for a quick response to the meds, but instead, their foreheads were hot to the touch and their eyes were beginning to have that glazed look very ill patients have.

They tried to be happy about supper in bed, but it was obvious they felt too awful to enjoy their surprise. Nevertheless, I tucked a pillow at their backs so they could use the soup spoon to bring the warm chicken soup to their mouths. Jenna tried several spoonfuls of soup then nibbled at the grilled cheese sandwich. She swallowed and grimaced. One bite was all she could manage. Her throat was too raw and painful for more. Nyna skipped the soup and went for the grilled cheese, bit into it, then looked up in disbelief as if her favorite sandwich had betrayed her by causing her to feel pain instead of the expected pleasure.

I gave the girls more Tylenol and hoped that sleep and the medication would work. The night brought no rest to any of us. I tossed and fell into a restless sleep, one ear open for a moan or a call from the girl's

54

rooms. Around midnight I stopped trying to sleep and went to take the girl's temperature one more time. In spite of the second dose of Tylenol, both girls' temperatures had continued to rise. I told Jim the next morning that we needed to get them to the embassy doctor as soon as possible.

Jim and I prepared Jenna and Nyna for the trip to the embassy. I asked the girls to show me their sore throats. They opened their mouths, and I tried not to gasp. It was a scary sight. Both had bright red-hot color down their throats. I could see white streaks of infection peeking through the redness. I recognized the culprit. Streptococcus. The white blotches left no doubt in my mind that my diagnosis was correct. Our little girls had contracted a bad case of Scarlet Fever.

As scary as it was, I reminded myself that a quick dose of penicillin would wipe out the disease in no time. I had seen a few cases when I worked in Children's Hospital back in the '50s. Scarlet Fever had become rare in the US due to the abundant use of penicillin. The disease had essentially been eradicated from the general population.

We felt terrible about taking Jenna and Nyna out of their beds that morning. They were burning up with fever and their throats were so sore and painful they didn't even try to talk. Jim pulled into the embassy parking lot, and checked in with his office while I rushed the girls to the Infirmary.

The US Embassy maintained a small but adequate infirmary for emergencies. The staff consisted of a nurse, a lab tech, and a doctor. This embassy doctor was young. Right out of med school, I suspected. He couldn't have had a lot of experience with children's diseases. But he looked smart enough and proceeded to perform a proper exam. He looked into each girl's throat and noted that it looked like a strep throat. I was relieved to see he recognized the symptoms, and I took the opportunity to share my own diagnosis. "I'm so relieved you agree that they have strep throat." I walked over and pulled Nyna into my lap. "Thankfully a shot of penicillin and they will be on their way to recovery."

The young man had turned and was preparing for the next step in the procedure. I expected him to return with the penicillin in hand. Instead, he was holding a swab and an empty vial. He must have seen the look of disbelief on my face. He insisted that a culture was necessary and he began a litany of caution about the use of penicillin. I was already aware that the medical professionals back in the States were promoting the idea that penicillin was to be used only in worse case scenarios. They made the case, the legitimate case I might add, that overuse of penicillin had created strains of bacteria that had become immune to the antibiotic. I stared at him, speechless.

I couldn't believe what I was hearing. He gave me the company line once more. "The latest studies show," blah, blah, blah. I stopped paying attention. "Penicillin should only be used in dire circumstances. Foreign service protocol," he said, "does not permit the use of penicillin for sore throats."

Huh? I knew a 'dire circumstance' when I saw one. And this was a dire circumstance. My children did not have a simple sore throat and I told him so. He nodded to indicate that he had heard me but nothing I said had changed his mind. Quite the contrary. The young doctor assured me that the broad-spectrum antibiotic he had just injected into their arms would take their fever down by nighttime. He instructed me to continue the Tylenol, apply cold compresses, and to call the next morning to report the progress the girls had made.

The next twenty-four hours were a nightmare. Our poor sick little babes' fever increased. For the second night, Jim and I took turns administering meds every four hours and applying cold wash cloths to their flushed and glassy-eyed bodies. They were restless, tossing covers and falling in and out of sleep.

By morning, Jenna's fever had remained steady. Nyna's fever, on the other hand, had continued to climb. I had a hard time choking back the knot in my gut as I placed the thermometer under her tongue. Even asking Nyna to open her little mouth caused her pain. Her fever was dangerously high.

I put down the thermometer, picked up the phone and shouted to the embassy nurse that we needed to treat the children with penicillin, now. I literally begged for penicillin to be administered as soon as I could get them to the infirmary. The young doctor took the phone and for a brief moment I felt a stab of hope. 'Young Doc' agreed that we must bring down Nyna's fever as quickly as possible. My spirits rose. Maybe he was finally listening to me.

My hopes morphed into despair when the doctor quoted the company line once again. Insisting that penicillin was not indicated. Instead, he gave me useless instructions. I was gob smacked once again. His instructions were to fill the bathtub with ice cubes as quickly as possible and put Nyna's tiny feverish body into the tub. I wanted to crawl through the phone and strangle the man. The very thought of shocking Nyna's little body that way made me shake.

I hung up the phone and took a long breath to absorb the news. I was in a terrible bind. I couldn't risk Nyna's fever becoming higher. I rejected the idea of putting Nyna into an ice bath. Yet, I couldn't just do nothing.

As painful as it was, the doctor's instruction was the only thing I hadn't tried. I choked back tears. I didn't want to leave Nyna for even a minute, but Jim had gone to work, and Jenna was still sick in the other room. There was no option. I told Nyna I would be just a minute and ran down the stairs to the kitchen. I emptied the ice trays from the freezer into a large pan and climbed back upstairs to the bathroom. I dumped the ice into the tub and told Nyna what we were about to do. I struggled to keep my voice steady. I didn't want her to hear the heartbreak in my voice.

I assured Nyna that she would be back under the warm covers in no time. I pulled back the covers and carried her shivering body to the tub. I removed her pajamas and gently laid her down on the ice cubes. Nyna screamed and I no longer tried to hold back the tears. I kept telling her it would be ok as I picked up a handful of the ice, preparing to sprinkle it onto her naked body. I stopped. I couldn't do it. Not for even one minute. I scooped her out of the tub as gently as I could, wrapped her in a soft blanket and hugged her to my chest.

There had to be another way. We had tried everything we were told to do, still, Nyna's fever continued to rise. I became frantic even thinking about the alternative. I tried to think what to do. A thought jumped onto my mind. I had become acquainted with several British women who had raised children in Nicosia. I called the British woman I knew the best and told her of my dilemma. I was convinced that Nyna would recover quickly if only I could find someone to give her penicillin. My friend gave me the name and phone number of a local pediatrician whose services she had used for her children when they were young. I thanked her profusely and wasted no time getting through to the doctor's office.

I rang the office and hurriedly described the symptoms to the receptionist. I was relieved to be transferred to the doctor without delay. He was a good listener and began asking pertinent questions. I could feel a sliver of hope creeping into my heart. Had I finally found someone to listen to me? I was frightened and tense but trying hard to keep the panic from my voice, worrying he might think I was a hysterical mother. After all, we had never met in person.

Much to my relief, his response calmed me. He was confident, he said, that we could bring the fever down quickly. I realized I'd been holding my breath. My shoulders had raised halfway up to my ears. I tried to relax. I took a deep breath. I listened with relief as the doctor told me to bring the children to his office as soon as possible.

I tried to be gentle as I pulled little arms through soft pink robes. They were in so much pain. Every touch made their skin burn, yet, neither of them uttered so much as a squeak. They looked at me with glassy eyes and slipped their little feet into house shoes and I walked them down to the car. The doctor's office was located in an unfamiliar section of town, and I was aware of being anxious and tired. I had to force myself to focus on the directions the doctor had given me. I became hyper alert to the lanes, careful to drive on the left side of the road.

Almost twenty minutes later, I spotted the white stucco house and helped the girls out of the car. We were ushered straight into the doctor's office. The staff obviously expected us. The doctor entered and introduced himself.

He was an elderly Greek man with white hair. Lines crisscrossing his face were a testament to his kindness. His presence calmed me almost immediately. I no longer felt alone. The doctor nodded reassuringly as I gave a brief report of the illness. He moved to sit in front of Nyna and asked her to give him a look at her throat. He spoke English with an accent, but his deep voice moved the words along smoothly. He looked back at me and nodded. No need for a culture. No need for explanations. This doctor had seen Scarlet Fever before.

He left the room for a moment, returned with vials of penicillin and syringes. I'd never thought I'd be happy to see my children with needles in their arms. I had an urge to go up to this stranger and give him a hug. I managed to contain myself.

Jenna's fever was gone by the evening that day, and though Nyna's fever didn't break for another twelve hours, she too was back in school the next week. I was able to sleep that night knowing that my girls would be awake the next morning.

I will never forget the kindness of that Greek physician and the lessons I learned that week. I would always seek a second opinion if I don't get the results needed with the first doctor. And I would persist pursuing what I knew to be right. That it was okay, even imperative, to step out of the pleasant woman's persona when necessary.

EIGHT
Surprise, Surprise

One Saturday morning after the girls had recovered from their traumatic illness, we looked out the window from the top floor of our house. We could see snow gleaming on the distant mountaintops. Jenna and Nyna began jumping up and down. Begging to go play in the snow. We were ready for a new adventure. I packed the warmest clothes we had and we were on the road to the Troodos mountains before noon. We drove for an hour with no signs of snow. We began to wonder if the snow on the mountain was an illusion.

The girls were restless but became perked up when Jim pulled off the highway and over behind a parked car. The hood of the car was up and a young man was standing over it. Jim went to speak to the driver. I watched for clues as to what the problem might be. I couldn't hear what was going on, but I could make out that the young man and Jim were involved in a discussion. The girls were itching to be on our way and had just asked if we would have to wait long when we heard a burst of laughter.

Jim was still chuckling when he returned to the car. "It's not the bonnet, it's the boot," Jim said. "What's funny about that?" I said, "I have no idea what that means. Explain please." Jim chuckled, "Europeans put engines into the rear of some of their cars rather than the front. There was nothing wrong with his car. The young man was looking into the trunk of his car which was in the front of the car. The engine in his car is in the rear."

Our lesson of the day. 'It's not the bonnet, it's the boot' became one of our favorite mantras between each other when we put our foot into a stink pile or mistook something for what it was not.

As we climbed up the mountain, snow began to cover the road. Excitement filled our car. We stopped at the entrance of the small mountain top hotel and the girls got into their jackets, mittens, and rubber boots. Warmly clad, Jenna and Nyna ran to the front lawn and fell to the ground. Snow angels were in the making before we could check into the hotel.

There was not a large amount of snow on the mountain that day, but there was enough to make a skinny snow man and slide down a small hill on a plastic bag. We could hardly convince Jenna and Nyna to come in for lunch and a potty break. Everyone slept well that night.

The next morning the sun was shining, and the girls begged for one more romp in the snow. They took a few turns sliding down the hill but the winds on the mountain were high. The wind pushed the cold through our lame attempt at winter weather clothing. We were soon saying our goodbyes to our fun mountain adventure.

Halfway down the mountain to Nicosia I began to feel queasy. I asked Jim to pull over to the side of the road. I threw up. That was my first clue that Melinda was about to join the family.

We were excited about having another child. We had planned to have a third back in the states, but pregnancy was postponed due to the change in Jim's career. I had not prepared for the possibility of being pregnant overseas. The reality that I was indeed pregnant required some creativity. I ordered a few blousy outfits from the Sears catalog and put out an SOS to embassy and AID women friends.

A friend whose husband was stationed at a small military communications base close to Nicosia loaned me her used maternity ensembles. I felt somewhat awkward as the woman was friendly but very secretive in a way that I could not understand. Jim informed me of the existence of the small US listening post on the Island. The mystery was explained. The awkward conversations we had at times finally made sense. I was grateful for my friend's wardrobe support despite the mystery surrounding our friendship.

Making meals and cooking for dinner parties became a source of torture for about a month. I was relieved when my hormones settled down and I felt comfortable enough to make To Do lists for the next nine months. I researched birthing possibilities and soon became a patient of the most prominent English-speaking obstetrician in the city.

Dr. Talidoros was trained in London. A man in his early 50's, he was blessed with classic Greek features. He had a full head of black hair and steady brown eyes. A crumb of a biscuit lay forgotten alongside an empty coffee cup on his desk. He had a very proper bedside manner as he explained the birthing facility and treatment plans for the next few months.

I drew my attention away from the crumb and back to Dr. Talidoros. I explained that the Navy had given me no choice in the manner of delivery I was to have with my other children. I wanted him to know that I was choosing to have this third angel without medication of any sort. I wanted to be fully present to my child with this pregnancy. Dr. Talidoros agreed that since this was my third pregnancy and the other two had been uneventful he had no problem with my choice of natural childbirth. I was thankful I didn't have to fight for what I wanted. I purposely didn't tell my parents about my choice. They were already concerned that I was having a baby overseas. I wrote a letter home every two weeks and kept them informed as to my good health. I assured them that all would be well.

My pregnancy in Cyprus gave me an unexpected peek into Greek culture. Some things can't be learned from reading a book. Or for that matter, in conversation with Greek women. In spite of the language handicap, and under the category of 'no one ever told me about this,' I learned of an unusual tradition early on.

Soon after I began to wear loose clothing to social gatherings, Greek men at cocktail parties felt it their responsibility to do their 'magic' and predict the gender of our baby. Much to my chagrin, I became the 'main event' at dinner parties. This required that I be comfortably seated onto a soft chair as the rest of the dinner guests gathered around my big round belly. One of the Greek male guests would stand over me holding a watch hanging from a gold chain. I hadn't noticed so many men wearing watches attached to gold chains before pregnancy. Dinner party guests stood quietly by, watching, as the gold watch slowly began to swing, first left, then right, over my belly. The watch would gradually find its course and continue its direction only one way. The lore was that if the watch swung left the baby would be a girl, and if the watch veered to the right, a boy was destined to appear.

As much as I didn't like to be the 'after dinner entertainment,' I remained committed to my responsibilities as an AID wife, and managed to attend cocktail and dinner parties to the end of my pregnancy. 'Gender prediction' or voodoo as I came to think of it, was a routine ritual on social evenings until the baby arrived.

Summers in Nicosia were unexpectedly hot. I grew more uncomfortable in the heat with the baby tucked snugly inside my body. Breezes from the Mediterranean rarely reached as far inland as Nicosia. There was no air conditioning.

The girls were out of school and activities for children were scarce. Lacking TV or movies, I searched for summer activities to entertain the children. I played musical soundtracks on the new record player in an attempt to provide some fun. We haunted bookstores in search of new reading material for Jenna and for books appropriate to read at bedtime. Play dates became scarcer as school friends were on vacation or out of the country. I grew more desperate and searched for a solution to our uncomfortable dilemma.

We were visiting a friend in her home in Kyrenia when I was struck with an idea. I loved being in my friend's home. The Kyrenia home was built with thick walls that trapped the cool morning air well into the afternoon. The house had no connecting rooms. In order to walk from one room to another one had to walk outside under a covered portico. At the back of the house a green lawn was open to the winds coming off the Mediterranean Sea. A house like hers would be the answer.

I was sitting with my friend and enjoying the cool breezes and view of the water when I decided to confide in her. I was miserable in the Nicosia heat. I'd thought of a way to get through the heat so I asked my friend Marta for help.

Perhaps it was the British influence apparent everywhere we went on the Island, or being around so many British accents, whatever. I could not get enough of our friend's gracious company. Her husband was a British CIA type and it was easy for me to imagine him as the prissy sleuth from an Agatha Christie novel. Ed was graced with a head of thick white hair and a full mustache to match. Our relationship was purely social and therefore he remained a mystery in both real and imaginary ways.

Jim and I were fortunate to be invited to their home on a regular basis. We enjoyed many evenings there sitting on the patio with a cold drink in hand, watching the sun slide into the Mediterranean Sea. Marta, his wife, was a strong role model. She poked the rebel in me.

Marta was unlike the other British friends I had in Nicosia. Most of them were proper in dress and proper in speech. Properly behaved.

Not Marta. Marta looked like a hippy. Her thick blond hair was always tied back into a loose bun and framed by a colorful silk scarf. Her ample figure was cuddled in colorful caftans that billowed softly around her legs when the breezes from the ocean reached the patio. She rarely came to the International Women's luncheons and more than once I heard a swear word escape her mouth. It was easy for me to imagine, when I was with her, that years of occupying middle eastern countries could somehow cause a genetic mutation, enabling British people like her to be extremely comfortable adjusting to any culture beyond their own. Marta was very comfortable in her own skin and was a very positive role model for me.

One particularly hot day I asked my friend if she knew of another house like hers, knowing her house was one of a kind. Marta agreed I needed to get the children out of the city's smothering heat. She was excited to help, and we began to explore the availability of rentals in Kyrenia on the ocean. For weeks after school was out, I loaded the girls into the back of the Vauxhall and followed up any leads my friends relayed to me.

It was not long before I presented Jim with a surprise. My friend and I found a house close to Kyrenia village that held some promise. Only after Jim had agreed to take some time off and look at our find did I confess to him that the house had a few glitches. They were, admittedly, important glitches. There was no indoor bathroom, no running water, and the master bedroom was full of worms.

I had freaked out when I peeked through the windows of the small empty house. It was obvious no one lived there, but one of the rooms was especially weird. A frame of wire spanned the entire room. Green leaves thickly covered the entire frame. An army of creepy, crawly caterpillar-like worms were munching away at the leaves. The frame was so packed with caterpillars, their crunching could be heard through the walls. Aside from these minor details, the place was perfect.

I was notified that the owner of the prika house by the sea had agreed to meet us. Jim ran out of logical arguments against my idea of moving to Kyrenia for a few months and took time off from work to drive out to Kyrenia with us. An AID driver came along for translation purposes.

The small white stucco house with blue shutters was obviously unfinished. There were no flower beds around the house. No garden at all. Just sand. But the rooms had lovely windows open to the ocean breezes and the house sat upon an open space away from other houses. The most important and redeeming feature was a direct path winding through a barren pasture down to the seashore.

The owner greeted us as we drove up to the house and the three men sat on the porch steps to discuss the possibility of a rental. I stayed in the air-conditioned car. While I pondered the significance of a room full of weird worms, Jenna and Nyna explored the barren area around the house. They were looking for a place to make a playhouse.

I was lost in thought and jumped when Jenna knocked on the car window. I opened the door and Jenna proudly held up a long black object. "Look what I found across the street," she said.

"Jenna," I gasped, "That is beautiful. I think you have found a snake's skin." I didn't add that I was fairly certain it was the skin of a dangerous Cypriot variety. It certainly looked frightening. Almost three yards long. "I suggest you stay close to the house until we know the grounds are safe." Jenna took the skin back across the street and motioned Nyna to follow her for a peek into the windows of the cottage.

I remained in the car and out of the conversation but I was silently jumping with joy at the possibility that a house deal could be made. Sweat ran down the tunnel between my blossoming breasts. I tried to stay calm. Trying not to show my excitement. I didn't want to appear too anxious for the deal to go through fearing my enthusiasm might effect the price of rent.

I was not kidding myself. There was always a possibility that the house couldn't be fixed. A sinking feeling invaded my stomach. Of course, we couldn't get by without a bathroom. And what would we do without running water? I struggled to come up with something creative to make it possible for us to live there. But nothing practical occurred to me. Still, I didn't want to give up hope.

Jim, the homeowner, and the AID driver were in discussion for what seemed like ages to me. The morning became noon and the small bit of shade from the scraggly grape vines that covered the arbor began to shrink. I was staying cool enough ensconced in the air-conditioned car, but I was not blessed with endless patience.

I shifted from one cheek to the other in an effort to settle the baby to a place where the kicking under my ribs would be less painful. The talks were going on and on. And on. Conversation, no matter the topic, seemed to be a major Cypriot pastime, and sometimes it appeared 'talk' was more important than the topic of the day.

I perked up when the owner suddenly became animated. I suspected we had made a breakthrough of sorts. I couldn't contain myself any longer. I stepped from the car and cringed when the heat hit me. Jim gave a slight nod in my direction, and I almost blew the cool front I'd tried so hard to display. Jim informed me that they had arrived at an answer to the mystery of the wiggly worms. They were silkworms. Silkworms spent their lives eating mulberry leaves and spinning silk threads from their bodies.

We had already guessed that the house was a prika house. The father had three daughters and had been unable to finish the house for lack of funds. Jim had suggested that we pay the summer's rent in one lump sum. Hence the smiles and animated display from the farmer. Three months' rent paid in full was the simple answer to the owner's dilemma and to my problem. With money in hand, the owner could buy the necessary tools to build a bathroom with running water.

I could hardly contain myself. I wanted to give Jim a great big hug. And the farmer and the driver too. The elated farmer assured us that the water situation would be solved. I didn't realize how tense I'd been until I took a deep breath. We had done it! We would have a cooler place to live for the summer and the children could swim and play in the cool waters of the sea.

There was a huge downside. Jim would only be able to stay with us in Kyrenia for long weekends. He would have to suffer the heat in Nicosia alone. He could stay cool while at work. Embassy offices at least had air conditioners, but he could be in for some uncomfortable nights. Our dear Jim was willing to make the sacrifice.

The deal was done, and two weeks later we arrived at our summer place. A barrel on the roof had been rigged to hold water and piping installed to enable flushing and showering. A brand-new toilet sat in the middle of the small room where silkworms had previously been chomping and weaving their sparkling webs of silk. We went from room to room, becoming acquainted with our new house, then stepped outside to breathe in the cool ocean breeze and feast our eyes on the beautiful Mediterranean just a short path from the house.

Stepping into the warm, clear water of the Mediterranean was like stepping into an emerald blue cloud. We fitted the children with water wings and blow-up plastic tubes so they could frolic to their hearts' desire. I grew larger every day and feared I'd sink if I tried to swim, so

I stayed cool, sitting with my feet and legs in the water and letting the gentle waves wash over me.

During the week when Jim was away at work, I tied a piece of butcher's twine to the girls' blow-up rings so that they couldn't float beyond water over my head. I kept them always in reach if they got into trouble.

On long weekends, Jim swam with them at least once every day. Two times a day if the heat was particularly fierce. It was a summer of growth in many ways. Jenna learned to swim in those waters that summer, and Nyna learned how to float on her back without her dad holding her.

I learned something about myself that summer that I hadn't admitted before. I felt a guilty jolt of joy when I realized how much I loved upsetting the status quo. I didn't divulge my guilty secret to Jim that summer. I was a bit ashamed of my behavior, but not all that much. My secret was the glee I felt as we walked the short path from our cottage to the sea every day. I had ordered a bathing suit specifically designed for pregnant women. The suit had a blouson top of blue and white stripes, over a solid blue tight-fitting bottom.

I donned my suit and rubber flip flops and waddled down the path each day, watching the girls race each other to the shore. It was our private daily parade. Or so I had imagined until I realized the girls in their pink and yellow swimsuits carrying blow-up toys and me in my pregnancy suit had become a village affair. In the beginning I occasionally encountered one or two village women walking on the other side of the path as they carried their morning shopping home from the store.

Gradually, our audience increased. There was no longer any pretense. Every day we could find a row of village women gathered along the path unabashedly watching our procession to the beach. We must have been quite a shocking sight. There were no pregnancy bathing costumes in their wardrobes. That was certain.

I had never observed any Greek women swimming in the sea. Pregnant or not. I must have been the topic of great gossip and hilarity. Dressed in traditional black dresses and their heads covered, the women stared. Every morning I would greet them. There was never a response. Maybe a few giggles when they thought I couldn't hear. Crazy Americans. Even the Brits never did anything like this. Bare arms and legs showing. Not to be done by village women for sure.

I admitted another guilty secret to myself. I enjoyed creating a challenge to a social taboo. That confession, the sea of stunning blue, and the yellow sand scattered with dusty olive trees, those things combined to make the healing balm I needed to get through the uncomfortable last months of pregnancy.

~

On October 24th,1963 contractions began. I was ready to meet this island baby.

It was the middle of the week when I called Jim and he left his office without delay. We arrived at the Talidoros Clinic in record time. Admission was fast and efficient, and I was ensconced in a private room without delay. The room was plain and clean, of medium size and comfortable enough to have a chair by my bed and a table for my knitting and a book. Jim called a friend to pick up the girls from school and stayed with me throughout the afternoon.

We made a plan. Jim was to inform our concerned parents that I was in labor. He was to find carpool help to get the girls to and from school. We imagined the fun they would have with a baby. We joked about how we would have to find money for a 'prika' house if the baby was a girl. And together, we counted contractions.

I was impatient. I always minded being heavy and uncomfortable in the last months prior to giving birth. So ready to get the baby into my arms. The contractions settled into a pattern of 'start and stop'. Around dusk, Dr. Taliadoros examined my progress and announced that I continued to progress but slowly. He predicted he would not be delivering the baby until the next day. Jim and I agreed that he should go home to feed the girls and get a good night's sleep.

For the first few hours after Jim left, I counted contractions alongside the stitches on my knitting needle. Knitting became too difficult after a time. Everything I tried to distract myself didn't work but irritated me instead. I was tired and tried to rest but loud noises coming from the birthing room across the hall invaded my space. Unlike any hospital I'd been to, this place was rocking with groans and an occasional scream. I realized this might go on for some time and I strained to make sense of the constant cacophony of sounds issuing from the room across the hall. But to no avail.

I couldn't make out what I was hearing and finally couldn't stand the mystery any longer, I held my hospital gown together, struggled out of bed, and cracked open my door. The racket was coming from across the hall. I followed the noise and cautiously peeked into the room. I was surprised to see how large the space was. Six beds were lined up against one wall of the room, four were occupied by a very pregnant woman. On the wall across from the beds were chairs. The chairs were filled with what appeared to be relatives. Aunts, uncles, grandmothers, and one Greek Orthodox priest. The room reeked of stale bread and cheese. An olive pit had escaped and was hiding under a chair.

As the cacophony of groans grew louder, the visiting 'chorus' chimed in and added to the verbal lament. As the groans ebbed low, so did the 'chorus.' The groans of pregnant women and their visitors morphed into a melody of highs and lows along a musical scale. The mom-to-be was never left to groan alone. The sounds became a spontaneous song of pain and hope.

I later learned that the 'music making' across the hall came from a tradition among some Greeks on the Island that friends and family participate in the birthing process. Grandmothers, aunts, uncles, and friends came to give voice to the contractions mother and baby were enduring. 'It takes a village to raise a child' was obviously a slogan taken quite seriously in Nicosia that night.

I returned to my solitary room to spend the night alone. I felt sorry for myself that lonely evening, wishing Americans were a more community-oriented sort. We were the 'pull-yourself-up-by-the-bootstrap' kind. True to type and stoic to the end, I put my head under a pillow and tried once again to sleep.

My Greek language skills provided me with enough vocabulary to talk with village women about their babies and their recipes, and to ask questions about their lives, but I had not thought to include medical words in my lesson plan. Doctor Taliadoros spoke excellent English. It never occurred to me I would need Greek words to get through the birthing night.

Dr.Taliadoros checked my progress again around 7:30 that evening and confirmed his previous diagnosis. He was certain that the baby would be arriving after breakfast the next morning. He wished me a good night, told me he was in his quarters upstairs. I settled in for a long, lonely wait.

I talked to the baby snuggling in my belly. Not certain if Melinda or Daniel was listening. Around 4:00 in the morning I noticed a drastic change in my contractions. There was no doubt in my mind that the baby had decided to prove the doctor's diagnosis wrong. I called the nurse and used all the Greek words that I knew to alert them to my progress. I'll never know what the pretty little brown eyed night nurse thought I was saying. She kept nodding as I tried to tell her that my contractions were arriving closer together. She smiled and nodded and quickly left the room. I assumed she had gone to wake the doctor.

Another hour passed and the door to my room remained closed. I rang the bell more vigorously, but I got the same response. Nothing. I tried groaning in unison with one of the families across the hall. It made me feel less lonely and lonelier at the same time. I comforted myself between contractions by imagining Jim getting the girls out of bed, having breakfast, and helping them dress for school. I watched a brown spider crawl up to the corner of the ceiling and weave an intricate web. I was tired, bored and ready.

Time and again I rang for the nurse and time and again nothing happened. I was quickly losing patience. I supposed the nurses had bought into the doctor's 'after breakfast prediction' as to the time of birth. Ok for him to say. I became more and more cranky with the pain. The relief between contractions began to come less often. Enough was enough. It occurred to me that perhaps my quiet stoicism was sending the wrong signal to the staff. I began to wonder if the nurse thought I was making no progress because I was not groaning with the contractions. Maybe she thought no groaning meant no progress. That was the answer. The nurse was paying no attention to my growing urgency because I was too quiet. I decided to scream.

I couldn't wait any longer. I could feel Melinda's head crowning. I screamed in Greek over and again, "my baby is coming," until the nurse appeared at the door. I spread my legs and pointed. "My baby is here." The situation finally got through to the nurse. She could see Melinda's head beginning to crown. She turned and ran from my room. I could hear her rousing sleeping staff into action. Another nurse appeared at my bedside with a gurney and I was wheeled into the delivery room just as Dr. Taliadoros arrived.

Dr. Taliadoros was a mess. His black hair was tasseled and his blue pj's were rumpled from the hot night. He quickly appraised the situation. Melinda and I had already done the work. Dr. Taliadoros had simply arrived in time to catch the beautiful, red-haired, tiny baby and place her on my stomach. She looked up at me, totally awake. Perfect love. I tried to choke down emotion, the miracle of that moment, but realized I didn't care. I sobbed in relief, love, and delight and didn't care that tears were streaming down my cheeks. Stoicism be damned.

The baby and I were cleaned up and transferred to a bright sunny room with plenty of space for visitors. Melinda was swaddled and placed into a basket by my side. I could not stop looking at her. I rubbed her little fuzz of red hair and giggled to myself as she struggled to keep her eyes on me. We were both exhausted, still, I was filled with awe at the miracle of that moment. Melinda had arrived on the day between my sister Reesa's birthday and my own. Another Scorpio in the family.

Jim was informed, and by the time he arrived at the clinic he had sent telegrams announcing the happy news to our parents back in the States. How I wish we had Facetime or cell phones those days. It would have been fun to share the moment with our family. Telegrams and a promise of photos to follow had to do.

After Jim had broadcast the good news, he brought the girls to see their new baby sister. They looked over the basket where Melinda was swaddled and asleep. Fascinated. They giggled when her tiny fingers curled around theirs. Jenna, the first to hold baby Melinda, sat on Jim's lap. Jim's arms cradling them both. Nyna was most fascinated by the tiny toes and feet. She wanted to touch and examine each little digit. She would touch a little toe and look up at me with those brown eyes and a smile and tell me how each one was so very tiny. She wanted to know when we could bring the baby home with us.

Melinda had arrived two days before my 30th birthday. Our little family was now complete. For three nights Melinda and I remained in the bright, spotless room at Talidoros Clinic. I was far enough from the birthing wing that nothing kept me awake. I slept. Melinda learned to nurse and sleep and to look around her new world.

Friends and acquaintances arrived at the hospital to meet the newborn. Every somber face peeking into the door alerted me that condolences on the birth of our third girl were forthcoming. After about the third visitor, I got tired of the condolences and fed up with the 'boys are better' attitude. I must admit that no one who watched our beautiful baby lying in a basket next to my bed kept a gloomy face for long. One woman held my hand, and with a solemn look reassured me that Melinda would be ok because she was so beautiful.

A second Greek friend echoed the sentiment. "Melinda is so pretty," she said. "She will have no trouble marrying a lawyer or a doctor."

This woman's prediction for my baby's future was too much. Diplomacy could go to hell. I told her plainly and more loudly than I should have, that Melinda would choose the partner that she desired. She could be a doctor herself, I told my friend, or a lawyer or whatever she wanted to be. My feminist gene could remain submerged no more. I understood about the strain on Greek families burdened with girl children. I did, however, make it clear that an American girl child had no such cultural constraints.

I felt guilty for a short minute knowing I had not been diplomatic. I didn't mention that Melinda had dual citizenship. She might even be president of Cyprus one day. Just a thought.

Every time I introduced the baby to our Greek friends, I could see the issue of financial cost popping into their minds. No one had to say it out loud but the prika word was in their thoughts.

I had seen firsthand the burden a village family endured. It was around noon one Saturday, our first spring in Nicosia. I was preparing dinner for a small number of State Department friends when the doorbell rang. I was inclined not to answer. My hands were sticky with cake icing.

The bell rang once again, and I hurried to answer. A man of an indeterminate age, one I'd never seen around the neighborhood before, was standing at my door. I assumed he was a villager by the wear and tear of his dusty black trousers and blousy white shirt. He didn't exactly have a scowl on his face, but he was a very solemn looking man. I was not frightened but didn't quite know what he wanted until he nodded his head slightly and held a bouquet of anemone flowers to me. I decided that he was selling the flowers and I asked how much. He held up three fingers and stood, waiting. I'm not certain, but he seemed a little taken aback that I had spoken to him in English. He probably had thought he'd rung the doorbell of a Greek family.

The flowers were lovely. Some were white with purple centers snuggled among red ones with yellow centers. Several blue buds were in the mix. The small bouquet was wrapped in brown paper. The flowers were the perfect addition to my dinner table, and I motioned for him to wait while retreated into the house to find my purse.

That was the first of many transactions I had with my very own florist. As long as the wild anemone grew in the countryside, the man appeared unannounced at my door with a small bouquet of anemones. He never spoke to me. He never smiled. Not really. Maybe a tiny grin toward the end. He held out the flowers, and I asked how much money he wanted. Depending on the number of stems included in the bunch, he held up fingers to tell me the price. I looked forward to my weekly delivery of fresh wildflowers and the anemone became my favorite flower. They provided a lovely centerpiece for countless dinner parties.

On the last day we met, I almost didn't recognize him. He had arrived much earlier than usual. I opened the door and I could see straight away that something was different. He didn't look like the same person. He appeared to be younger than I'd thought him to be. Dressed in a clean shirt I'd never seen before. The most striking change, he was smiling from ear to ear. His face was glowing with excitement and happiness. It was obvious that something very good had happened to bring him joy.

He spoke to me in Greek and managed to explain that he would not be coming again. I raised my brows and wondered why? He smiled even broader and let me know with gestures and words that I could understand, he had finished paying for all the prika debt for his daughters. They could now marry. He stood straight and proud, his cap in his hand while telling me in Greek that from now on, the money he made would be his own. I told him I would miss the flowers while attempting to let him know that I was happy for him. I asked how much he wanted for the flowers that day.

He simply bowed, tipped his cap, turned and skipped down the walk to the road without a glance back at the house. The heavy burden of duty had been drained from his shoulders. He was a man reborn.

NINE
Dark Times

Jenna and Nyna were excited the day we brought Melinda home from the clinic. They held and caressed her, as much in love with their new baby sister as were Jim and I.

We had adjusted to having another member of the family when one beautiful sunny morning I was snuggled in my comfortable bed with Melinda at my breast. Melinda was an enthusiastic eater and I had ample milk. The morning sunlight was flooding the room. Scents from the lemon trees outside my bedroom wafted through my open window. Jim was helping Jenna and Nyna dress for school. This was what I'd imagined family life would be.

The phone next to my bed rang and I leaned over to answer. Becky Toner was on the phone. "Turn on the BBC. Immediately." I was stunned. I'd never heard her voice sound so weird, then I realized Becky was sobbing. Before I could ask what was wrong, Becky said, "President Kennedy has been shot." The phone went dead.

I pulled Melinda closer to my chest and stared into the room. Seeing nothing. I couldn't move. Even breathe. I could feel the blood rushing through my body as I gasped for air. My world fell apart for a moment. Melinda, obviously feeling the change in my body, stopped nursing and looked up at me. Tears flowed down my cheeks.

I called out and Jim came running into the room. The distress in my voice had alerted him that something was wrong. I choked out the news. We held each other. I was in shock. I must have put Melinda in her crib. I don't know what we told Jenna and Nyna at that moment. I have some recollection that the school van arrived as usual to take them to school that day. Jim and I were glued to the stereo, listening but not wanting to believe what was being reported. Not long after Becky's call, Jim was rushed to the embassy for a briefing.

That first day the world held its breath. The news that followed that moment stood in sharp contrast to the blue bright Cypriot sunshine. Life as usual stood still.

Americans and Cypriots alike were glued to BBC radio, desperate to know if the President Kennedy would survive. We searched for news of the assassin. So many questions.

After hours of praying and waiting for any bit of good news, an official announcement arrived from the embassy. John F. Kennedy had died. Diplomatic communities all over the world would observe official mourning protocol for one month. Memorial services were to be held at St. Paul's Cathedral in Nicosia.

The week after Kennedy's death, the Catholic Cathedral was packed with diplomats, heads of state and regular citizens representing every nation in the world. It seemed as if the whole population in Cyprus was determined to cram into the building. Kennedy was very popular among the Cypriots. Jim and I waited in line under the hot sun for a very long time. I hadn't thought to bring water. The day was hot. The sun was shining brightly, I began to feel faint. I was debating whether to stay or leave when we were ushered into the crowded Cathedral. We were fortunate to be seated in the diplomatic section. I was present but absorbed little about the service. Present but numb. In a traumatic fog.

The President's death was personal to me. I had worked as a block captain for John F. Kennedy's campaign back in Silver Springs MD, and I had ruined my only dress suit sliding down a hill to shake Kennedy's hand at a campaign rally. He was truly 'my president.' My whole being had gone into shock when Kennedy died.

Official mourning lasted a month. The day after the official mourning ended I was busy with household chores when I heard a frightening noise. It sounded to me like gunfire coming from the old town. I wasn't wrong. Fighting had broken out between the Greeks and the Turks. It was as if the Turkish and Greek governments had waited to start a war the minute the official mourning period ended.

I ran to the phone and told Jim what I thought I'd heard. Wondering if he knew something I needed to know. Jim confirmed my fears. He assured me that the children and I were ok. The embassy had information as to what was happening and were assured it was under control.

That evening Jim was able to tell me that the gunfire signaled an end of peace talks between Turkey and Greece. The gunshots didn't reoccur for some weeks, nevertheless we remained on alert. No matter what we were doing we had one ear tuned to any sign of gunfire. Fearful the trouble would begin again. We didn't know what to expect. We pretended to go through our days as if they were regular work and school days, but Kennedy's death and its aftermath had changed everything and everyone. Our life in Cyprus was never the same.

~

The first week of December the embassy notified us that our new president, Lyndon Johnson, would be visiting the Island on a diplomatic mission. All State Department and USAID officers were to gather at the embassy to greet President Johnson and his wife, Lady Bird.

The official reception took place inside a large hall in the US Embassy building. The greeting line was arranged according to rank. The Ambassador and wife, the State department officers and diplomatic corps, including the Toners, stood at the head of the line. Jim and I stood amidst other ranking officers of the State Department. We stood, and stood, and stood. Waiting.

My feet hurt, and I was still grieving for Kennedy and not happy that Johnson was taking Kennedy's place. I shifted from one foot to the other, speaking only when someone addressed me. It must have been time for Melinda to have a snack because I felt the milk begin to fill my breast. I was a sad, disappointed, unhappy camper.

A Marine guard finally stepped through the doorway, followed by a couple of men in black suits. Secret service men I assumed. Lyndon Johnson ducked his head in order to enter the room, his tall imposing frame filling the space. He was not a handsome man, but oozed strength and authority. An embassy person accompanying the President called each of us by name. When my name was called Johnson glanced at my forehead and smothered my hand in his huge paw, eyes already moving ahead to the person next to me.

I didn't expect anything different from him. My Dad worked with Sam Rayburn and Lyndon during their Texas politicking. I had heard stories of his infidelity, his power in the congress and his ability to get things done on a national level and, naturally, his conflicts with the Kennedys. Yankees he called them.

I was already cross because we had been told the meeting was late because the plane bringing Johnson and his entourage had to be turned back to Ankara. It seems Johnson's favorite brand of Scotch was not available in Nicosia and the plane had flown back to Turkey in order to get the particular Scotch that Johnson required. I was, in spite of all I had been told about him, impressed that he was taking the time to be seen in US Embassies all over the world.

I turned to see Lady Bird Johnson standing in front of me. She was dressed exactly like the Southern Texas woman that she was. Just like my mom. She wore a pale blue light weight suit that sported an abstract patterned silk blouse of cream and blue. She had a matching blue hat and her left gloved handheld its white partner. She reached out to shake my hand as the embassy guide read out my name. "I'm happy to meet you," she said. "I'm told you are from Lubbock Texas."

Surprise must have shown on my face because she rushed to put me at ease. "How are you doing?" she asked. I found my voice and answered without hesitation, "We are okay." That sounded so lame. I was searching for a respectful response when she asked if it would be alright if she contacted my folks in Lubbock to tell them she had seen me and give them the news that I was ok. I told her I would appreciate that very much.

That moment of human connection imprinted itself on my heart and brain. I had heard about Lady Bird and how she was the power behind her husband's career. President Johnson was not known for his social skills. The more I learned of Lady Bird, the more I realized the rumors were true. She truly did walk behind Johnson and smooth over his gruff mistakes.

I thought nothing of President Johnson's curt greeting after the brief moment with Lady Bird. She did, indeed, follow through with her promise. Several months later I received a letter from my parents saying that a person from Lady Bird's office had called to say she had met me in Cyprus and that my family and I were well.

December arrived and we began planning for Christmas. Jim and I wanted to make this Christmas a special one. It was Melinda's first, and we had been through some rather gloomy months. We broke open boxes of Christmas decorations we had brought from home. The girls had been making Dear Santa lists for weeks. Jim and I read the list and wondered what we could do. The toy requests on the girl's Santa list were not to be found downtown in the British shops. Jim and I began scouring the Sears and Ward's catalogues for items they had asked for. We were lucky to find a few desired items at the Security Station PX.

I have to admit we took creative license with some of the requests. Jenna and Nyna requested roller skates. They were easy to find, but Barbie dolls and clothes were impossible. They would never arrive from the States in time for Christmas. We substituted some weird little troll figures. As it turned out the little figures proved to be a blessing. They were not only easy to pack but provided the same creative imaginative play that the dolls promised.

No matter the country in which we were living, Jim and I managed to keep our family holiday rituals intact. After Thanksgiving, I searched the area for anything resembling an evergreen. Even allowing for 'artistic license,' I found nothing remotely resembling a fir tree. As a last resort I brought home a succulent pencil tree. They were prolific on the island. The pencil tree had fat, three-and four-inch stems. Just long enough and strong enough to hold a glass ornament. We set about decorating its pencil-like branches with lights and Christmas ornaments that had arrived in our shipment from home. At least the plant was green.

It didn't really satisfy me. When I found a fake tree at the PX made of silver foil fashioned into fir-like limbs I snatched it up. In lieu of strings of colored lights, a lamp rotating four different colors was set up in front of the tree and the tree shone like a rainbow as the light caressed its silver branches. Jenna particularly loved the tree and sat cross legged for hours watching the colors dance on the shiny sparkling leaves. We set the fake tree up in the foyer at the top of the stairs next to the beautiful stereo Jim had proudly purchased soon after we arrived in Cyprus.

A week before Christmas Jim called to inform me we were to have guests for Christmas. He stumbled around, which was very unlike him, until he managed to admit that things were becoming more unsettled in Cyprus. The news was a real downer, but I tried to push away speculations as to what it could mean. Before the week was over, orders were issued from the American Embassy declaring American personnel were to be withdrawn from all villages. Americans were recalled to the capitol to wait for the decision as to whether to send them back to their work in the villages or send them home to the US.

Our guests were two young men from the Peace Corp. Both young men had been living and working in villages outside of Nicosia. We explained this unusual Christmas situation to the girls who immediately began practicing their 'hostess roles.' They participated in preparing Nyna's bedroom for the boys. They were concerned about the young men having no Christmas presents under the tree on Christmas morning and got busy with their crayons and craft materials to remedy the situation.

The young Peace Corps men, John and Paul, arrived filled with hope that the armed conflict would soon be resolved and they would be allowed to return to their posts. The men were in their early to mid twenties. Good looking American boys. They expressed disappointment at having been jerked away from the progress they had made in the villages. They talked of their Cypriot friends and the projects they had started. Despite their disappointment, they put on a brave face. They were very polite and dear to the girls. They understood our efforts to create as 'normal' a Christmas as possible and joined in the spirit of planning the day.

Christmas morning arrived and the girls were up early as usual. We cautioned them to be quiet until the young men woke, but that was a near impossible request. Melinda was awake, fussing to nurse and no matter how hard they tried, the girl's whispers were not fooling anyone. The young men didn't keep the family waiting. Wrapping paper soon littered the floor as packages were opened. Paul and John were kind to show surprise and appreciation when presented with the handmade gifts the girls brought from under the tree for them to open. They played with the girls' Christmas toys like a big brother would.

I hesitated when the girls wanted to go outside to try out their new roller skates. I had heard sounds of gunfire echoing up the hill from the old town. Nyna begged, "Just five minutes. Please."

I relented when tall blond John promised to watch after her. It was, after all, an unusual Christmas. I was anxious the whole time they were out under the portico. My body was a knot of nerves when I heard a burst of gunfire coming from down below. Jim spoke to me in a calm voice, "The guns are too far for the bullets to reach our drive." Soon after, Jenna, Nyna, and the young man came back into the house. Nyna proudly announced that the outing was a success. She had learned to roller skate.

The next few weeks the political atmosphere became more complicated. It was obvious that the outbreak of violence between Greece and Turkey was escalating, not waning. The young Peace Corp men received word to return to the US. We bid them a sad goodbye, trying not to think about their departure as an omen. We hadn't yet heard evidence of fighting near our own neighborhood, but it had been unnerving when Turkish fighter planes started flying over the city. Some of our embassy friends tied US flags on top of their flat roofs hoping the Turkish bomber pilots would pass over American homes and do no harm. Others thought it not a good idea to draw attention to American homes. Jim and I talked it over and decided not to post a flag.

That didn't mean we became lulled into thinking nothing had changed. On the contrary, we continued to be hyper-alert. We hunched over the stereo every day to hear any news regarding the conflict in Cyprus. The days dragged on and we became exhausted as we waited to see what would happen next. There was discussion in Washington, D.C. as to whether to close the AID mission in Cyprus or to leave personnel to keep a skeleton crew intact.

I felt the stress as did everyone in the foreign service community. Melinda was nursing and I worried about losing my milk entirely. I jumped anytime a car backfired or a garbage can turned over. Each day my hyper-alert state increased. Melinda's waking in the middle of the night for a feeding didn't help. I was certain the baby could feel my tension.

Sleep became more chaotic. Jim and I had fallen into a half-awake sleep one evening when we both sat straight up in the bed, startled by a loud crash outside our bedroom window. We were simultaneously alert and unsure what to do. I quickly tiptoed across the hall to check on the girls. Jim motioned to me, "Stay quiet and do not turn on the lights."

We felt somewhat safer having our bedrooms on the second floor. I was hoping Melinda would not wake and crept back into bed. A stained burp cloth lay on the carpet next to my pillow and my milk glands reacted. Jim crawled to the window and looked out into the dark yard below. He shook his head indicating no sign of any movement outside. There was no moonlight that night and no streetlights.

We sat side by side in bed, trying to breathe quietly, listening intently for any sound of footsteps or evidence of a home invasion. Any hope of rest dissolved, Jim decided it would be a good idea to put some lights on downstairs. We quietly made our way to the kitchen, brewed coffee and sat at the kitchen table waiting for Melinda's cry for breakfast.

After the sun was up, Jim went outside to see if there were footprints under our window. He discovered our garbage barrel had been overturned and trash scattered across the yard. Dogs probably. My heart slowed down a bit and I relaxed into a bright sunny day.

A few days later, I received a message from Jim's office that some Turkish wives of Cypriot government officials would like to visit me. I was surprised but honored and thrilled. I had been shut at home for weeks, my forays into the old town severely curtailed by the troubles. I let myself hope, for a moment, that their visit could be an indication the conflict was cooling down.

I prepared an afternoon tea and dressed Melinda in a light blue onesie. The two women arrived with small baby gifts and ogled over Melinda. I was truly amazed the wives had come through the streets from the old town up to the Greek section simply to see the baby. It was particularly impressive that they visited despite the uneasy atmosphere laying like a cloud over the city.

The next day I was even more impressed when I was informed bombs had exploded in the old section of town. Thinking back on the ladies' visit that day, I realized that they had dropped hints throughout our visit that the situation in the old city was deteriorating and we might never meet again.

After breakfast the BBC announced that fighting had begun in downtown Nicosia, confirming the escalation of the Greek/Turkish conflict. The roads to the old town were closed. The Turkish Cypriots had taken over the old town and were barricaded there. I remember to this day the gratitude I felt for their show of friendship and kindness in a time of unrest in their city. The brave gesture by my friends marked the first time I felt we had made some progress in bridging the conflicts between political factions on the island. Sadly, I was never to see my Turkish friends again.

Not long after visits from my Turkish friends, the USAID office received instructions to shut down projects across the Island. Jim received a phone call from Director Toner that evening asking him to fly to D.C. and speak to a congressional committee in charge of USAID affairs in the Middle East. Director Toner and Jim were against closing the AID mission completely. They argued that it made sense to keep a skeleton crew for the AID program in place until the international skirmish was over. Joe and Jim made the case that the progress our teams had made in the villages and towns need not be wasted.

Jim was eager to take on the assignment but uncomfortable about leaving me and the girls on the island without him. He came up with a plan. I was not thrilled, but Jim was persuasive. He pressed the importance of his errand and how he would worry if I did not have help. He spoke to a couple from the agriculture department with a proposal. He asked that they move into the house with the children and me while he was away. It would be safer for both of us, he argued.

I first balked at his idea. I didn't know the couple well. I felt as if I would have more work if they moved in. I'd be taking care of the children and elderly guests who were near strangers. I relented in the end. I knew it would make Jim feel more at ease.

The couple was probably in their late sixties at the time, but to my 30-year-old mind, they were old. In reality, they were a healthy, active couple. The wife had lovely streaks of gray in her hair. The man was a little older and loved playing with the girls. They were blown over by Jenna's reading skills and charmed by Nyna's cheery disposition. I think they missed their grandchildren back home.

We settled into a routine, and I was happy to have their company. Less spooky than being alone. The couple helped by playing with the girls, while I continued to take care of the house and prepare meals. Schools had been suspended until the troubles cleared. Just as I'd expected, the couple's presence did very little to ease my workload. I could hardly offer them peanut butter sandwiches or mac and cheese every night.

Soon after they arrived, Nyna came down with a tummy flu. Her frequent trips to the bathroom added more stress to an already stressful situation. I grew more grateful for the couple's helping hands as the days unfolded. I had my hands full holding Nyna's little head over a pot, feeding Melinda, and preparing dinner. I was grateful they were there to keep company with Jenna and Melinda.

Jim had been gone almost two days when I received a call from Becky Toner. The embassy had issued orders for all USAID families to be evacuated from the Island. I was informed that a plane would be waiting the next day to transport the families to Beirut, Lebanon.

Our instructions were brief. Pack a warm blanket for each person, our pillows and eating utensils along with suitable clothes for cold weather. We were told we were being sent to one of the luxury hotels perched in the hills around Beirut, Lebanon. These hotels were fancy summer resorts but not equipped for winter guests. Hence the necessity for blankets. A specific weather report was not included in the evacuation information. It was January 1964 after all, and it was safe to assume the weather would be on the cold side.

The minute I put the phone down I went to the living room to inform my guests of the notice to evacuate. I hadn't expected their immediate reaction. Fear and anxiety were written all over their faces.

The wife began asking me questions to which I had no answers. She wanted to know about how they would get their possessions sent back to the states. She wanted to know if they would be allowed to go straight home to the US and skip Beirut. I was surprised to hear the intensity of concern in her voice. I was young and naive and trusted our government would take care of us, but the older couple was truly frightened.

The next morning, I managed to keep my voice calm and told them I'd decided it would be best if they went home to take care of their affairs. It was obvious they were very concerned about their belongings, and we all needed time to organize our evacuation plans. Those good people made a few lame objections. I expressed my appreciation again and did my best to reassure them that I would be ok. I was certain, I told them, that Jim would be coming home on the next plane. The discussion lasted less than an hour before they packed their overnight bags. I thanked them for their help and the girls and I waved them on their way.

I never saw them again and imagined they caught the first flight available back to the States.

I closed and locked the door and stood in the hallway for a moment. I had mixed feelings. I was alone with the children now. I took several deep breaths, grateful I was no longer responsible for the older couple. That moved my stress level down a peg.

But the fact was, I had a child who was throwing up and I had a nursing baby. Jenna was as helpful as a six-year-old could be. But too young to help make travel decisions. I was overwhelmed with the choices I needed to make. I had to choose clothes for an unknown climate in an unknown destination. A mountain hotel without heat? Away from amenities of any kind? Away from medical services? The instructions from the embassy were to pack bedding and the cooking utensils for each person. How would I manage to carry all of that and three children?

So many questions. What if this evacuation meant walking away from the life we had built in Nicosia? What would happen to the dog we had been fostering for a British couple? We had collected a small number of Cypriot artifacts. Memories of our tour on the Island. I hated having to leave them behind. But taking an extra trunk was not an option.

I didn't have much time to mull over my dilemma before I heard Nyna call for help, again. I was relieved that Jenna was feeling ok and could look after Melinda. It would not be long before the baby would be asking to nurse again. I calmed myself and explained to Jenna that I needed her Big Girl Help. Needed her to watch Melinda while I attended Nyna. Nyna called for more help. That made the decision for me. I had to focus on the children's needs. I couldn't think about the packing dilemma at that moment.

I made a halfhearted attempt at packing clothes for the children before I dropped into bed that night. Exhausted. I lay thinking about what to do and realized that leaving the next day was more than I could handle. Nyna's tummy problem graduated from throwing up to a low-grade fever and diarrhea. I couldn't see putting her onto a plane in that condition. I reasoned with myself that it was safer in our home than taking the risk of a feverish Nyna being ill in a cold hotel room somewhere unknown.

After all, I rationalized, I felt safe. Two weeks ago when the troubles began, my neighbor from across the street had come to me and told me not to worry. She confided that EOKA fighters lived in our neighborhood and patrolled our streets every night. She assured me that they knew I was home alone with children and that they would be guarding us. I believed her.

Jim and I had watched from my darkened bedroom window every night since Christmas and we could see men outside walking in pairs and gathering in small groups on the dark street corners. We were curious as to what the men were about. I had noticed the activity in the street had become more intense. My neighbor had confided that the nightly patrols had been in place all the time we'd lived here. In the beginning the men were careful not to be seen. Since the fighting had broken out in the old town, their surveillance activity was more out in the open. I was safe.

TEN
Stepping Into the Unknown

Reassuring myself of our safety helped me to sleep that night, but it didn't mean I had any idea what was going on. I was given no information as to the level of danger we Americans were facing. I had no idea if this evacuation was considered a temporary assignment. Would we return to Cyprus one day? I made the assumption that our personal belongings would be packed up and sent back to us in the US. But that was only a guess. The phone call I'd received said nothing beyond evacuation instructions.

Rumor had it that USAID personnel were being shipped immediately out of Beirut back to the US. I worried that might be my fate. Would I be sent home after a short stay, alone with the children and separated from Jim? Was this the end of Jim's diplomatic career? Should I pack our home movies and photos of our tour in the Middle East?

So many unknowns. I worried about the kind of medical attention available in the mountain resort. I decided I would need a first aid kit no matter where we were sent. Was Lebanon a good friend of the US or would they want us out of there soon after we arrived? What language was spoken there? What kind of money would I need while we were there? Would there be someone with us who could translate? What kind of food would be available?

Questions and more questions.

The lack of information was bringing me face to face with too many unknowns. I took a deep breath. I had no choice but to stop the 'what ifs' and make a decision.

Early the next morning, I called the AID director, Joe Toner, and explained my dilemma. I made the argument that Nyna was ill and I did not want to take a sick child to some cold hotel in the mountains surrounding Beirut. I added that I wasn't certain it would be a good idea to take a three-month-old baby into such an iffy situation.

Director Toner must have heard the stress in my voice because he wasted no time before speaking to the right person in the embassy who, thankfully, gave permission for me to stay until Jim had returned to Cyprus. I breathed a sigh of relief. For a brief moment I wondered, was this evacuation being used as a political tool rather than a clear and present danger? I dismissed the thought when the sound from an airplane flying low over our house rattled my dishes. I pulled out our suitcases and began packing. Again.

I had only the vaguest idea what we would need for clothing in the cold weather. Nor how long we would be living out of our suitcases. I packed what I did know we would need. I gathered vaccination records and passports and Melinda's birth certificate, my address book, a few children's books and toys. I did not have American money but assumed that I would be given some credit to use until Jim joined us in Beirut. I piled Melinda's baby things into my suitcase. For the first time since Melinda was born, I substituted a package of disposable diapers for the usual cloth. I packed cans of dry baby formula, bottles and nipples. Just in case I had to give her extra feedings.

Even though I was operating in an information vacuum, one thing was clear: I didn't want to be sent back to the States without Jim. I didn't like to admit it, but there was no guarantee I would have any say about where the children and I ended up. But I couldn't waste time thinking about what might happen. I had gained some time by staying another day and set about making lists and packing important items into boxes that I assumed would catch up with us, eventually. I stopped for just a moment the next afternoon and listened as the plane carrying American women and children to Beirut flew over our house. I said a silent goodbye to my friends.

I felt a sharp pang of regret and a nagging feeling of guilt that I was not on the plane with them. I rationalized, once again, my decision to stay behind. What if I'd made the wrong decision? What if something happened and we could not get off the Island before fighting reached us? Joe Toner told me that Jim had been informed of the evacuation and was already on a plane back to Cyprus. I prayed I'd done the right thing. I glanced at the clock. The evacuation plane had left the airport. All second guessing was useless. Jenna, Nyna, Melinda and I were staying put at home in Nicosia.

ELEVEN
Evacuation

That morning as non-essential AID families were being evacuated to Beirut, Jim was in Washington D.C. speaking to a foreign affairs congressional committee. He was making the case as to why it would be best to only pause the AID mission rather than shut it down entirely. Joe Toner and Jim were outraged that the carefully laid groundwork of the past one-and one-half years could be destroyed. They were thinking how the inroads into agriculture, commercial and structural projects would be cut short. Not to mention the waste of the money poured into the projects.

His talk was paused when an aide entered the room. The man apologized and informed Jim that an evacuation order had been issued for diplomatic families living in Cyprus. Jim didn't waste a moment. He made apologies to the Congressional committee, explained the situation and left the room. A government car was ready to rush him to the Washington airport where he boarded a waiting Pan Am plane headed to the Middle East.

Jim's m.o. was to maintain a calm exterior, but he later confessed that he was an anxious wreck on the inside. He sat back in the airplane bound for Beirut, hoping to join us there as soon as possible. His heart sank when the pilot announced that all passengers would be asked to disembark in Rome. The pilot said that the plane had been rerouted to Cyprus to evacuate American personnel.

Jim was frantic to reach Beirut as soon as possible. Searching for another flight to take him to Beirut would mean more wasted time before we could be united. Jim requested permission to stay on the plane. He explained to the airline personnel that he, too, was headed to Cyprus. He was overjoyed by the possibility that he could arrive in Cyprus in time to greet us hello and hug us goodbye at the same time. Unfortunately, even his diplomatic status and his smooth talking couldn't convince the airline to let him stay on the plane. They were firm. Under no circumstances could they permit any passenger to continue on to the Island. Jim was disappointed and frustrated but had no option except to find the next available plane from Rome to Beirut.

After a frantic few hours, Jim procured a seat on a plane bound for Lebanon. He was calmed by the news that the girls and I were being carried away from danger and ensconced safely in Beirut. Jim knew more than I about our final destination. He was informed that families were to be housed in city hotels. No mention of mountain resorts.

On disembarking in Beirut, Jim wasted no time calling the major hotels. He was disappointed. No one had the name 'McGraw' in their registry. He turned to the US Embassy. He was certain the embassy would know the whereabouts of all evacuees. He found his way to the American Embassy and was stunned when he encountered impossibly long lines of weary, stressed people. Americans and Europeans alike were not only seeking information, but anxious to get the important papers necessary to enter other countries. The scene was chaotic and tinged with panic. Jim became more and more worried and decided to track us down on his own. He took possession of a phone booth and spent anxious hours calling government offices and hotels seeking information regarding Cypriot evacuees.

He searched for hours and hours until he found Becky Toner. He was relieved and excited and gave her a big hug. Becky shattered his newfound sense of relief when she broke the news to him. I was not in Beirut. She rushed to explain my decision to stay in Cyprus.

Poor Jim. He was expecting to hug his little girls after his long tiring, anxious flight and it turned out we were not there to hug. He couldn't believe that his family was still in danger. He was frightened.

Anger was easier to deal with than fear and helped to fuel his determination to be on the next plane to Nicosia. His anger continued to build during the short flight, so by the time he arrived at the house, he could hardly contain himself. Tired, angry and rumpled, he didn't bother with hugs or greetings of any kind. The first words out of his mouth were, "Get ready. You are leaving this afternoon." I didn't need a psychic to tell me that he was upset. I didn't argue. Guilt overcame me and I left the room to hide my tears. And to finish packing our bags.

Later that evening he told me about how difficult it had been to find us. I tried to apologize. To tell him how deeply sorry I was to have put him through the trauma of the previous two days. The mood in the room was thick with pent up emotions. I wondered again if I had made the wrong decision.

It had never occurred to me that Jim would fly to Beirut to look for us there. I had been told he was on his way back to Cyprus. My emotions were as raw as his. I saw the pained look on his face. Regret mingled with relief, thankful that my partner and I were together again. The strong woman persona I'd worn in front of the girls vanished.

My tears seemed to touch his heart and we melted into a huge hug. We were relieved to be able to express our feelings and began to wonder aloud as to what might lay ahead of us. We reverted to our usual way of communicating. I told him how ill Nyna had been that night and how reluctant I was to take the children to a cold hotel somewhere in Lebanon. We breathed again, happy to be able to express our feelings. We began to wonder aloud with each other as to what might be ahead of us.

We held each other that night until we could no longer fend off exhaustion. Early the next morning Nyna's temperature was normal, and she had stopped complaining about her tummy. The trip was a 'go.' The suitcases were packed and loaded into the Vauxhall. Jenna and Nyna were in the back seat, no seat belts at that time. Jenna clutched a backpack stuffed with books and Nyna held a plastic bag containing a family of little plastic gnomes. Melinda snuggled in my arms in the front seat.

We set out for the airport. The roads were eerily quiet, no cars in sight. We were only a few blocks from our neighborhood when I sensed a change in the atmosphere. Everything around us was not only quiet, but still. There was no movement. No dogs on the streets. No children playing in the front yards.

Jim drove carefully, taking his time. Trying not to call attention to ourselves. No cars on the road. No cars ahead of us or following us. We pulled onto the main highway and came upon a stream of Cypriot military trucks. The trucks were headed away from the airport and into the city. I held my breath as the soldiers on the trucks glared down at us as they passed.

Jim continued to drive slowly, showing no interest in the soldiers. We relaxed when they didn't pause but drove on down the road.

The drive seemed safe until we reached the Greek monastery. The large building with its warm brown exterior and blue painted door and window frames was one of my favorite structures in Nicosia. A cross over the front door marked its purpose. It was a beautiful old building with green lawns and well tended flower gardens. That morning the monastery brought me no comfort. The peaceful exterior had morphed overnight into a menacing threat. Every window facing the street was filled with an armed soldier holding a gun out the window. Pointed at the road. I didn't say anything because I didn't want to frighten the girls, but I glanced over to the driver's seat to see if Jim had seen what I had seen. He gave a small nod as he drove ahead looking neither left nor right.

I glanced in the mirror above my seat, looking to see if the girls had seen the armed soldiers. Nyna and Jenna seemed not to have noticed the guns pointed down at us. Though they were quiet, no doubt sensing tension in the car. We had talked with them about a new adventure coming up, and it had not occurred to them that the adventure might be a frightening one.

My mind turned to our poor parents and how worried they must be. The news of the conflict and the evacuation of Embassy personnel had been broadcast around the world. Jim reminded me that the American Embassy had sent telegrams to our parents assuring them of our safety. Jim planned to follow up with phone calls to the States as soon he was certain we were safely in Beirut.

We boarded the Pan Am plane. The girls pressed their faces against the window and waved down to Jim standing on the tarmac below. We were saying a temporary goodbye to Jim and, sadly, a final goodbye to Cyprus. Jim would stay in Nicosia. He had the difficult job of closing the AID mission. In his time off he would supervise the packing of our household goods. I checked to make sure the girls were properly strapped into their seats for the short flight to Beirut.

I was engulfed with a strange empty feeling. This must be how it feels to be homeless.

TWELVE
Beirut

The flight from Cyprus lasted about two hours.

Culture shock hit when we entered the airport. The brightly lit, shiny halls in Beirut were decidedly different from the plain walls in Nicosia airport. The passageways were crowded with people from all over the world. It could have been a convention hall at the UN. Businessmen in western suits and ties, Arabs with turbans and flowing robes, Asian workers dressed in brown loose garments.

I would have liked to stop and take in all the different sights, but I spotted a driver holding a sign high above the crowd with 'MCGRAW' written in large letters. The Embassy rep guided us through the security line and we were escorted to a waiting car. I was impressed when the driver helped me settle the girls into their seats. A welcomed act of kindness in a foreign country. The driver gave a nod of approval when Jenna asked to ride in the front seat. I settled in the back with Nyna and baby Melinda. Our belongings were loaded into the trunk of the van and we were taken to the American Hotel.

It didn't take long to settle in. Circumstances required we make do with a couple of suitcases for each of us and an inexpensive folding baby stroller we had picked up at the PX. These were to be our only possessions for the duration of our visit. It seemed strange. One night we were in our fully equipped comfortable home, and the next morning, we were refugees stepping into a strange new world. I tried to reassure the girls, and I suppose myself as well, that we were arriving in Beirut for an exciting new adventure. I told myself we were simply writing another chapter of our story.

Beirut in 1964 was one of the most beautiful cities I have ever seen. The buildings were modeled in the style of European capitals with accents of eastern architecture. It was obvious why Beirut was known as the Paris of the East. Our rooms in the modern, seaside hotel were spacious and inviting. The children couldn't wait to see what was beyond the balcony off the living room. I gave them permission to go on the balcony to check out the view. They came running back into the room, excited. They were both talking at once. They wanted to go for a walk that very minute. The promenade that ran along a shining Mediterranean Sea was inviting us all. They pulled me to the windows so that I could see what they saw.

They were right. The scene outside our room was stunningly beautiful. Just past the green lawn and walking path, we could see a collage of smooth large rocks scattered along a sandy beach. The rocks were a perfect size for climbing.

The hotel room was furnished in an up-to-date Western style. It was comfortable and familiar. The children ran from room to room exploring the space. Shortly after our arrival, the middle-aged hotel owner and his wife presented themselves at our door to welcome us to the hotel. The American couple was gracious and kind and offered their assistance if ever I needed it. What a relief. I went on to explain, "Melinda is only three months old and I am unsure how a change of water will affect her digestion. I need to ask a favor. I need to boil water for the girls, and to have a way to boil the bottles and nipples for the baby. What do you suggest?"

I could hardly believe my ears when I was granted full permission to go down to the hotel kitchen and use the facilities there. I breathed a sigh of relief. Their kindness overwhelmed me for a moment, and I choked over my words of appreciation. Throughout our stay in Beirut, the hoteliers were generous and helpful. I was saddened to hear that the hotel was destroyed in a war some years later.

By the time I arrived in Beirut, Becky Toner and all AID wives had been shipped to parts unknown. It was somewhat unsettling when I realized I could be the lone AID evacuee remaining in Beirut. I would never learn if that was the case or not. The first weeks my focus was on the children. I didn't have time to miss adult conversation. Once a week phone chats with Jim and the paperback adventures of Miss Marple and Hercule Poirot kept me sane.

I gradually came to grips with the reality that our stay in Beirut would not be a short one. I grew weary of the isolation, and I began to explore the hotel for a solution. I discovered that a ritual was held every evening. A large patio overlooking the sea was set up with tables, chairs and umbrellas, and an intriguing buffet filled with exotic middle eastern fare. Mezze': meaning small dishes. Plates of goat cheese, bowls of hummus, olives, eggplant and grape leaves, served with warm slices of pita bread. The beautifully appointed table aglow with candlelight was a far cry from the trolley table delivered to the room each day. I felt like a real adult as I sat tasting a plate of the offerings enhanced by a cold gin and tonic with a slice of lime.

This quiet time alone was the one restoring moment of each day. On particularly trying days, I felt guilty when I found myself checking my watch more frequently than usual. Wishing mezze time would hurry and arrive.

All in all, I managed okay. I missed Jim terribly, but I had the children. That didn't mean I had any idea what to do with the three of them in a hotel room for a long period of time, but I settled the girls into their room as best I could. Melinda slept in a crib next to me. Each day I was faced with time to fill. Each day the children and I created something to fill the hours.

I lay awake at night with the same questions popping up in my mind. How long would we be in Beirut? In the hotel? If or when would Jim be able to join us?

Like all the evacuated families, I had been offered tickets to return to the US to wait there for our husbands to join us. I declined. I wanted to stay close to Jim. For one thing, I had no urge to travel miles back to the States with three small children. I would wait. That was my decision and my choice.

The time passed more quickly after Jim and I arranged weekly telephone calls. The children and I were eager for him to visit Beirut and we began to make a plan. The 'Daddy' calls were the highlight of our week. Jim's life was not a bunch of cherries. No easier than mine. He, too, was lonely and missed being with us. He wanted to hear every detail about the girls. What they were doing and saying.

Jim's daytime job kept him occupied. He was busy shredding documents and filing reports at the AID offices in Nicosia. The nights when he stood duty along with other officers guarding the Embassy were lonelier. There were spurts of gunshots in the city from time to time. The situation remained tense. One night an intruder was able to get close to the Embassy building and set off a small explosive device. Jim was not wounded and there was little damage to the building, but it was frighten-ing. He didn't tell me about this incident until we were safely reunited in Turkey.

By the third week, I understood that the Cypriot USAID mission was, indeed, shutting down. I found the courage to take advantage of our situation and began to explore our host country of Lebanon. I grilled the hotel personnel as to activities children could do or see. Where was Google when I needed it? I was fast coming to the end of my efforts to keep Jenna and Nyna interested in indoor activities.

Melinda was easy. She ate and slept and laughed with her sisters. Thankfully, we all loved playing with the baby. The first few weeks, Jenna and Nyna made playhouses for the little squatty, stringy haired gnomes. They went on scavenger hunts to collect items to create a world for their gnomes. They used toilet paper to make clothes for the trolls, menu cards to create furniture. Any found object became a decorative item for their troll houses. Within a month, fascination with the trolls began to wear thin.

My American hosts provided me with some valuable resources. Small steps first, I gathered the courage to venture out of the apartment with the girls. Once a day I dressed the children and took them out for a walk. Melinda in the stroller and Jenna and Nyna walking ahead of us, we walked the beautiful promenade that lined the space between the Sea and hotel lawn. One day the girls suddenly stepped off the path to do somersaults on the grassy lawn in front of our hotel. The girls loved their 'backyard' and couldn't wait to show it to Jim when he came to visit. They didn't have to wait long. Jim announced his plans to visit Beirut the first of the month.

Each outing, I ventured farther away from the hotel and deeper into the city. I learned that Beirut, while it was a Middle Eastern city, was similar to the West in some respects. There were wide streets, beau-tiful shops and architecture, a combination of western and eastern de-signs. I agreed with those who had named Beirut the 'Paris of the East.'

The streets were crowded with men wearing white robes and headdresses called kaffiyeh, white scarves wrapped many times around their heads and tied down with a black cord. I explored farther along the path to the center of the city until, at last, I felt comfortable enough to ask our American hosts for the name of a guide and driver.

A whole world opened up to us once we had transportation. Our driver/guide—he said to call him John—was a real godsend. I bought travel brochures and local history books and learned about the ancient and famous sites close to the city. We took a tour down the coast of Lebanon to the ancient villages of Tyre and Sidon. These were places I'd read about in the Bible since I was a child. Years later I felt horror and sadness as I watched on television as many ancient historical monuments being destroyed by ruthless ISIS rebels.

The streets in the city were crowded with cars and the occasional man-propelled bicycle taxi. Every car seemed longer than the next as limousines vied with small European cars for parking space. Many extremely wealthy Arab men visited the shops with veiled women walking a few steps behind. People dressed in flowing robes, their white head scarfs held in place by black braided rope, rushed from shop to shop. Women in flowing silk caftans and faces covered by scarves were drawn to windows decorated with precious jewels. Eastern women never wore costume jewelry. Only gold and silver and precious stones would do. Famous brand names found in New York, Paris and Rome lined the streets of Beirut.

The big difference between shopping in Paris of the East and Paris of the West was the number of gold shops tucked in between. I became aware of another important difference as I toured the town; a man would occasionally stop and stare openly at a woman. I was a young woman with two small children and pushing a baby in a stroller. I thought I was safe, however, there were times I felt uncomfortable when walking on the busy street. When I got that weird feeling, I ducked my head and turned my attention to the girls. I mentioned the experience to the hotel manager's wife one day and she reminded me that Arab men thought a woman who did not cover her face when out in public was a loose woman of ill repute.

One day after an unusually long jaunt, I answered a knock on the door of our hotel room. A middle-aged Arab man was standing at attention. He was in full white robes with the traditional white scarf and black braided rope on his head. He had a full beard and alert dark brown eyes. I assumed he had made a mistake and knocked on the wrong door. He bowed slightly, then in broken English, he introduced himself. Mohammad ben... I didn't pay much attention to the name. He said something to me in broken English. I couldn't understand. I assumed that he had made a mistake and motioned to a door down the hall. He shook his head and kept talking and pointing to the gold rings on his fingers. He managed to find the words to tell me that he had many riches to offer and would like me to come with him to join his other wives. I caught on to what he wanted from me and couldn't hide my shock. The expression on my face conveyed my answer in no uncertain terms. The poor man backed up and hastily retreated down the hallway.

It hadn't occurred to me that a man would follow a thirty-year-old woman, with a child in each hand, to her home. The incident was a heads up. From that moment I was more aware than ever that I was in a strange land that I knew too little about. I had more questions. What had I done to make him think that I wanted to join his harem? Had I been on the wrong street? Had I worn something that made the man think I was for sale?

I never went out on the streets again without a scarf large enough to cover my head and part of my face and my chest when in public.

~

My friends at the hotel gave me the name of an agency that specialized in caring for the children of diplomats. The owner of the agency spoke impeccable English. She was a trained nurse. I agonized over the thought of leaving four-month-old Melinda in her care but with her safely in a crib, warm and fed, I could take the girls to see the countryside and the learn about historic places around the city. I needed the history lessons to exercise my brain. I had become intrigued with the country of Lebanon. I was woefully uneducated about the Middle East and more and more curious to learn about our temporary home.

Not to mention that I was running out of ideas that would keep the girls occupied while living in a two-bedroom hotel suite.

The first time I left Melinda to stay at the agency, I was nervous every minute we were away. I had booked her for a two-hour stay but couldn't wait that long. I was not able to focus on our history lesson that day. All I could think about was Melinda. And all of the 'what-ifs'. What if she missed us? What if something happened that she didn't understand? What if someone took her, or importantly, what if no one paid attention to her and she was scared or in pain?

I conjured up all the 'what-ifs' I could possibly think of until I couldn't bear it another minute. I called a halt to our outing. Jenna and Nyna were disappointed but didn't complain. The driver returned us to the nursery. We found baby Melinda safe, laughing and waving her arms, kicking her legs in joy as a young Lebanese attendant made funny noises over her crib.

Melinda became famous in the nursery. The head of the agency told us stories about how everyone in the place adored the baby girl with red hair and a ready smile. I was cautious about the specific hours I would leave the baby. I purposely kept our destination a secret from the nursery staff in case there might be a plot to kidnap her. Still, I grew to trust the staff and consider the agency reliable. Convinced that Melinda was in a safe and happy place, I planned sightseeing adventures for Jenna, Nyna and me. Beirut was within driving distance to many wonders of the world. Each venture out into the wider world, I became more comfortable about leaving Melinda with her caregivers. With our tried-and-true John at the wheel, Jenna, Nyna and I visited ancient structures and heard about the myths that they represented. The ancient ruins and monuments were not Disneyland, but they relieved us of hotel boredom.

John, the driver, and I grew to know each other. He had children of his own. He listened to our story about the troubles in Cyprus and how we missed being a family. As we became more relaxed with each other, John began to tease the girls. I could see him stifle a chuckle as he listened to their exuberant chatter. It was obvious he liked Jenna and Nyna and could see how much they missed their father. One day he pretended there was an urgent errand he must attend to. He asked permission to go out of the way to a particular shop. I thought it was more likely a kiosk belonging to a cousin. He went into a small shop and we could see him speaking to a man behind the counter. He returned to the car with a container of sweet brown dates for each of the girls.

Every trip after that, John would pretend he had an urgent stop to make. He would enter a kiosk and return with cardboard cones filled with nuts, or candied fruits. I was convinced he smuggled an extra sweet to them when I was not looking. I caught him at it once, and gave him a 'no, no' look. He simply ducked his head, gave a sly smile and a wink in the direction of the girls.

I was not really angry. We were all happy to be out of the hotel room. For me, the outings were a godsend. One of the few activities I had to keep me from going brain dead.

The weeks plodded on with Jim across the sea, alone and in danger. He was always on my mind. Evenings after the children were asleep Jim and I visited over the phone and encouraged each other to 'hang in there.' We didn't have much news to share. Jim was either uninformed about what was going on with the conflict, or didn't choose to talk about it over the phone. We tried to be optimistic, shoring each other up when one of us was down. The primary question of 'when' was always on our minds but unspoken out loud. The question lurked in the background of all our evening chats.

When. When will we be together again? Week after week, the answer was the same. We wait.

Jim didn't complain about being asked to stay behind to guard the embassy. But I could hear by the tone of his voice that he was lonely. Director Toner had already shipped out to join Becky in the States. All but a few AID personnel had been sent home or reassigned to other countries. We supposed Jim was asked to remain to help protect the Embassy because of his Naval Security clearance.

Every morning, the girls and I looked at the calendar and counted the number of days that had passed since we had seen their father. I pointed out that January 1, New Year's Day, was an important holiday in the States. I taught them about the special days in February. George Washington's birthday and Valentine's Day. They liked the idea of Valentine's Day and pulled out paper and crayons to make cards for Jim. That special day came and went in Beirut without notice. Until one day in early March, the doorbell rang. I opened the door to our suite and was presented with two identical packages. One addressed to Jenna and one to Nyna. I had a surreal moment when I noticed that the packages had come from a department store in Lubbock, Texas.

Jim was as surprised as any of us when he discovered he could send Valentine gifts to his little girls from Texas to the Middle East. Clearly he had no access to children's gifts while being stuck in a foreign city under siege. He was feeling extra sad when he came upon the idea of contacting someone in the States. Long distance telephone calls alone cost a small fortune on our low-level government salary, but to Jim, it was worth the price. He made a call to Hemphill Wells, our favorite department store in Lubbock. He was directed to a store shopper who was happy to find gifts for Jenna and Nyna.

He explained the situation and his dilemma to the unknown West Texas woman who, in her broad Texas accent, was eager to help. He almost choked up as he described the five-and-seven-year-old girls and told her how brave they were. He explained how they were living away from him in a foreign country while he was in another, guarding the American Embassy. The response was gracious and immediate. The buyer at Hemphill Wells assured Jim they had the perfect gifts. "Not to worry," she said, "we will take care of it. And thank you for representing America abroad." A rare acknowledgement by the public at home.

The girls grabbed at the parcels, tearing at the wrapping helter skelter. They hadn't had a new surprise to open since Christmas. Inside the boxes they found a small red case with a brass clasp on the front. It was fun to hear them oh and ah when they lifted the lid of the box. Each red case was fitted out with pretend makeup. Lipstick, rouge, and face cream. Everything a girl needs to compliment her wardrobe. What a joy! Jenna and Nyna spent hours pretending they were grown-up ladies using the items from the small red cases.

That evening I told Jim the surprise had arrived and how happy the girls were. The next day, they made thank you cards from the wrapping paper to send to him. Jim couldn't believe his idea had paid off. He was genuinely astonished at the quick and gracious response from Hemphill Wells.

He told me the story more than once about calling the department store and explaining our predicament. To a perfect stranger. He never ceased to be amazed at the thoughtful service he received from a small, family-owned department store in a West Texas town. Jim and I had attended Texas Tech University in the city and had first met there, but we had never considered Lubbock our home. We had often wondered if people at home cared about the world outside their own states.

My parents sent us a copy of the human-interest story in the Lubbock Chronicle telling how Hemphill Wells had taken part in making children of a 'hometown diplomat' happy.

Jenna and Nyna were as excited as I to chat with their Dad when he called. We never knew when the call might come. They wanted to tell him about what they had seen and about how the driver had tricked me once again. How John had become good at sneaking them yummy treats.

Jim and I planned and fantasized about getting some time together. Soon, he would say. Soon.

And then one day the doorbell rang and there he stood, suitcases in hand. The girls jumped into his arms, hugs and kisses galore. They pulled him over to Melinda's crib to show him how big she had grown. Jim pointed to one of the suitcases and explained it was for them. I had asked him to bring some clothes more suited to warmer weather, as Lebanon was beginning to feel more spring-like. Jim had included some books and toys. Becoming reacquainted with old belongings was, as before, like having another Christmas. The girls pounced onto their suitcase, screaming in delight at the things he had chosen to bring. Happiness filled the room.

Jim lowered his voice and asked me how the girls were getting along with each other. Jenna was seven and half, Nyna five. I can't remember any fighting or arguing during that time. There were, quite naturally, disagreements now and then. I told him that most of the disagreements were over whose turn it was to order dinner for the day. But those disagreements didn't last long.

The reunion was memorable. We hadn't been together for a month. That evening, Jim and I sat talking, trying to fill in the blanks of our time away from each other. The girls became absorbed in the new toys and Jim took me into his arms. I hadn't realized how uptight I had been until I felt the tension seep away. I simply hadn't let myself dwell on the danger Jim was facing while in Cyprus. I had tried to brush away scary thoughts as best I could. I had my hands full with the children. No use worrying about something over which I had no control. My motto remained steady through any discomfort I experienced: 'Do the best you can with the equipment you've got.' That was my focus.

When at last the girls were fed and calmed down, I introduced Jim to my evening ritual of mezze' on the veranda. Every evening that I was alone I had fantasized having Jim join me on the beautiful balcony overlooking the blue Mediterranean Sea. That fantasy had sustained me throughout the long evenings without an adult in my life. I was thrilled that my fantasy had finally come true. I could at last introduce Jim to the mouthwatering wonders of mezze'.

Small bites of baklava, flaky paper-thin dough filled with pistachios and soaked in syrup, finished our evening treat. I was embarrassed to confess to Jim, but this evening ritual was responsible for my weight gain. It wasn't just the baby fat. He made some comment about having more of me to hug and we ate our fill that evening.

We were as starved for conversation as for good food. We fell over each other in an effort to catch up with our adventures. Jim described what it was like to take his turn and sit at the Embassy at night with only a few Marine guards for company. I asked for news of our

Cypriot friends. What did he know about Kormakitis? Did he know what had happened to Ellen? So many unanswered questions.

We had two weeks to be together. Jim suggested the possibility of a trip to the Holy Land. I was hesitant because, while we could take the older girls, it meant leaving Melinda at the childcare agency for several days. Jim pointed out that this was a unique opportunity. We were so close and would probably never get the chance again.

After wrestling with the pros and cons, we decided that the licensed, embassy-endorsed agency had proven to be safe. We were to be away for only two nights and three days. Our American friends at the hotel had agreed to check on the baby every day.

THIRTEEN
Trip to the Holy Land

Jim arranged for a small public van to take us from Beirut through Jordan to the Holy Land. The car looked as if it could be an exhibit in an antique auto museum. Or the local dump. There were four Arab men travelling in the van. We were the only English-speaking passengers on board.

The hotel had packed a small picnic for us which was fortunate as the other passengers were clearly also prepared for 'luncheon-on-the-go.' Every hour or so the aroma of fresh bread, olives and stinky cheese from a passenger's lunch bundle wafted through the small van. Several hours into the journey, the van stopped at a small hut and the other passengers disembarked. Minutes later, our family was travelling a bumpy road through miles of desert.

There was nothing to see for miles around except sand dunes. And more sand dunes. The winds had picked up the sand and fashioned it into an ocean of rolling waves. The four of us had our noses to the windows next to our seats when Jim nudged us.

"There." He pointed to a scene outside the van to a cluster of dark objects standing out against the yellow sand. He whispered, "Those are Bedouin tents in the distance."

I squinted through the glass and could make out several camels and what looked like goats tethered to a cluster of black tents. Jenna and Nyna were excited. "Are they real?" Nyna wanted to know.

Jim put his finger to his lips to caution her to lower her voice. We didn't know if we might offend the driver. "Yes," he said. "They are nomads. Tribal people. They live in the Saraha desert all their lives."

The girls looked at each other and rolled their eyes. A desert life did not seem appealing to them.

The tent sightings were rare. We saw plenty of sand. Miles and miles of desert sand baking in the hot sun. Seemingly forever. Only once did we encounter more Bedouins. A caravan of tribal people appeared on the horizon. A line of camels swayed back and forth carrying large loads on their backs. We watched a parade of horses and camels and brightly clad riders until they were only dots against the horizon.

Our bus ride was tiring and beginning to test the girls patience. We did our best to distract ourselves by playing games but it did not take long before the games we played became as boring as the sand. You can only play 'I Spy' for so long when the inside view was limited and the outside was a big sandpile. One and then the other, Jenna or Nyna would ask how much longer it would be before we arrived.

We had traveled for several hours when the bus finally came to a halt. I looked at Jim wondering what was happening. We seemed to have stopped in the middle of the desert. The girls and I strained to see something besides sand from our bus windows when the driver of the van, who obviously did not speak English, motioned for us to exit the bus.

I was instantly on alert. Was it possible we were about to be robbed by rogue Bedouins? Perhaps the Bedouin encampment we spotted a short time back had caught up with us. We remained glued to our seats until Jim went to the door of the bus and stepped outside to talk to the driver. He nodded and the girls and I followed him to the exit door.

We stepped out. As suspected, we were not alone. To our surprise and the girl's delight, men with horses and donkeys appeared. A man in striped robes stepped over to Jim and had a short conversation. The girls and I were perplexed when Jim put money into the man's hand. The Arab man nodded to the donkey drivers. Jim spoke to the children and me and said that we were about to make a short detour.

It was hot under the desert sun and I hoped whatever Jim was planning, it included lemonade. Jim assured me that it was a good thing to be doing. That helped me feel a little better though I was still baffled as to where the animals had come from. There was no building in sight. There was no watering place that I could see. There were no cars or buses. It seemed to me that the donkeys and men had just magically materialized. It was spooky, but Jim assured me I would be happy with the detour.

The donkey handlers motioned to us and directed Jenna and Nyna to the smallest animals. Jim and I were mounted onto horses as the girls were helped onto blankets that had been piled atop the donkey's backs. I felt the skinny backbone of my horse poking into my behind. I was hoping Jim was right and this would be fun because I was fairly certain I would be sore tomorrow. I checked the girls to see if they were ok and both grinned a yes. Each had their own donkey driver holding the reins of their ride. The head man raised his hand and signaled forward.

We were about to enter the ancient city of Petra.

Jim rode in front and Nyna followed, sitting proudly on her own donkey, very pleased to be treated as grown up as Jenna. Jenna sat atop the red and blue striped blankets on the donkey's back as if she rode a donkey every day of her life. I brought up the end.

We moved, swaying and bumping, toward a towering wall of red rock. We arrived at a place so narrow that I could almost touch the walls on each side of me. I had another twinge of doubt as to what we had bargained for. We turned a bend in the rock and stopped. The scene ahead of us was astounding. Unbelievable. A building had suddenly come into view. The building was nothing like we had even seen before. It was as if an ancient skyscraper had been carved into a wall of a mountain.

The Red Rose City of Jordan grew out of a mountain of pink rock. I could imagine travelers down the ages being as much in awe as I.

The city has since been designated as one of the Seven Wonders of the World. And what a wonder it is! Towering buildings with pillars, and stairways leading to wide doors tall enough for camels to pass through, had been carved into the red rocks up and down a wide thoroughfare.

It was said that the Nabataeans were great traders and anyone traveling through the desert to the sea had to go through the narrow streets of Petra. The luxury trade was therefore controlled by the ancient city. The enormous, magnificent structures were not built in front of the rock but have been carved into the rock. Bedouin tents were said to have been clustered around the entrance of the narrow rock pathway into the city in the old days.

Aside from the men holding the reins of our mounts, we were alone in the ancient city that day. The huge facades were ours to explore. Today, busloads of tourists make their way across the desert to visit the site. I understand that the Bedouins run camels alongside the donkeys and the entryway is clogged with beggars and souvenir salesmen camping around the entrance to ply their wares.

The sight of the ancient three-story buildings carved into red rock made us forget the heat. We were tiny shadows looking up at the fantastic structures. The experience was so out of this world, we forgot to think about the discomfort of our bumpy, donkey rides.

And the sight of Nyna and Jenna running from structure to structure and climbing the steps to the magnificent carvings that decorated the entrances was an Alice in Wonderland moment. They waved back at us, proud to have made it to the top. Jim and I stood in awe of the ancient city, curious to know how the carvings could have survived throughout time.

It was close to noon when we settled our tired bums into a hired car Jim had arranged for the next part of our journey. On our way to Jerusalem we disembarked for a brief stop at the Dead Sea. We sat under a small tree and I changed the girls into bathing suits. Jim took them into the cool water to show them how the waters were so salty that a swimmer would not sink. I was happy to sit under a shade tree and spread a towel to set out the picnic our hotel in Beirut had prepared for our journey.

We made our way to a small inn in Damascus where we spent the night. The day had been filled with fantastic surprises and fairytale images. We welcomed the cool shade of the garden outside our room. The next morning the car picked us up and we continued on our journey to Jerusalem.

So many of the sights we encountered on the way were unusual and fascinating. We visited Jericho where we ogled at women carrying large pottery water bottles on their heads. We stopped at the Jordan River at a site said to be the place John the Baptist was to have been baptized by his cousin, Jesus of Nazareth. It was nearly Easter and the hillsides around Jerusalem were covered with wild anemone. I thrilled at the splendor of the colorful hillsides. My mind went to my last meeting with the dear little man back in Nicosia who had brought those beautiful bouquets to my door each Friday.

We arrived in Jerusalem by mid-morning. The narrow streets of the Old Town were already filled with crowds of people. Women with scarves on their heads, their arms filled with bags of fruits and vegetables were shoulder to shoulder with venders peddling their goods. Religious clergy of all beliefs were identifiable by their colorful attire. Some wore special head gear and heavy gold crosses around their necks. Muslim believers were recognizable by the dark spots on their foreheads. Calluses formed from years of touching their foreheads to the earth in prayer. I imagined a group of young men dressed in blue suits with matching striped ties to be Baptist ministers from southern US. It was shocking when we realized there were no men dressed in black suits and wide brimmed black hats and sporting long black beards in the sea of pedestrians. Jews were relegated to a small section of Jerusalem at the time.

Jim and I held tightly to the girl's hands so that we didn't misplace them. We pointed and waved left and right identifying places and streets we recognized from Bible readings. Hardly believing we were actually walking the same streets from the ancient stories of our youth.

Jim told the girls the story of the Street Called Straight. He spoke to the girls of the history they were seeing while I was distracted. Jittery. I was dividing my attention between Jim's narrative and keeping the girls in sight. It seemed it would be way too easy to lose one in the crowded pathways.

We entered cathedrals said to contain sacred artifacts taken from Jesus' life. We stood in line to visit places marked as sacred sites.

One place was said to be the exact spot where Jesus was buried. Flowers, fresh and plastic, were placed along the walls of the cave like space. Black robed men guarded the spot marking the grave. Tourists from every part of the world crowded into the small dank place. Pungent incense was so dense my eyes watered. Religious artifacts from many different religions were placed around the cave. I felt extremely deflated. Religion had taken over the natural places I had imagined the Holy land to be. Protestant upbringing had not prepared me for the religious trappings that filled the shrines.

We hired a car to take us to Bethlehem, the place where Jesus was born. A robed priest directed us down into a dark, small cavern and we stood in line waiting as people prayed for a moment then moved on. That small dark cavern was filled with candles and incense, and statues of Mary with the baby.

Most places we visited were more like a movie set than a place where people would live a day-to-day life. I continued to be put off by the whole Jerusalem scene until we were leaving Jerusalem's inner city. After the long day of touring the streets of Jerusalem, we made our way back to a small Inn outside the Old City. We enjoyed a dinner of lamb stew, rice, pita bread and hummus before settling into our cool, quiet rooms.

The next morning we made an early start. We wanted to be ahead of the tourist crowds. Jim spoke to our driver and soon we were making our way around the Old City to the Mount of Olives. I took in the sights as we passed the beautiful domed churches and mosques that dotted the hillside. We reached the top of the hill overlooking the city. The driver guided us to the entrance of a path leading to the Garden of Gethsemane. Jim and the girls walked ahead, Nyna skipping happily in the lead.

I followed at a more measured pace, taking in the colors of the dusty green leaves of the ancient olive trees. I came to a small grove where a tree with a thick gnarled trunk was highlighted by a ray of sunshine breaking through the overhanging branches. I had a strange moment of déjà vu. An image of robed people sleeping on the red earth under the olive trees in the grove was so vivid I took a step back. There was no doubt that I was standing on the same ground where Jesus had walked and prayed. My chest clutched and I was surprised to feel a tear running down my cheek.

We were able to visit only one part of the Holy City. To arrive at the other part would have meant abandoning baby Melinda. Jerusalem was a divided city in 1964. Across an invisible line was the country of Israel. To cross into Israel from Jordan meant having our passports stamped. Lebanon did not recognize Israel at the time and we would have been unable to return to Beirut where Melinda was staying in the nursery.

I was eager to return to my baby. I couldn't get back to Lebanon fast enough. My mind was focused on Melinda. My arms ached to hold her. While I was grateful to have had the opportunity to be in the Holy Land, I was relieved when we boarded a plane taking us to Beirut and baby Melinda.

FOURTEEN
Ankara

Four months after we left our home in Nicosia, Jim received his new assignment. He spoke to me over the phone with instructions about leaving Beirut. I was to pack our bags and be ready for the girls and me to be taken to the plane bound for Ankara, Turkey. On leaving the hotel room, the girls and I went through what had become our ritual. We walked from room to room in our hotel apartment saying goodbye to each one. And we repeated our goodbyes as we looked out of the windows of the plane, waving farewell to the beautiful beaches of the Paris of the Middle East.

Jim met us at the airport and took us directly to an apartment that the State Department had rented for us. The apartment was located on a busy city street that looked quite like a street in New York. The apartment was nothing fancy. Adequately furnished with nondescript government furniture.

The day after we arrived, I opened the small travel bag and arranged our candle holders, and placemats onto the dining table. Another country, another ritual 'hello' to mark a new home.

A secretary at the embassy had hired a cleaning woman to help us once a week. She was an older woman, gentle with me and with the girls. She always kept a scarf on her head and though she spoke little English, she had no difficulty understanding our needs. I always felt a bit sad because I didn't know enough Turkish to learn about her life. She was a real jewel. Without her I could never have found the right place to buy fresh food. I was relieved to find that she was willing to stay with the children when Jim and I needed to be out in the evening.

Turkey was a very different experience than Cyprus, Beirut or Syria for that matter. We were in a whole different environment. Ankara, the capital of Turkey, was very like many Western cities. It had paved streets and tall buildings housing offices and apartments. It was our first introduction to a Muslim country, and we soon became accustomed to the sound of the Imam praying from the tower of a nearby mosque. A tradition practiced by Muslims for centuries. Ankara was an interesting mixture of West and East.

We were happy to settle into the apartment and did what we were able to do to create a 'normal' life. The girls were enrolled into the American school as quickly as possible. No school uniforms were required. The girls were able to attend school in their own clothes for the first time.

The American military school experience highlighted the glaring differences between the British schools they were accustomed to and the American way of educating children. Jenna was so far ahead in reading and writing that the teacher asked her to read to the class a couple of days a week. We were told this served the purpose of giving the understaffed teachers a short coffee break.

Jim went to the office at the American Embassy every day. It was not clear to me what his role entailed. I, on the other hand, was back to being the homemaker, cook, and grocery shopper. I was within walking distance of a fresh food market. The markets in our neighborhood were outdoors under tents. Fruits, vegetables, vats of olives in oil and water, dates, dark brown and some slightly green varieties I hadn't seen before. Mangos piled high forming golden towers of sweet perfume. There were exotic vegetables and fruits I didn't recognize, and some that I did. We were fortunate to have fresh green beans in abundance. One of our family's favorite dishes became the Frenched beans with onion and tomato which our housecleaner taught me to prepare.

I didn't try to learn the Turkish language. I learned a few words out of necessity but was again grateful to have conversations simply by using pantomime and sign language.

~

In Turkey we added to our growing list of rare and amazing sights. One evening a colleague of Jim's invited the two of us to a nightclub downtown. The place was packed with men. The few women diners that I could see in the dimly lighted room were dressed in beautiful silk saris similar to those worn by women I met in India. I was fascinated by the tall willowy men in white suits, some wearing white scarves for a headdress. Others wore suits that could have been seen in the streets of any Western nation. I enjoyed watching the people at the tables placed around the small center stage.

My delicious meal of lamb and vegetables was left half eaten when a couple of drum and cymbal players took to the stage along with men carrying a variety of stringed instruments. The music began and a spotlight highlighted a belly dancer. She was dressed in a fuchsia silk skirt and a matching bolero. The skirt rode low on her hips and her flat stomach had a gem attached. Brass beads rimmed the long-flared skirt and jingled to music with her every move.

There is something mesmerizing about the traditional belly dance. The music began and a woman's beautiful thin body gyrated from one unattainable position to another. I spent a moment trying to analyze her moves. How anyone could possibly get their hips to move like she did I'd never know. The constant hypnotic beat mirroring the bumps and grinds of the dance captured every ounce of my attention. The meal was quickly forgotten.

My curiosity about differences between cultures was, fortunately, shared by Jim. We immersed ourselves in as many sights and cultural experiences as we possibly could with the time we were given. In keeping with our pledge to educate the girls about the people and different cultures in the world, we ventured out into the countryside whenever possible. We were thrilled that Jenna and Nyna took interest when we visited a new place.

On our first weekend out to the countryside, we were driving through a small village when I shouted to Jim, "Slow down."

Poor Jim. He was so startled he almost ran off the road. "What in the world is that huge bird circling that roof?" I wondered. Jim pulled off the road and we all looked back at a brown stucco house with black trim.

On top of the house, next to the chimney, was a huge nest. The nest of a stork. The nest was about six feet in diameter and stood around ten feet atop the roof of a house. And it was substantial. Comfy and roomy enough for a mamma stork and babies. Our lesson of the day? Turkey is an ideal place for storks to have their babies. The birds fly to Turkey to lay their eggs every spring reminding the Turkish people of new birth. We made our way through the countryside that day counting the number of stork nests on our way.

The highlight of our tour in Turkey was a trip to Istanbul. A classmate of Jim's from Columbia School of International Affairs was very gracious and brave to have us in Istanbul for a visit. Tom Buchanan was a bachelor Foreign Service Officer stationed in Istanbul. He was young to be in such an important post.

We arrived in Istanbul and Tom treated us to a geography lesson and patiently explained to the children that they were to visit a special place. He took us to see the Dardanelles Straits. He made the Straits, said to separate Europe from Asia, seem very mysterious when he promised the girls they would see the water dance.

He promised there was another treat to Jenna and Nyna when we landed on the Island.

We boarded a ferry for a short ride across the Bosporus to the Island of Batucada. Known as the big island. Batucada was a restful paradise after the honking and rushing of city noises. No cars were allowed on the Island. We were all delighted when we stepped into a horse drawn carriage. The ride took us past elegant homes surrounded by lush green lawns and mounds of red bougainvillea. We stopped at an outdoor cafe to have lunch and Tom's promise of a treat arrived. It was a special mango ice cream made from mangos that could only be found on the Island. My treat was a tour of the beautiful gardens in full bloom.

Back in the Istanbul, we visited the spectacular Blue Mosque. Our necks ached from looking up at the spectacular mosaic ceiling. Nyna went round and round until she got too dizzy to stand. We toured museums from the pre-Ataturk (prior to 1923 and the creation of the Turkish Republic) era. It was the most exotic city I'd ever seen. The city was crammed with beautiful, impressive mosques with tall walls and ceilings covered with intricate mosaic patterns. Those stunning art and architectural works were on display everywhere we looked. Exotic art and exotic foods.

Eastern and western tastes co-mingled in the fancy restaurants. There were shops that reminded me of the posh streets of Beirut. Those shops were for window shopping only on our budget.

Then, a special treat for me. Tom introduced us to the Grand Market. That was a market dreams were made of. Miles of alleyways filled with shining brass and copper pots and pitchers, etched platters and kiosks filled with semi-precious jewelry. Hand woven carpets and fabrics from all over the middle east were on display. Antique items, or at least they were touted to be old, were set out on tables to be examined.

I pleaded with Jim and Tom for more time than we had allotted for shopping in the huge, wood-covered, dark market. I'm not a particularly enthusiastic shopper, but I was enthralled by this place and it was one time that I remember totally turning the girl's care over to Jim. I didn't want to multitask at that moment. I could see how easy it would be for the girls to become disoriented in the crunch of people. I needed time to purchase gifts for family back home.

The goods on display did not have price tags. A shopper was expected to bargain for each item. I had grown accustomed to doing business in this way in other countries, but here in Turkey, it was an art form. I haggled and discussed and walked away and returned as I bought pots and platters of the copper and brass. They were so very organic, and earthy somehow. I realized their golden, warm patina said a lot about my taste in beauty.

I could have stayed in that Turkish bazaar for days. To me it deserved to be declared one of the great wonders of the world. The Grand Bazaar covered miles, well, acres of space. The rows and rows of brass and copper trays and fancy urns and ornaments gave way to glass boxes filled with gold jewelry and exotic stones in all sorts of settings. There were shelves of brightly colored silk laced with gold threads. Another stall contained a mixture of spices and herbs and the aroma of burned sugar filled the cavernous hallways.

Jim gently reminded me that I had to pay to mail all the purchases home and I had to agree I hadn't thought of that little item. But it was when he reminded me that I would someday be polishing the brass pots without help, that I left the arena peacefully. Fascinated as I was with the Turkish world, I was also aware of our impending travel back to the US for home leave and the organization that would be required.

Back in Ankara, I turned my attention to making the all-important 'To Do' lists. It was time to organize the trip back to the states. I stared and stared at the page and finally, I had to admit that my mind was empty. I was weary. Six months of living out of suitcases was beginning to get to me. My pen paused way too long over the paper. I was stuck.

One evening as Jim and I settled in for adult time, I was feeling more discouraged than usual.

"Do you realize," I challenged, "poor Jenna won't have a birthday party again this year?" I was almost in tears. Jim reached out and pulled me into a hug.

"I know," he said. "We will think of something." I snuggled in. It was such a relief to be together again. A reminder that I no longer had to solve problems alone.

"I may have an idea," he said. I took his comment to mean progress.

I focused on gathering our belongings to pack into trunks. A few days passed and I was beginning to wonder if Jim did indeed have an idea for Jenna's birthday when he came home from work at the AID Mission and presented me with a white envelope. He had such an impish look on his face I knew there was something important inside. I tore at the envelope and found tickets for travel on the Orient Express. What a great idea and what a lovely surprise.

I was happy to let the list-making go until another day. Jim had booked us on a train, not just any train, but the famous Orient Express. We would take the train from Ankara to Istanbul! I planted a happy kiss on Jim and ran to tell the girls the news.

That evening I had no problem making plans for Jenna's special day. First on my list was birthday cupcakes. I wondered if candles would be allowed on the train then remembered there would be smoking allowed somewhere on the train. Cupcakes would surely be ok. I added a box of birthday candles to the list. Jim and I had already ticked off number two on the list. Her special birthday gift; a grown-up camera of her own. It would be a family-only birthday party but it was sure to be a memorable one.

I giggled with excitement as we waited to board the Orient Express. The scene was right out of a movie. The Express was not the newest of trains. Its age was its attraction. The brass fittings were polished and shining brightly against the black exterior of the cars. The windows were shockingly void of fingerprints. I didn't understand how that could be. A testament to the care given by the workers I assumed. The multiple tracks were filled with trains bound for mysterious ports unknown. Foreign languages blared over a system announcing the arrivals and departures to cities across Asia and Europe. People of different nationalities were rushing to and fro along the corridors to the trains. A porter directed us to our small compartment and we hurried to settle in.

The compartment, though a bit worn looking around the edges, was clean and elegant. The walnut paneling along the walls had been polished to a shine. The benches were wooden with thin cushions covered in a worn fabric. The compartment was closed off from the aisle by etched glass doors. We settled into place and I leaned back against the hard seat.

It was easy for me to imagine Christie's characters occupying the compartment across the aisle. Poirot was probably next-door busy grooming his fancy mustache and keeping an eye out for any hanky-panky that might need attention. And Jane Marple was definitely sitting in the dining car having afternoon tea with a well-dressed retired Raj from some mysterious country. The train was a relic, a bit run down and not as elegant as in the movies, but for me, the Orient Express taking us from Ankara to Istanbul was perfect.

We had a two-day layover in Istanbul waiting for the plane that would take us to Europe. Jim knew I was intrigued by the mystery and exotic atmosphere of Istanbul. He surprised me on our layover night by taking me for dinner at a restaurant rumored to be a gathering place for international spies.

We arrived at the dining room and I sat sipping a dry martini, taking in the luxurious decor. The floors were strewn with vintage oriental carpets. Plush red velvet covered couches and stuffed chairs were placed in groups around tables set for four. Heavy curtains framed the tall windows and paintings of famous rulers looked down on the room. The room was filled with elegant, comfortable, old-world furnishings.

The restaurant's signature bowl of Russian borscht did not disappoint. As we ate, I looked around at diners sitting at nearby tables and wondered which of our fellow diners were the spies. The middle-aged man with a thin mustache on his upper lip and a British haircut, sitting alone with his Pimm's cup? The old man with the eye patch and the young wife? Or mistress? Who would know the difference? All my Agatha Christie instincts came to the fore and I inwardly hugged myself in disbelief that I was actually living a real-life Agatha Christie moment. A night on the town in Istanbul was a wonderful beginning of our journey back to the states.

FIFTEEN
Home Leave

A travel book touting a fun trip through Europe on five dollars a day was all the rage that year. Jim and I poured over the pages time and again. We counted our assets and in spite of the average government salary, we decided we had the means to take a week and make the 'Grand Tour.'

Jenna lobbied for a trip to Denmark. She had read about Tivoli Gardens. In her own persuasive way she explained that Tivoli was the only place in Europe she truly and dearly wished to go. She has always been clear about her desires. No other place would do. Our first stop, Copenhagen. We booked into a low-cost hotel with just enough room for the four of us. Melinda was snug in the bottom of a beautifully crafted chest carved out of local wood.

We were pleased to discover that Tivoli Gardens was as thrilling as Jenna had dreamed. We arrived late afternoon at the park and as soon as the afternoon light faded, the park came alive with beautifully colored lights. There were booths of tasty sweets to eat and fun games to play. There were rides upon which Jim, fortunately, enjoyed accompanying the girls. I was happy to stay with Melinda and the stroller.

The children were happy and tired and ready to crawl into the fresh sheets when we returned to the hotel. Jim and I went to the dining room for a quiet supper. The waitress arrived and Jim ordered glasses of wine for us. The woman straightened her back, and peered at us through thick black rimmed glasses. "Monsieur," she huffed. "This is a Temperance hotel. We do not serve alcohol on these premises."

Jim and I struggled to hold in a giggle. Jim managed to get the words out to apologize and asked for water. After the waitress left our table we looked around at the other diners. It was true. There were no glasses of wine on the tables. We had unknowingly booked ourselves into a non-alcohol hotel.

We had not paid attention to the temperance part of the hotel but we had made great efforts to choose something affordable, within walking distance of a local bakery. Copenhagen was the best! Soon after Melinda woke for her morning sip, Jim dressed and walked a block down the street to buy freshly made buns, milk and coffee. By the time Jenna and Nyna roused, we had a morning picnic set out on a small table.

The day was packed with stories by Hans Christian Anderson and trips to places around the town that honored his memory. Jenna and Nyna recognized the statue of the Little Mermaid from their bedtime story books. Seeing the statue in person was a fun surprise.

We took a boat ride on the central canal and made note of the outdoor cafes as we passed by. Sidewalks were lined with buffet tables laden with beautiful open-faced sandwiches. Dark and white breads were spread with rich yellow butter and decorated with fish and cucumbers and small salty pickled vegetables. We walked the streets in search of lunch items the girls might enjoy. We passed row after row of the open-faced sandwiches. They were on display everywhere we looked.

Jenna and Nyna practically gagged. The strange looking fish morsels decorating the sandwiches looked 'weird,' according to them. They were hoping for a big bowl of mac and cheese, or a peanut butter sandwich at least. We hadn't thought about the fact that their daily diet for the past three years had been scarce in fish dishes.

We had been surprised that there were no fresh fish to be had in Cyprus. Legally. When we voiced our surprise and disappointment, we were told that the government had put a stop to the fishing industry, in large part because local fishermen had begun using underwater explosives to reap larger catches.

The girls did not go hungry in Copenhagen. The breads and pastries, and a large variety of cheeses, were more than enough to keep their tummies from growling. And the milk was rich and filling. The pastries were like having Christmas every day. There was more than enough to suit their palates.

Next stop, the Netherlands. The weather was cool and a little damp. We were enthralled with all there was to see in the city of Amsterdam. We boarded a fancy tourists boat and glided by rows of beautiful, immaculate homes painted soft pastel colors.

We hired a car for a drive through the countryside. Surprised when we turned a corner in the road and caught our first glimpse of tulips. Acres and acres of tulips. All colors, red, yellow, orange, pink, were on exhibit as we passed. I could have driven around the tulip fields until there was no more light in the sky, but that was not the children's idea of fun. It was only when they spotted one of the tall, graceful windmills that dotted the countryside, that Jenna and Nyna began to pay attention. Their noses pushed onto the window glass as they ogled and pointed at the huge blades.

Nyna, true to form, asked if we could go up in one of the structures. Jenna, ever the big sister, explained in her school marm manner, the danger of such a wacky idea. Jim and I grinned at each other. It was such a joy to be together and privy to our children growing up.

Jenna broke off her 'education of little sister' role when she spotted a sign of a shoemaker's shop. She didn't have to read Dutch to know the shop sold shoes. There was a large, bright yellow shoe carved out of wood hanging by a chain in front of the store.

We peeked into the shop window and marveled at the sight of shelves filled with brightly painted wooden shoes. Shiny red, yellow, and blue shoes. Some had tulips painted on the toe and some were plain with no decoration at all. Jenna and Nyna jumped up and down. They sat to be fitted for wooden shoes. They had a great time clomping up and down the store, trying to walk in the wooden shoes. Melinda watched from her stroller with a serious expression on her face. Probably thinking her sisters had gone nuts. But then, she had that expression on her face a lot.

We left the shop, new shoes in hand. That night in the hotel room they practiced walking in their new shoes as we read the story of "The Boy and the Dyke." Being a tourist was tiring, and the girls were asleep before the story was finished.

It was hard to contain my excitement as I thought about showing baby Melinda to our parents for the first time. I had visions of happy Jenna and Nyna basking in the loving attention of their grandparents. I was ready to board the next plane out of London but we had promised Jenna one more treat before we headed home.

Jenna had dreamed of watching the changing of the guards at Buckingham Palace ever since she had heard of Christopher Robin and Pooh. She was so excited the morning after we arrived in London, she could not stop singing the Pooh song over and over: "They're changing the guard at Buckingham Palace."

She was driving us all crazy. After a short breakfast of scones and marmalade, we took a taxi to join the small group of tourists who were gathering in front of the Buckingham Palace gates.

The morning was a bit damp and chilly but Jenna and Nyna didn't seem to mind. They stared at the guards standing in front of the golden gates that separated the castle grounds from the outside world. The guards looked splendid in their bright red uniforms and beehive black fur hats. Very regal.

We had explained before we arrived at the castle that the guards were not allowed to talk to visitors. It was still somewhat unsettling when the guards didn't move an eyebrow, but stood still as if they were statues. Jenna whispered that she wanted to try and make the guard smile. She walked a few steps closer to the guard, looked up at him and stuck her tongue out. She waited for his response. Nothing. She shrugged and returned to stand beside us. Exactly on the hour, new soldiers marched in to take their places. After the changing of the guards was done, we walked down the boulevard to the park, words of the song reverberating in our minds.

Sunday morning was our last day in Europe. We dressed in our best Sunday attire and made our way to visit a small Anglican church that was located on the outskirts of London. The church looked exactly like most Anglican churches we had seen in other parts of the world. Built with stones carved from the land it sat upon.

The building was surrounded by a beautiful lawn and rows of well tended flowerbeds. I stood taking in the view, entranced by the bucolic scene, thrilled that we could see past the church walls all the way to the banks of the Thames River.

Inside, its dark beams and white walls reflected the decor of every other Anglican church we had visited. Well oiled but uncomfortable wooden pews showed a slight dip where hundreds of bottoms had made a shallow bowl in the wood. They had obviously been sat upon for eons.

I tucked a blanket around baby Melinda, reluctant to cover her Sunday attire. I had dressed her in little white tights and a pink dress that Jim's mother had sent her. The girls once again had donned their best dresses, white tights and black patent Mary Jane shoes. I was reminded that Jenna's arms were sticking farther out of her sleeves and Nyna's coat was beginning to resemble a short jacket.

We settled into the back pews, about to give the Priest in Charge a huge surprise. The girls were trying not to giggle at the thought of participating in such a surprise. I winked at them, and shushed them, joining in on the joke. I turned my attention to the window across from our pews and watched, mesmerized, as men in sculls rowed in rhythm, a dance that moved them swiftly down the Thames.

The organ music began, and a small choir made their way down the aisle to their seats flanking the altar. Our Anglican priest friend from Nicosia, Rev. Farrah, brought up the procession. He reached the front of the altar and turned, then broke into a huge grin. He had spotted us. Nyna was so pleased she waved. He opened the service with a welcome to his friends from Cyprus.

After services, he told us he was so shocked by our unexpected appearance that he almost forgot what his sermon was about. He had to close his eyes and take a second look to make sure we were truly there in person.

I soaked up the unique feeling of reuniting with good friends miles away from home. It was as if we had become a more integrated part of a larger world. As if all the unique and strange experiences of the past three years had been leading straight to this moment of belonging. That moment of connecting with friends from a different country, and with whom we had shared a piece of history for a time, brought another dimension to my life's experience.

We spent the last night in London with another of Jim's friends from Columbia University. The couple had two small boys and lived in a typical British flat with no central heating. I could hardly wait to get out of their uncomfortable place. London was damp and cold and I was yearning for a taste of hot, dry, Texas weather.

We arrived in New York City in June 1965, and stayed a few nights with Jim's cousin, Peggy and Mike Piemonte. Nyna was not herself but she didn't dare complain because we were scheduled to take her and Jenna to the World's Fair. It was being held in New York that year. I wasn't fooled and saw the sore throat she was trying to ignore. The cold flat in London didn't help to cure Nyna's sore throat but neither was it the cause. It turned out that Nyna had to have a tonsillectomy. At that moment in New York, we were all sad that Nyna would miss the day trip to the World's Fair but happy that Jim's cousin made such good spaghetti as a treat for the girls. We were thankful for Peggy's help and proceeded to take Jenna to the Fair.

Our flight from New York to Lubbock gave me a chance to reflect on the past three years.

Jenna and Nyna had grown in so many ways. I watched as they settled themselves into adjoining seats on the plane and reached for the buckle. They were pros at this flying business now. Nyna no longer had to run up and down the aisle and Jenna looked out at the runway to watch the take-off. No hurry to bury her head in a book. We had left the states as a family of four. Now we were five. Eight-month-old Melinda snuggled sleepily in my lap.

I felt sad for the loss of friends and people and jobs left behind. So many unsaid goodbyes stuffed down inside myself. I hated that the troubles interfered with our AID work in the Cypriot villages. I hoped that, in spite of our abrupt departure, we had been able to make some small differences in the amount of time we had there.

I was more convinced than ever that a life lived only for the sake of feeling good did not make a life. Only through serving others could meaning be found. We would never know what effect we had on that country or as individuals on the people we went abroad to serve. But there is no question as to the effect that service had on us as a family, and as individuals. We had discovered a larger world than we ever dreamed, and awakened to a new identity as 'world citizens.'

I was eager to arrive back in Texas. Eager to show friends and family our beautiful grown-up daughters and red-haired baby, Melinda. I was fully aware that we would be in an uncomfortable limbo kind of space until our next overseas assignment. Another two months of not knowing.

I didn't have much time to dwell on the limbo part. Home leave was a whirlwind of visits.

The first week back in Lubbock, Jim set about arranging a cookout for his college friends. We were pleased when so many of his best friends from Texas Tech came to welcome us back. Or we assumed they would welcome us back.

We arranged card tables and chairs on the back lawn under my parent's pecan trees. We served Texas sized hamburgers from the grill and settled back to fill in the gaps from when we said our last goodbyes three years ago. Two of Jim's closest friends who were present that evening had been groomsmen in our wedding. They greeted us warmly but as the evening wore on, Jim and I realized we didn't feel quite the warm welcome home we'd expected. Our friends politely asked a few questions about Jim's work and our lives overseas then turned the conversation to the latest football scores.

We asked about their lives and about their families. We found their lives hadn't changed a lot. We heard the same woes about the West Texas drought and the same complaints about the "wetbacks" (as they called the undocumented workers) as before. Their focus, like ours, was on creating family and career. Our connections were bound only by time.

Jet lagged, I realized I had dropped in and out of the conversation. No worries. Our Texas friends' conversations hadn't changed since we last met. I was relieved when they finally departed. Jim and I sat for another few minutes, not saying a word, just listening to the crickets calling to each other in the dark.

Jim took a deep breath and turned to me with sadness in his eyes. Those friends with whom Jim had discussed philosophy, politics, religion, and careers had continued their lives. Had become more conservative. Less open to events outside their hometowns, uninterested in people or cultures outside their local bailiwick.

Jim linked my arm into his as we made our way inside. The quality of our friendships had changed, leaving us with feelings of profound loss.

~

The first week in Lubbock passed quickly. Our next stop was a trip to Middlesboro, Kentucky to visit with Jim's sister, Mona, and family. Jenna and Nyna were thrilled to spend time with children their own age. They were old enough now to understand a cousin was different from a friend. And much to their surprise, they had cousins! They were practically giddy with excitement.

There were five children to play with. Melinda and Robbie were just beginning to walk. They stared at each other for a bit, then played around each other. Nyna and Katie played with the toys Katie brought for Nyna to share. Jenna and Mark mostly ignored each other. Mark remained focused on his mother. Kim, Mona's oldest, spent some time trying to keep track of the six mobile children, then gave up and went to her room to read.

The first few days were a blur. So many things to become used to. The weather was hot and dry. The milk was creamy and sweet. Not an ocean or a lake in sight. Lawn sprinklers began their swooshing songs in the middle of the night. Jet lag created havoc with sleep habits. There were no strangers in the home, only parents and grandparents. There was always something kids liked to do.

As soon as the girls had learned to be on USA time, my Dad took Jenna and Nyna out to a farm where he went to ride horses. Maybe it was his way of teaching them about their Texas heritage, or maybe for making memories with their seldom seen grandfather. Whatever it was, he found great joy in teaching them to love horses.

I went along to watch and stood by the paddock with Melinda in my arms. Dad settled Jenna into a saddle and showed her how to hold the reins. He walked alongside the horse around the paddock a couple of times.

Melinda leaned back onto my chest and watched. Fascinated by the horses. I was less relaxed and tried to deal with the twinge of anxiety lurking around my gut. Horses were big and unpredictable, though I knew they were safe when my Dad was in charge. I rode horses throughout my childhood, but still, watching my small children was different. My anxious twinges only went away after both girls had their feet on the ground.

Dad lifted Jenna from the top of the horse and she ran to us, grinning from ear to ear. "That was fun!" She begged, "Can I go again, please, please?"

I told her it was Nyna's turn and she had to wait. A pout began to show on her face, but was immediately erased when my Dad reached over the fence and lifted Nyna onto the horse. Nyna took the reins as Dad instructed and looked over with a proud smile as the horse walked calmly around the paddock. The first riding lesson with their grandfather, Papa, cemented their lifelong love of horses.

We were eager to visit Jim's parents in Midland, Texas. We drove into the driveway of the little white house in Midland and Mama Mac came out to greet us. She was all smiles. Her thin white hair pulled back into a bun and her blue eyes a little moist behind her rimless glasses, Ruth was the very image of the warm, snuggly grandmother depicted in children's books. Jenna and Nyna piled out of the backseat of the car and ran into her arms. Jim and I choked back a tear and waited until Ruth could free herself from little arms. Her face melted into a smile as she moved to get a better look at baby Melinda.

The dusty backyard, the mosquitoes, nothing could overshadow the fond memories of the visits to Mama and Papa Mac's.

Jim's dad sat in his reclining chair and joked with the girls. A bowl of hard candy sat on the coffee table in front of him. Both girls looked at me for permission to take a piece. I shook my head, explaining to Ruth that we didn't like the girls to eat sweets. I reached to remove the candy from the table when Mama Mac stopped me. "No," she said. "I only have my grandchildren for a short time. I am their grandmother and I will give them candy when they visit our house."

I was literally speechless. Ruth had never before objected to anything I had done. Or said. I backed away from the candy bowl and nodded ok. She was right. The bowl of candy on Ruth's table was a special treat at their Grandparent's house in Midland.

Visits at Mama and Papa Mac's house were even more fun because Midland had Dennis the Menace Park. The park was exactly the kind of place we had wished for when we took the girls to Larnaca in Cyprus. There were swings that were quiet, merry-go-rounds that didn't wobble, and slides that were slippery. And a bonus. A fountain had been set into the ground. When a child got close enough, water would spray high into the air.

On hot sunny days, the girls could visit the fountain spout between sweaty playground rides. They took joy in pretending they 'accidentally' got their clothes wet. Jim and I knew the wet clothes were no accident. We pretended we were unhappy with the soggy clothes. We put on a fake frown. Jenna and Nyna laughed at our faces. They weren't fooled.

Interspersed with horseback rides, visits with relatives, trips to the dentist and pediatricians and trips to the shoe store, Nyna had to undergo a tonsillectomy.

She was a little brave six-year-old when we told her of the operation. She tried not to cry and we tried to make the news easier by telling her she could have all the ice cream she could eat. She came through the operation without any trouble until the first bite of vanilla ice cream reached her sore throat. She was full of disgust with Jim and me. She exclaimed in a voice that could be heard in the next ward that we had tricked her by giving her the wrong ice cream. Nyna recovered and we prepared for our home leave to come to an end.

It was morning and Jim and I were sitting at the kitchen table in

Lubbock, discussing the possibilities of our next move. Jim had received two intriguing job offers.

We turned first to the Paris, France post report. Paris was an obvious choice. The idea of the girls growing up in Paris seemed too good to be true. I had studied French in college and was itching to try my skills. I could almost taste the warm croissants I would have with my coffee every morning.

Paris was not a third world country by any means. The post report either did not make the job clear, or Jim downplayed important points. Some of the Embassy women I'd met in Ankara had alluded to the idea that France was 'spy central' in Europe. I wondered if that was a decision-making factor for having USAID officers posted there.

The second option on the table was Dacca, East Pakistan. We began to read the post report. A few minutes in, we were shaking with laughter. It wasn't long before we were struggling to stay in our seats. The report was divided into questions and answers. "Do you like to drive?" And then the answer: "It is possible to have a car in East Pakistan but colliding with a cow or a person drawn rickshaw could result in being attacked physically by local bystanders." "Do you play golf?" The answers continued, "There are golf courses. It is advisable to bring a large supply of golf balls as birds frequently catch the balls before they reach the ground."

The post report also gave a brief history of the creation of East Pakistan. The country was originally a province in India called Bengal. In 1947 The British partitioned Bengal into East and West Pakistan. The two regions were formed because the Muslim populations were concentrated into those two regions. There was ongoing religious tension between Hindu and Muslim populations. (East Pakistan became the nation of Bangladesh in 1971 when it won independence from Pakistan.)

The report went on to explain that East Pakistan is a tropical country with land level with the sea. Every year the fields flooded with water killing the rice crops. The result was an annual famine throughout the country. It seemed everything listed in the post report was a bad joke. The big question? Why would anyone in the world want to serve in Dacca, East Pakistan. As far as quality of life in East Pakistan, the report had little to recommend it.

Jim and I mulled over the report and thought over and again about the pros and cons of taking our children to the Middle East. We discussed our motivation for accepting another post. Jim had a multitude of job options. Another tour overseas was only one of them. We sweated over the decision for several weeks.

Jim took his career trajectory into consideration. He explained that as a junior officer in Paris, he would most likely be relegated to the roll of coffee boy. In Pakistan, he would be a part of the agency's policy making team.

I was torn, pinching myself at the thought of living in Paris, practicing my French, and exploring other European countries on long weekends. On the other hand, I was intrigued with the Middle East. The mysterious cultures and religions, the ancient civilizations.

In the end there was no toss up.

The deciding factor for Jim was how best he could serve and make a difference in the country of choice. It was clear to me that Jim would be happier, more fulfilled, and rise in the Foreign Service ranks if we chose Dacca. In the end, Pakistan provided us with the best opportunity in which we could contribute. A way to make lives better. That was the bottom line for both of us, the deciding factor.

The biggest immediate drawback was the vaccinations we faced in order to travel to the new region. We renewed our regular vaccines and added yellow fever, cholera, and several others painful exotic deterrents. Home leave came to an end. Shopping was done for the girls, we had endured the vaccinations, and had packed the quinine pills we needed to protect ourselves from cholera. We made our way for the second time to Rome and flight connections to the Middle East.

SIXTEEN
East Pakistan

Our arrival in Pakistan brought with it an immediate transformation in the way we experienced ourselves in the world.

We stepped off the plane and into the airport terminal and stopped. We were brought to a standstill at the sight of so many people. The terminal was packed with people. Shoulder to shoulder with people. People dressed in white, collarless tunics worn over flowing trousers. We learned to call them lunges. Some wore matching white turban-like scarves around their heads. A few women in bright jewel-colored saris, their black hair pulled tight against their head mingled with the crowd. Most women were covered head to toe in black gowns with only a small slit where their eyes were supposed to be. Burkas. Children and men of all ages dressed in tunics and blousy white trousers.

Our little family intuitively moved closer together forming a pale white blot in a sea of brown. We were easy to pick out in the crowd. The presence of so many people would take some getting used to.

We hesitated, unclear what our next move was to be when Jim spotted an embassy driver standing at the back of the crowd holding a sign marked McGraw. Jim grabbed a carry-on bag in one hand and Nyna in another. I held Jenna's hand and pushed Melinda in her small folding stroller and we headed in the direction of our driver. Curious faces turned toward us as they moved aside to make room for us to pass.

Our driver whisked us through the security lines with ease. Adherence to the caste system was enfolding right in front of us that morning. It was clear from the beginning that white European-looking people were given a very different treatment than most of the folks around us. I felt embarrassed and tried not to look at the crowd of people left waiting in line.

The drive into town was a visual testament to the veracity of the post report. The day was sunny and moist. A grey-green moss covered the concrete buildings that bordered the road. Even new buildings wore patches of green. Buildings were packed close together, making use of every bit of land available. Narrow alleyways emptied teeming crowds of people onto the busy thoroughfare. The main road through town was paved and our car vied with pedestrians and rickshaws drawn by men riding bicycles. The rickshaws were open on both sides and covered with a fringed canopy. Most were decorated along the sides with bright colored paint and shiny patterns of stars and moons cut from tin cans.

As we were driven through town, bright colored tropical plants caught my eye. Mounds of red bougainvillea vines spilled over compound walls and large trees sporting red fuzzy blossoms shaped like bottle brushes provided shade along the street. Smaller trees sporting yellow tulip like blooms, and purple jacaranda trees lined the street between buildings. A whiff of white jasmine broke through, now and then, adding a sweet flavor to the smell of the damp moss-covered exteriors of the buildings.

Somewhere along the way a strong, pungent aroma of curry came through the open windows of the car, tickling our pallets and making us all hungry. One of the girls asked if we had eaten lunch yet.

The post report described East Pakistan, "Excluding its river area, East Pakistan has a total area of 51,921 sq. miles and an average population density of 979 persons to the square mile. This density is considerably greater in areas such as Dadd, Comila, and Noakhali."

The report describes the people, "It is said that the Bengali is truly a child of his country: dark moods of fatalism, philosophic resignation, and fear of the unknown, are as deep and erasable as jungle shadows, while his self expression in song, dance, and art and religious festivity are as naturally quicksilver as the sunbeams that spark the paddle-ruffled waters about his boat."

"Dacca, the capital city, is situated on the Buhri Ganges River, near the confluence of the Brahmaputra and the Ganges. The surrounding area is low lying delta lands with an altitude of only a few feet above sea level. The climate is semi-tropical with most rainfall occurring during the monsoon season." We had arrived at a place where the people were poets and Scotch was cheaper than water.

East Pakistan was basically a farming community growing rice and jute. Rice was their main food source and jute their largest export.

USAID averaged around 92 families in Bengal at the writing of the report. Other Americans employed by the government worked at the Consulate General. Around 70 Peace Corps employees were scattered in the surrounding villages, and American Foundations such as Ford Foundation, Christian Missions, and Fulbright Foundation created another 200 Americans in-country. Jim was joining a much larger, more established AID mission than he had worked in before and our family was becoming a part of a larger community than before.

We had been informed that a fully equipped house was awaiting us. If for any reason we were not pleased with it, we were free to find another place. What a joy! I was tired and unashamedly relieved as our car drove up to a gate opening into a fenced compound. On the left was a lovely white house enclosed in a well-kept compound.

On the right side of our compound, the scene was strange. There was not another compound. Instead a straw hut with a tin roof was set back from the road. In front of the hut sat a group of bare breasted men dressed in long skirts with scarves on their heads. The men squatted under umbrellas wielding mallets above their heads and beating yellow-colored bricks into pulp. We were mystified until we were told there were no rock formations in East Pakistan. Crushed mud bricks were broken into pieces and sold for gravel. The gravel was used in the construction of houses. The sound of hammers against concrete blocks was a daily constant for the whole time we lived in Dacca.

Servants had been hired and were lined up along the driveway to greet us. First in line was Lucy, the ayah. Lucy was a Christian and therefore did not have to cover herself in a burka. She had smooth brown skin, dark brown eyes, and black hair pulled tightly into a neat bun at the back of her neck. She looked lovely in a blue sari and had brown sandals on her feet. She may have been fifty years old. Not more. It was hard to tell but I did spot a few gray hairs mingling with the black ones around her temples.

Akbar was the head bearer and stood next to Lucy. He was slight of build, not much taller than I. He had wavy, black hair and sported a thin mustache across his upper lip. His main helper was Mohammad. Mohammad was thin, also, but taller, clean shaven. He was shy and I suspect he did not know much English. Both Akbar and Muhammad were Muslim.

The fourth in line was a young Hindu man, Maudun. Maudun smiled from ear to ear when he spotted the girls. He radiated happiness with every smile. His hair curled slightly around his face and his dusky skin was smooth and clean. Maudun was the sweeper and the only Hindu in the household.

The Buddhist cook was not introduced with the rest of the household. We were to meet him later.

I had objected when I'd been informed we would be hiring servants. I made it clear that I didn't want to use servants, but I was quickly and firmly informed that we had no choice. If we didn't hire the staff we would be cheating large families out of their livelihood.

It took some adjusting to feel comfortable having people as our constant companions in our personal lives. I soon appreciated the luxury of free time they provided me. I admit to a certain twinge of guilt as I went about playing with Melinda and the girls while the sweeper and cleaner, the gardener and ayah and cook took over tasks that were usually mine. I was not clear exactly how to act at first. I felt at a loss as to what role I was to play in the household, if I had one. I soon learned I did indeed have a role.

My role was that of manager. Every morning I met with the head bearer to discuss menus, to plan dinner parties, or explore garden ideas. I planned table place settings and recipes and seating arrangements for the many dinner and cocktail affairs we hosted. My primary job was to keep the head bearer informed as to our family schedules so that the staff was fully prepared for the events of the day.

Living in a fishbowl made us all clumsy at first. The loss of privacy was uncomfortable for what seemed a very long time until bit by bit we relaxed and grew to be ourselves. We gradually learned to leave our public personas at the door when we came home from our busy days.

I was wary in the beginning of having strange men going about their daily chores when the girls were home. I was alert for any suggestion that the men paid too much attention to my sweet girls. I checked with Jenna and Nyna to ask if they felt ok with having the men around. They didn't seem bothered one bit. I had no worries in regard to ten-month-old Melinda. She moved to ayah Lucy's open arms and snuggled. It was love at almost first sight.

All the staff had been well trained in their roles and my worries fell away as I observed that they set clear boundaries. Each day was carefully organized into a household routine. Everyone had a job to do and each person knew their job. The work was done like clockwork.

Every morning I met with the head bearer to go over plans for the day. After the children went to school and Jim left for work, Maudun swept the floors using a Bengali broom. A short stick with a brush made of grass on one end. Beds were made and lunch was prepared. Jim returned home for lunch, much to our surprise and delight. As soon as the lunch table was cleared, siesta began. For two hours each day, Bengalis rested. Offices shut down, except for the Americans of course, and merchants in the town pulled the iron gates across their doors. The pounding of bricks next door ceased. Midday heat ruled the hour.

The house was functional and spotless and quite pleasant. The floors were made of light-colored ceramic tiles. The front door opened into a spacious living room that was attached to a dining room with a table large enough to seat ten people. The master bedroom was off the living room and attached to an oversized bathroom. Green tiles lined the walls of the bath and the tub was as wide and long as any six-foot plus cowboy might require. A smaller bedroom was opposite the master and perfect for a nursery. A crib was already in place for Melinda to take a nap. Jenna and Nyna each had a bedroom on the second floor. A marble stairway added a graceful architectural element to the room.

Akbar gave me a tour of the house that first day. We had been through all the rooms when I spotted the door leading off the dining room. I assumed the door led to the kitchen and I was interested in seeing what it was like when the head bearer rather shyly guided me away from the opening. He stammered a minute, then explained that I need not concern myself with that room.

I thought for a moment that I had misunderstood. Surely I would be able to see the kitchen. How would I make a peanut jelly sandwich for the children or heat a bottle for Melinda if I didn't know the kitchen? Akbar's behavior was curious and I was determined to go into the kitchen. I brushed him aside and pushed open the door.

Oh my. I almost gasped aloud as I took in the situation. The counters along the walls were covered with a metal of some kind. I suspected it was tin. Open shelves above the counters reached almost to the ceiling. The whole kitchen was painted brown. A small window allowed light to reveal a dent in the metal sink. There was a large black stove with heavy doors and well scrubbed gas outlets. Nothing in the room looked new. There was a large walk-in refrigerator in the wall opposite the stove.

The kitchen had not yet been totally stocked with food necessities, but it was easy for me to see there was no way I could have reached everything necessary to make a meal. I would have been unable to even reach the necessary tools to cook a meal in that place. The kitchen, for all intent and purposes, belonged to the chef. It was part of the staff's quarters.

As I stepped into the kitchen that first day, a man was sitting on a stool. He jumped off the stool, a surprised look on his face. The poor man was shocked to see me there. He made an attempt to look at me while trying not to look at me.

He was a larger man than Akbar. Not to say he was fat, just more substantial. He was dressed in the usual white spotless pants and shirt but with a difference. His head was covered with a white scarf blocking all his hair from being seen. The head covering reminded me of a helmet. He bowed graciously when introduced to me, but never uttered a word. In all the time we lived in Dacca I never heard his voice. I said hello and left the kitchen. I couldn't bear to bring any more discomfort to Akbar, or the shy Buddhist cook, than I already had.

Akbar rushed to explain. He told me that all the best cooks in Dacca came from the Hill Country. The hill country was populated by people from Burma and were Buddhist. I'd heard about the forest area famous for training elephants, but had no idea the people who lived there were so different from the lowland Bengalis. I'm fairly sure our cook could speak no English. All communication I had with him after that first day was through Akbar or Abdul, the Head Bearers. I don't remember seeing him more than two or three times during our two years living in the house. It was obvious that he was there. Delicious meals that appeared on our table every day were not down to magic. Cook was an invisible but welcomed asset to our household.

While we were accustomed to having help come from outside the family for a few hours a week, we were totally new at living with strangers 24/7. Were we just to ignore their very presence? We found it difficult to ignore someone working in the same room with us as we were reading or chatting or playing games. It was Jenna and Nyna who broke the tension early on. They began asking the servants questions about their families. They asked Maudun why he was using the stick and grass to sweep the floor. They asked Lucy where she went on her day off. Their friendly curiosity began to turn the servants into friends.

At first, their questions only served to make the servants confused and embarrassed. The British, who had controlled the whole Indian territory in the past, were more reserved and comfortable integrating their caste system into a similar practice in the East. I gathered from other American families that the British remaining in the country were of the opinion that we Americans were ruining years of servant/master norms. There was some grumbling among them that we Americans failed to maintain strict enough boundaries between servants and 'masters of the house.'

The Brits were also unhappy when we upset the pay scale they had established way back before India was split into Muslim and Hindu countries. As far as we were concerned, the amount we were paying for our help seemed inadequate considering all they did for us. When Jim and I learned what we paid each person each month we were happily ready to raise the salaries. In the end we complied with the status quo. We were told that Americans had already caused enough problems for westerners living in Dacca. We discovered the meager salaries we paid the five staff working in our household were supporting the lives of fifty people or more. That was some small consolation at least.

Jim and I had chosen the Dacca post over Paris because we wanted to be in a position to make a difference in the lives of people in this underdeveloped country. I admit to being intrigued by exotic Eastern cultures but I was looking for an opportunity to contribute to the community as well.

I had much to learn in that regard. Work with women in the Bengali community was loosely organized and very limited. Few Pakistani women felt free to attend social gatherings. Most remained true to the Muslim religion and were enclosed in a burka when they left their own compounds.

An International Women's Club did exist and once a year an annual potluck luncheon was held. There were some upper-class women who were a part of the club. The annual gathering took place in a beautifully designed hall in the American Consulate. Each participant was expected to bring a dish from their own town. Tables were placed end to end to form a long buffet. Dishes were arranged so that the least spicy dishes were on one end of the tables and the spiciest dishes at the opposite end.

I remember bragging with one of the participants about our spicy dishes in Texas. The Bengali woman was beautiful and her dark brown eyes gleamed with mischief when she asked me if I'd try her curry. She guided me down the tables explaining the differences in the area dishes as she went. We arrived at the end table and she explained that people in her part of the country were known for cooking the spiciest food. She dared me to taste. I don't know what I was thinking at the time, but I took her up on the dare. She didn't take her eyes off me as I took a small bite of her curry. I gasped for air as every pore in my body began to weep. The woman laughed. Not in jest but in sympathy, I hoped. I would have joined in the joke but I could hardly breathe, much less talk. That encounter made me somewhat wary of Bengali women but by and large, I found them to be pleasant, soft spoken, and intelligent.

I was disappointed when I learned that Pakistani women did not attend social gatherings. It meant lunches that Jim hosted at home were of the 'men only' variety. I planned the menu for the cook, informed the servants about the arrangements, and greeted his guests at the door. I excused myself and went about my day.

I enjoyed being a hostess but the job I most enjoyed was working with the hospitality group of AID women who arranged houses and staff for incoming USAID families. We looked for living quarters that would be suitable for Western families. We worked with the Consulate to secure rentals, and see that the appropriate furniture was delivered before the families arrived. The women responsible for arranging our house could not have made a better choice. I hoped to pass the favor along.

Our pink stucco house was enclosed in a compound and set back from the road so that there was space for a small lawn both in front and in back. Just enough grass for the girls to have a place to play. There was a large banana tree in the backyard. I wanted to make life as normal as possible for the children and decided a playhouse would be fun.

I spoke with Akbar and a grass hut was erected in no time. Jenna and Nyna were deciding how to decorate inside the playhouse when I arrived to inspect the hut and discovered a slim green poisonous snake already making a home there. Akbar informed me it was probably only a banana snake, but I was too scared to listen. We had been warned about numerous dangerous species of reptiles living in Bengal, East Pakistan, and I wanted to take no chances with our daughters. The grass hut idea was not my best.

I was more successful in providing Melinda with a place to play.

We had a wooden frame built and Maudun went to the market to find bags of clean sand. Lucy brought out a container of water and Melinda would sit in the sand and make mud pies every chance she could get. Lucy didn't approve of her getting her clothes dirty, but she could see that Melinda was full of joy when running her hands through the dirt. That turned out to be an ok idea. We just had to watch Melinda every minute. She liked to taste her mud cookies from time to time.

The sandbox was placed between the house and the paved drive which led to the staff's quarters. I never ventured inside those quarters. The staff had their own lives and culture, of which I was not a part. I was never called upon to discuss living conditions at the quarters. I have no idea how they allocated space among them. My hunch was that they maintained the strict caste system with the head bearer claiming the best space and down the line. The ayah had her own quarters on the bottom floor of the structure and away from the men who lived in rooms above.

The staff used the house kitchen to make large batches of curry every other day or so. On curry days our whole house was filled with the delicious aroma of the spices simmering slowly from early morning to evening. I never asked if the staff shared meals or cooked separately. Contrary to my natural inclinations, I learned that some things in the Middle East were best left unknown.

Jim settled in quickly with his new assignment. East Pakistan's problems differed drastically from Cyprus and Turkey. Poverty was the norm throughout the country and a food crisis occurred every year. AID work in Bangladesh was the story of American generosity and arrogance.

The arrogance manifested in our 'know it all' attitudes. For instance, we arrived in the country certain that we could introduce a kind of rice that would survive the annual floods and produce enough grain to keep the population fed throughout the year. USAID had contributed the new strain of seed and the whole of Bengal was waiting for the crops to grow. If successful, hunger could be almost eliminated for the Bengali population.

Alas. When the rice crop grew and the floods came, the American rice could not withstand the floods. The Pakistani rice, on the other hand, grew rapidly to keep its head above the fast-rising waters. The yield was not adequate to feed all the people throughout the winter months, but the rice yield was adequate to stave off starvation for many. AID personnel were discouraged at the failure of our grand experiment, but that didn't deter us from working harder to find a solution to the national hunger crisis.

The girls were enrolled in the American school and we set about getting to know their teachers and friends. Early on we met a family whose parents had grown up in Texas like Jim and me. We had a lot in common. The Weavers had a girl, Kate, a year older than Jenna and a boy, Mark, the same age as Nyna. Beth was an artist and a teacher before coming to Dacca. Mark Weaver was an architect teaching architecture classes at the University of Dacca and designing buildings for their campus. Our families became close and we spent many evenings watching plays the children wrote and acted out for our pleasure. Many nights after dinner together, we sat around the family compound singing folk songs while Mark played the guitar. Much to our delight, our sense of community developed quickly over the months that followed.

Our household fell into a comfortable routine. The girls went to school. Melinda was a constant joy for her ayah. Lucy dressed Melinda every day after nap time and took her for a walk in the stroller. She would gather with the other neighborhood ayahs at the corner of our street. Each ayah arrived proudly pushing their baby in its pram. Each baby was bathed, groomed, and dressed in their morning going-for-a-walk outfits. It was a virtual baby fashion parade. Every day the ayahs and babies could be seen parading down the street and back again, but not before a gossip session at the corner.

The ayahs were the nerve center of the neighborhood. They knew everything about the families they served. Gossip was the topic of the day but only after each ayah reported the 'smart or advanced' progress their baby had made that morning. One bragged that her baby slept through the night for the first time, and I'm certain Lucy glowed with pride when Melinda began to crawl.

I learned of the session when Lucy proudly announced that Melinda was not only the most beautiful baby among all babies, but she was also the smartest. It seems the ayah brigade had agreed that Melinda was impressive. It was as if Melinda had won a Miss American Baby contest. Lucy beamed with happiness. Having the smartest, most beautiful baby in the neighborhood raised Lucy's status among the ayah community.

More importantly, Lucy and Melinda bonded deeply in the first months after we arrived. Lucy glowed with pride when Melinda spoke her first words, and when she took her first steps. Melinda has memories to this day of being two years old and playing a trick on Lucy. Lucy fed Melinda her lunch of cereal and pureed peas and fruit, changed her diaper, and tucked her into her crib for a nap. She told Melinda to have a nice sleep and left the room to have her own lunch. Melinda purposefully peed into the clean dry diaper and began to cry. Lucy rushed back into Melinda's room. What could be the matter, she wondered. She checked Melinda for something poking or sticking her and found nothing. She had just changed Melinda's diaper and couldn't believe it when she felt something warm. Melinda had wet the diaper as soon as Lucy left the room. Lucy changed the diaper to a fresh one. She had a scowl on her face . It was her lunch time and she hadn't eaten since early morning tea. She couldn't believe if when Melinda began to laugh. Lucy told me that she was certain that two-year-old Melinda had wet her clean diaper on purpose. She and I had a chuckle together.

Lucy took care of Melinda's clothes, prepared her food, and dressed and bathed her. I was a bit miffed at first. But I realized that rather than lose time with Melinda, I was free to spend more time playing with her. Lucy was in charge of Jenna and Nyna's clothes as well.

We all benefitted from the time we could spend together without folding clothes or putting things away. We had more time to sit together at the table after the girls came home from school. We discussed our days together over cookies and a glass of the dread milk. The pace of our daily lives slowed down. Life grew to be in harmony with the slow rolling Burmaputra River.

Bengali dairy products were unsafe and our only option for milk to feed the children was to mix a powder with boiled water. The taste left something to be desired. We had to keep an eye on the girls at the dinner table. One of them was certain to try and empty their glass somewhere besides their tummies. Jenna and Nyna weren't the only ones playing games at the table. We were mystified when Melinda began turning down food at our dinner table.

I talked the matter over with Lucy but she had no answer. I began to notice Mohammed, our server at the dining table, ducking his head to hide a smile when Melinda turned down bites of food from the table. I had a hunch that something was going on that I didn't know about. Melinda was definitely not losing weight. She was as rosy and plump as ever. I decided to confront Lucy about my hunch. Lucy was more forth-right the second time. She confessed that Melinda had been eating lunch with the servants every day. She wasn't eating family meals because she preferred curry and rice. Mystery solved.

When Melinda learned Bengali words before English, the staff could not hide their delight. No doubt Lucy worked hard at coaching her in the Bengali language. The ever-present staff provided an approving audience for Melinda's speech development. Bengali people loved children and having Melinda in our family seemed to smooth the way for our servants to become relaxed around us. We gradually learned to relax around them. I suspected they were as uncomfortable with us in the beginning as we were having them around all the time.

The staff tried hard to carry out our wishes. They showed up every morning before breakfast dressed in clean white shirts and pants. I learned a lot about each of them by watching and listening to the way they engaged Melinda. Lucy and Abdul were the only ones who were brave enough to hold Melinda's hand. The others made funny motions or talked to her in Bengali. They were ready at any moment to pick up a toy she had thrown onto the floor, her favorite game just after we arrived.

We came to know each servant as a person. Lowest according to the caste system was Maudun. He was the only Hindu servant in the group and the youngest. He was a good-looking young man with a broad smile. The other servants treated him like a younger brother. His job was to sweep the floors, inside and out. I was as fascinated as the girls to watch him clean the floor with a Bengali broom.

One weekend Abdul, the man who replaced Akbar after an unfortunate incident, came to me with some troubling news. There was an uprising in the town. A group of Bengali men were going through residential neighborhoods, looking for Hindu people. Some kind of dispute had broken out between a small faction of Bengalis and some local Hindus. Abdul told me that Maudun would not be working that day because our servants wanted to keep him safe. They were planning to hide him in their quarters above the garage.

I could hear the concern for Maudun and didn't hesitate to give my blessings to the plan. I asked if Jim and I could do anything to help and Abdul assured me the servants would take care of the boy. For a few days we had no sweeper, but we had no complaints. Jim and I were pleased to know that our caretakers put care for others above politics regardless of their station in life.

The second bearer, Mohammed, dusted, cleaned and helped Abdul serve the meals. It took awhile for me to become accustomed to eating my dinner in front of Mohammed. He stood like a statue at the side of the room. He never said a word. He was there in case we needed anything. Mohammed was a kind, pleasant man, taller than the others, and shy. From time to time when he caught one of the girls pouring their milk into the other's glass he tried his best not to laugh. He would put his hand over his mouth in an effort to stifle his smile. But his most difficult challenge was to keep us from seeing him laugh when Melinda did something 'naughty.' Melinda's antics broke Mohammed up.

Jim and I played a guessing game as to why Mohammad always ducked his head or put his hand over his mouth when he had to smile. One evening Melinda did something that was just too much for Mohammad. We caught him unaware. We saw a wide gap in his smile where he should have had two front teeth. Another mystery solved.

Akbar had been trained well by British families and I was grateful that he had organized the household well. Everything seemed to be running smoothly. Every morning when I met with Akbar at the dining table to go over the daily schedule we discussed the business of the day. Nothing else. He gave me a food shopping list for PX purchases when needed. I knew nothing of his family. He didn't volunteer information and I didn't ask. I got the impression it was best to keep our relationship on a businesslike basis.

~

The children and I were settled comfortably reading books one Saturday morning when we were startled by a loud banging noise. Lucy came scurrying into the room and told us that we needed to come quickly. There was something we had to see outside at the front gates. She deftly plopped Melinda into her stroller and pushed her out the front door. The girls and I were right behind her.

There was indeed something to see at the gate outside. A Bengali man in white pajamas and a colorfully embroidered pill box hat was squatted outside the iron gate. He was beating a steady rhythm on a drum about the size of a soup tureen. A small brown monkey wearing a tiny matching hat was standing at the gate looking at us through the bars. The monkey was tied by a rope to the dance master. When the drummer began to beat a rhythm, the monkey danced around his owner.

We watched as the monkey jumped and danced around and around to the music. The dance went on for about ten minutes then stopped. The monkey took a cup from beside the owner's lap and held the cup through the gate bars to collect money for their performance.

As I left to go into the house for 'baksheesh,' I was interested to see that some of the other household servants had found a place from the front porch to watch the performance. I caught the shy smiles on Lucy and Maudun as they glanced at me, a little sideways, as if to see if I was enjoying this entertainment as much as they. I wondered if they were a bit anxious that I might disapprove. The servants didn't try to hide their own pleasure as they watched the girls being treated to the traditional Bengali entertainment.

We moved into the social scene with gusto. The usual cocktail and dinner engagements filled our weekly calendar. Jim's position as chief loan officer at the Agency meant we were expected to host Embassy folk as well as Bengali government officers. At least once a week I met with Akbar to arrange for a cocktail party or a dinner party. Guest lists had to be decided upon, and menus talked over.

We were lucky in this post to have a group of young idealistic couples from Jim's office to help entertain. They were financial types who became devoted to Jim from day one. Most were married and we grew fond of the lively discussions and comfortable camaraderie. Our young friends were a great help when we found it necessary to entertain a large group of diplomats.

One evening the work party had gone well. The evening grew late and we stood at the door expressing, once again, our gratitude to Jim's crew and wishing them a good night. Our guests had departed, and Jim and I sat for a while talking over the evening's success. It had been a long day and we were ready to retire but I took another minute to organize the liquor cabinet. That cabinet was the only one we kept locked. I was organizing the bottles when I spotted a bottle I didn't recognize. It was partially hidden at the back of the cabinet. I asked Jim if he recognized the liquor. It was something I had never seen before. It looked wicked to me, a very strange color. Jim didn't recognize it either and I reminded him to speak to Akbar about it before he left for work the next morning.

The following morning, Jim was surprised when Akbar couldn't look him in the eyes. We discovered that he had been taking small shots of liquor from each drink he poured the previous evening. He would pour one shot of liquor for a guest's drink and add one to a secret bottle. The concoction in the bottle was a mixture of gin, Scotch, vodka and any other liquors opened that evening. No wonder it appeared weird looking. And it was frightening to think of what might happen to a person who drank the stuff.

We didn't know what to do at that moment. We told Akbar we would talk with him later in the day. I couldn't think of anything else that day. I kept asking myself if I'd been overlooking something that was going on under my very nose. My thoughts and feelings ranged between anger and regret. I'd begun to trust the people in our house. I felt angry and betrayed and a little stupid. I regarded our domestic staff as friends. I wondered if they had been putting on an act all along. Jim urged me to try and relax. He assured me that he would ask advice at the office and take care of the situation when he came home from work.

The embassy liaison officer advised us to relieve Akbar of his job and search for another head bearer.

SEVENTEEN
Friends and Extended Family

We were grateful to have friends in Dacca with children the same age as ours. The AID director, Bob Johnson and his wife Betty had Eleanor, who was our daughter Jenna's age. And the Weavers of course. They were the only Americans in the program who could understand a Texas accent.

Our family began to find our place in the community. The girls entered the American school with their usual zest for learning. Jim was pleased with his young staff and respected Director Johnson's leadership and expertise.

Once I adjusted to having the housekeeping and cooking taken out of my hands, I joined the group of AID women whose task it was to arrange housing for newly arriving government families. I enjoyed being a part of a large community of women.

Not all of my new friends were associated with the US government. We were fortunate to live next door to an American engineer connected to a private international company. The Downing family had two children, both attending high school in Europe for months out of the year. Ruth and I became friends and she was instrumental in luring our new head bearer, Abdul, away from his present job to come work in our household.

This fortunate turn of events led to a lifelong relationship with Abdul and his family. He stepped in and made some minor changes in our routine, and to my relief and pleasure, my life became easier. I had struggled with Akbar at times. He responded to my directions with nods of agreement, but I always had a weird feeling my message was only partially understood.

Abdul, on the other hand, spoke impeccable English and came with a huge bonus; he could also read English. After Abdul arrived I was able to give him our favorite recipes which he would then translate for the Buddhist cook. I could make notes and grocery lists which saved both of us time.

Abdul was a slender man with a well trimmed beard. He was always immaculately groomed in white shirts and trousers. That he was highly respected in the servant community was obvious. He carried out his duties with a confident authority. Abdul was articulate and pleasant when dealing with our family.

Abdul's insistence that prayer times in a Muslim household be strictly adhered to made little difference in the daily routine. Abdul was a devout spiritual leader and a highly respected man, not only in our household but also in the Bengali community. Jim and I had no objection to his requirements as long as the household was running smoothly.

I had many fantasies about what monsoon season would be like. I had images of being stranded in our house for days with nothing to do but listen to rain pounding relentlessly on the roof. In my fear fantasy, the girls would be unable to go to school because the roads were flooded. The servants would be arriving each morning wearing soggy, limp uniforms because nothing wet would have time to dry. It was a relief to find that my fantasy fears were unfounded.

In reality, the monsoon season meant that we had an afternoon rain every day for a few months. Each morning the sun would rise as usual. Like summer afternoon in the Rocky Mountains, the sky would cloud over, the humidity would increase, and we would have a rain. This made for a lush, damp environment. Perpetual dampness on the outside explained the moss-covered buildings. Air conditioners on the inside kept the mold from invading our clothes.

The girls were happily engrossed in school and busy with play dates. Jim came home one day and asked if I was interested in joining the amateur theater group. In the 1960's television sets had not reached the subcontinent. Amateur drama groups provided the English-speaking community with their primary form of entertainment. Jim and I discussed the pros and cons of joining the thespian community. We both enjoyed being a part of a theater, yet we hesitated.

Jim's workload was heavier than expected and we hadn't been in plays since high school. But it came down to whether we could still memorize lines at the old age of 33 and 35. Then, the director called and offered us the leading parts in a comedy named *Mary, Mary*. We said yes.

Mary, Mary played three nights in front of a packed house. Jim and I had so much fun. The play was perfect for us. We joked about being typecast. Jim as the sympathetic gentleman and I as the sharp spoken wife. The production made us recognizable everywhere we went in the larger community. We were greeted after opening night like Broadway stars. We received fan mail and flowers in our dressing rooms. One unexpected pleasure of our tour in Dacca was to find ourselves a part of a large, integrated community so far away from home.

Working with the cast and crew was a hoot. Working with our British director changed our views about our British fellow travelers.

Our director was a good-looking middle-aged man with a strong British accent. He had been involved in theater while living in the UK and had been directing plays in overseas posts for years. He was well known for his expertise.

Jim and I would lie in bed at night discussing our lines. The production was progressing well until the monsoon season arrived. Humidity and heat affected every living thing. Even the plants sagged when the humidity index hovered around 100%.

One afternoon we were rehearsing and the heat on stage was breathtaking. I stopped for the umpteenth time to wipe away the sweat pouring down the back of my neck. My hair was plastered to my skull and I was fighting a losing battle trying to keep the sweat from falling into my eyes. I swiped at my forehead time and again. The heat broke into my concentration and I became irritable. I began messing up my lines.

The director, thinking I had forgotten my lines, broke in and gave me a prompt. That was like putting a burr under my saddle. I looked out from the stage. "I'm sorry but the heat is putting me off and I'm sweating like a pig," I snapped. All activity in the room stopped.

The director with his perfect British accent patiently replied, "Madame," he slowly replied, "Ladies do not sweat. They glow."

The cast waited silently, wondering what was about to happen. I stood for a moment, then broke into laughter. The tension faded, the spell was broken and I remembered my lines. I felt like I glowed a lot while under stage lights in Pakistan. But it didn't seem to bother me as much when I reminded myself that I was glowing, not sweating.

The temperature was more forgiving in the spring when we participated in a musical, *Annie Get Your Gun.* Beth Weaver took the role of Annie and I played her sidekick. The singing and dancing parts were adequate. Beth had a beautiful voice. My dance routines were simple. I required more rehearsals than expected. Dancing with someone beside Jim as my dance partner presented more of a challenge than I realized it would be. Jim didn't need to rehearse how to swagger like a cowhand. He had learned that firsthand growing up in Texas.

We learned there would be an Easter sunrise service in the town park the first spring we were in Dacca. We dyed eggs with the girls and added a few chocolate surprises and unpacked the Easter baskets. We had purchased a small hibachi from the PX and I pounded thin slices of beef to paper thin. My special Easter Sunday breakfast of steak and eggs were packed and ready for the grill.

We sat on a hillside just before dawn. A choir of around twenty people gather on a stage at the bottom of the hill. Just as the sun rose the choir began to sing. It was a cool, bright morning and we were enthralled. Melinda squirmed in my lap, ready to practice walking some more. She hadn't been at it long and didn't want to forget. The choir broke into Hallelujah, and somewhere in the distance a loudspeaker broadcast an Imam calling Muslims to prayer. A magical moment. As if the whole world had come together to celebrate the rebirth of life.

The morning prayers ended and we took the girls into the brush and asked them to close their eyes. I hid eggs while Jim fired up the grill and began making breakfast.

We said, "Open!" Jenna and Nyna scampered in and out of bushes gathering eggs. One at a time the girls would stop and lead Melinda over to an egg placed in plain sight. We asked to take a bite of steak and eggs before tasting the candy. A hard thing to ask, but it worked. Jim and I watched the girls scampering about and chuckled. We had hidden Easter eggs in lots of places but this one was the most weird.

KINDNESS

EIGHTEEN
An Ongoing Pledge

We were eager to uphold our pledge to each other and the children, to learn as much as possible about the countries we lived in. We decided on a trip to Cox's Bazaar, a shipping village located on the Bay of Bengal. The heat in Dacca made us all yearn for ocean breezes and cool water to swim in. We asked our friends the Weavers to join in our adventure. Beth and I talked over the logistics and decided that Abdul and Lucy should accompany us. Jim obtained permission from his Bengali colleagues to rent some cabins built for weekend get-aways. Our excitement grew as we packed the car. This was the first car trip we had taken since arriving in Dacca.

Just driving to the coast was an adventure. No need for a map. There was only one paved road leading from Dacca to the Bay of Bengal. The girls were beyond excited to be in the ocean again and wondered aloud if the water would be as blue as the Mediterranean. We piled into two cars and set off with fantasies of crowded beaches, umbrellas, and cold fruit drinks.

Traffic through Dacca city was moving at a snail's pace. We could only creep through the narrow streets. The girls grew impatient, complaining that we were losing sun time. I didn't mind. I loved to watch the crowds as we thread our way through throngs of women in burkas and men in shalwar kameez. Bicycle rickshaws vied for any small space around us, their bells jingling and sunlight reflecting in the fancy designs made from tin cans that decorated their cabs. We said little as the cacophony of sounds of teaming people and honking horns filled the car.

We had traveled a few blocks when the voice from the Mosque nearby called noonday prayer over a loudspeaker. Traffic slowed. Men dressed in robes, some in shalwar kameez, and some in western style clothes, formed lines on each side of the road. They kneeled onto their back heels and began to bend forward, touching their foreheads to the ground in concert with the Iman's voice. Traffic continued to creep along. The drivers paying no attention to the praying men.

We crept to the edge of the city and arrived just in time to wait. To the girl's disgust there was a line of cars in front of us. A train filled the road at that moment. The road served all forms of transportation. One at a time. After the train, cars took a turn. First into the city and then out of the city.

The road was only wide enough for one car at a time. We watched with interest as the vehicles going into Dacca passed us by. Some were crammed with families and children. Some looked to be carrying coconuts or mangoes. A packed bus was decorated with people hanging onto the outside of the vehicle.

It was finally our turn and we slowly made our way across the long ribbon of pavement toward our destination. The railroad track ran down the middle of the road. On each side of the road tiny spikes of green rice plants were poking their heads through acres of wet bogs, searching the sun. I took a deep breath, relieved to be out of the ever-present crush of people. A bit further down the road I spotted water buffalo munching on some low growing greens. They were impressive beasts with long curved horns. They slouched through the shallow water with an ease that belied their bulk. I wouldn't like to tangle with an animal that large.

As was our family custom, Jim began singing a Broadway song and we all joined in. This seemed like our ordinary, happy family time on the way to a beach holiday. Suddenly there was nothing ordinary about it.

We had traveled halfway across the long stretch of road when Jim slowed the car to a crawl. The children and I craned our necks to see what was causing the delay. Jenna and Nyna clapped their hands in delight. Coming toward our car was a caravan of elephants. Each elephant was topped by a turbaned man with a cane. We gazed up at them through the car windows and they gazed down at us from atop the animals that seemed as tall as a two-story building.

There were about eight huge elephants, beautiful, and well trained. We oohed and aahed as they rode past the car so close we could feel the road shake. A fitting start to an unusual trip to the beach.

The government cabin was clean and sparsely decorated. Abdul and Lucy had gone ahead to arrange the beds and kitchen. They looked relaxed and happy as we drove up. The ocean air already provided soft soothing breezes. Abdul welcomed us and began unloading the car. Lucy seemed relieved to have Melinda back within her grasp. I asked Lucy if she was excited abut being at the ocean. She replied that she had never been to the ocean before. I offered to lend her a bathing suit but she emphatically let me know that she would not be needing one.

The day was hot and sunny. We hurried to unpack bathing suits and crammed oversized towels and pails and shovels into beach bags. Before we left on our walk to the beach, Abdul met with me to discuss dinner plans. He would go into the village market and buy the meat and vegetables to cook our meals for the weekend. He and I agreed this was a perfect time to have kabobs over the outdoor grill. The girls giggled with excitement and wiggled into their bathing suits while Lucy changed Melinda into a little yellow bathing suit with ruffles across the bottom. Abdul had water and snacks prepared and we were all set.

We walked out into the fresh ocean air, filled with anticipation of what was to come. We stopped on the porch. We were being serenaded by an unexpected visitor. A barefoot Bengali boy, a little younger than Nyna, stood at the bottom of the stairs. He had black hair, big brown eyes, and a clubbed foot. He was playing a homemade instrument and singing along in Bengali. He had attached a piece of wire to both ends of a long stick. He pulled a smaller stick across the wire making a sound. It was his version of Bengali music. I seemed to detect a minor key but I'm still not certain what that key would be. The instrument was clever. I had to give him that.

I turned and asked Jim to go back into the house for some change but Abdul shook his head. "Saab," he said, "if you give the boy baksheesh for this serenade every child in the village will be waiting at our door when you come back." He explained that word of handouts would spread in no time. We listened to Abdul and thanked the boy for his song.

I assumed we would go on our way and never see the boy again. I was wrong. The boy's eyes were glued to the sight of two-and one-half-year-old Melinda. It's certain he had never seen such a white baby and certainly none with red hair. I realized, with a shock, the little boy looked like he had fallen in love. Every move we made for the rest of the weekend, the boy was there in the background, smiling. His eyes followed Melinda's every movement.

We settled onto the blankets we had arranged on the sandy beach. Miles and miles of white sandy beach and no one in sight. After about an hour we watched a very large fishing boat come ashore down the beach about a half mile away. We could see the fishermen unload baskets of fish onto awaiting rickshaws. Suddenly the men's voices rose to shouts and we craned out heads to see what all the commotion was about. We were astounded when a man dressed only in a wet lungi held up a small shark.

There was no other activity on the beach that day. The miles of beautiful, white sandy beach had no umbrellas erected to protect bathers, and definitely no tiny paper umbrellas atop a cold drink. We had the miles of beautiful sandy beach and cool ocean water all to ourselves.

Jim and Mark were the first in the cool water. Lucy took Melinda by the hands and duck-walked her up and down the sand in front of our pallets. I slathered the eager girls with sunscreen lotion and they ran whooping and galloping into the smooth surf. I took a deep breath and luxuriated in the thought that the crowds of people we usually encountered when we left our compound in Dacca were out of sight, if only for a weekend.

It was my turn to take the plunge. The water was refreshingly cool, and I leaned back and let the waves rock me back and forth as I watched a stray white cloud move slowly across the blue sky.

I returned to the blanket to dry off and play with Melinda. Lucy surprised me by walking across the sand and into the water, silk sari and all. She later told me that salt water is very good for silk. I watched as Melinda played with the sand and caught another glimpse of the young boy we had met on arrival. He was dressed in a dusty shalwar kameez and carrying his 'instrument.' He had followed us to the beach.

He was obviously enthralled with Melinda. He became emboldened and creeped closer to her. I wondered if I should be concerned and watched as the little boy seemed to be telling a story in Bengali. Melinda was not alarmed, she just looked at him. Something took his attention away from Melinda and he got up from the sand and abruptly disappeared. Melinda picked up a shovel and began moving sand from place to place. I wondered if the boy disappeared because it was close to his lunchtime. It would remain a mystery.

Beth and I were chatting and watching the children splash in the water. Lucy began waving and screaming from the waves, "Memsaab, Memsaab!" I looked out at her splashing through the water. Lucy was pointing to something behind me.

I turned to where Melinda was sitting in the sand just to the left and slightly behind me. A group of six men and women were standing in a circle around Melinda. I could barely see her through the gaps between the visitors' legs. The people were talking to Melinda and Melinda was smiling happily, digging her shovel into the wet sand. One of the women bent down and scooped her up. They were laughing and throwing her in the air and clapping to make her laugh. Melinda was responding with a belly laugh. She seemed to be having a marvelous time of it.

Lucy's shout shocked me into action. I realized the distance between Melinda and me had changed. The group had moved, very slightly, down the beach away from where I was sitting.

I jumped up from the sand and sprinted a few yards to pull Melinda out of the woman's arms. My heart was pounding. Lucy was running toward us as fast as a wet sari would allow. She must have had a huge adrenal rush to reach us as quickly as she did. She arrived just as I had my hands on Melinda. My heart was pounding so hard that I hardly noticed the Gypsies move swiftly away.

Lucy hugged us both and began to explain in a shaky voice, "Memsaab, those people are Gypsies. They roam the area and steal children. They cut them and send them out to beg."

I could hardly take in what she was saying but her fear was contagious. I stood still for a moment giving my head time to stop spinning. The fantasy of a relaxed, beautiful day at the beach had turned bittersweet. As soon as my heart stopped racing I hugged Melinda even tighter to my chest. I tried to control my shaky feelings so as not to alarm Melinda. Lucy could see how I was reacting and took the baby and began to interest her with the shovel and pail again. Melinda did not seem to have minded the Gypsy encounter in the least.

I, on the other hand, took a long while to shake off my feelings of dread. How could I have taken my eyes away from her? It seemed to me I had only turned my head from Melinda for one moment.

This lapse of attention was obviously the dark side of having an everyday baby care person. I was so relaxed when Lucy was around to watch Melinda that I had not been vigilant enough. The incident was a shocking wakeup call and a lesson learned. I realized I could never let my guard down when we were in a new place.

We'd had enough sun for the first day and returned to the cabin. We walked into the cool living room creating a path of damp sand on the floor. The salt water stung as our bodies began to dry. I took the girls into the back yard to throw tap water over them to wash off the salt and sand.

We were surprised by a cute little gray goat tied to a bamboo fence. Jenna and Nyna ran over to the goat and patted it. They interrupted each other as they tried to settle on a name for their pet. I don't remember what they decided on, but the goat immediately became their cherished beach mascot.

The Weavers arrived. Abdul had worked his magic. Over cocktails on the porch, the pungent aroma of rosemary and lamb shish kebob announced the time for dinner. Saffron colored pilaf dotted with bits of peas and fried onion was plated next to skewers of roasted meat. A basket of fresh pita bread was passed around the table. This was a perfect culinary treat at the end of our momentous day in the Bay of Bengal.

The children finished eating and asked for permission to play outside. It was just natural that they wanted to show their friends their surprise. A baby goat.

A minute later Jenna rushed back inside. "Mom. Dad, you gotta come! Quick. Someone has taken our pet!"

She ran to Abdul and pulled on his hand. "Come Abdul. You have to find the baby goat."

Abdul looked over at me. He wasn't sure how to respond. Jenna persisted. Abdul found the right words and told her he couldn't come right then because he had to clean up after dinner. Jenna began to insist and argue with him.

I stepped in to save Abdul. There was nothing to do but tell her the truth. Nothing to do but tell her we had eaten the goat for supper. Her face reflected shock as she took in my words. It took her a moment before she completely accepted that we had eaten their pet goat for dinner.

I hugged Jenna while she could absorb the reality of the situation. Nyna was disappointed she couldn't show the pet to their friends but full tummies, the sun, and the long day finally caught up with them all and they didn't complain when we called time for bed.

We were hesitant to give up a few hours at the beach but we were excited when Jim was able to get a permit allowing us to take a boat ride into the Bay of Bengal. We were headed to a small Island off the coast of Bengal that was legally a part of the country of Burma. Burmese people were heavily controlled by an authoritarian communist government.

A regime firmly opposed to Bengali democracy. The Island was one of the few Burmese places that allowed visitors from other countries. We were told that it was politically risky to visit the island but that the people there would be happy to see us.

The women on the Island were known for their rare and unique textiles. Beth and I were particularly excited to have a look at the art and we were all curious to have firsthand information about the lives and culture of these isolated people. The Island was only a short motorboat ride away.

Upon arriving we could see that we had stepped into a very different culture from East Pakistan. The streets were quiet and empty when we arrived at the wooden dock. It wasn't clear if that was in response to our visit or if it was the usual way of things.

~

The houses were huts composed of bamboo. This was a poor island. There were no large buildings. The empty dirt streets gave out an eerie feeling as our boat came to shore. One of the children said the word spooky out loud. Just saying what we were all experiencing. I glared at Jim to get his attention, wondering if we should turn back without disembarking.

A man, his face all smiles, stepped from one of the huts and greeted us. We were not surprised to learn that he was the head schoolteacher in the village. He waved us ashore, indicating that we were welcome to disembark. There was always one person in every village who spoke English and many times it was the schoolteacher. This schoolteacher, a man of uncertain age, wore a second hat in the village. He was also the mayor. The white cotton robe that he wore resembled a gown. He had a square shaped black cap on his head and a colored woven scarf around his waist. He was very eager to show off his language skills.

We explained we had come to see the famous fabric woven on the Island. There were some tense moments as the teacher/mayor hesitated. I was wondering if we were about to be sent away, if we had made the trip in vain.

Mark went on to speak to him of how we had heard of some famous women weavers who created beautiful fabrics here on the island and the man relaxed, his shoulders slumped into their proper place. Jim explained that we were eager to buy some of their wares. The compliments and the mention of trade seemed to do the trick. The mayor smiled and with a nod, he motioned for us to follow him down a dirt path toward a cluster of houses.

As we made our way down the road he grew more eager to tell us about his village. We continued to be uncomfortable about the empty streets. We reminded the children to stay close. The schoolteacher/mayor stayed even closer. It became clear that we were not free to explore the village without a chaperone.

We continued to move around the circle of huts with the street to ourselves. We tried to be unintrusive while we strained to see into the huts as we passed by. Every now and then, we were able to catch a glimpse of a women or a child peeking shyly from inside the dark spaces.

The guide stopped in front of one of the larger huts and motioned for us to wait outside. He entered the hut and spoke to someone. He must have convinced them we were safe, for he returned with the news that the famous weaver women inside the hut would be happy to show us their work. Beth and I took a few cautious steps inside the dimly lighted room. Four women stood behind looms large enough for weaving small carpets. Baskets of colored yarn were stacked along the walls. Rich reds and royal blues were in baskets next to yellows and greens. Each loom was filled with colored wool woven into unique works of art.

The Burmese women watched Beth and me with large, wary brown eyes and stared at our children as if wondering if they were some kind of ghosts. It was obvious they were not used to seeing small people with such pale skin and light hair. I was eager to speak with the women, to learn how they had acquired their weaving skills. The fabrics we saw inside were intricate and stunningly beautiful. I especially loved the yarns dyed bright fuchsia. Holy men all around the East dressed in robes of that color. I wanted to know how they made that particular dye and the other colors as well.

I was curious about the patterns they wove. I wondered if they ever added their own designs to traditional patterns. The mayor turned to the women and translated my questions. They answered. It seems every villager, female and male, was educated in the art of weaving and trained to pass the traditional patterns down from one generation to the next. Tradition was strictly adhered to. Any deviation from the tradition was forbidden.

One by one a new woman appeared in the hut. And then another, until the hut was full of women. They were wary, careful to move toward the back of the room so they couldn't be seen. Until curiosity drew them out toward the light.

Beth and I stood just inside the doorway, silent, waiting to see what was going to happen. A woman from the back of the hut approached us. She was holding some cloth across her arms. The pattern was made of black thread woven into a background of shocking pink. One by one, other women followed. The women were small of stature. Shiny black hair and dark brown eyes. They wore long skirts wrapped around their lower bodies. Like a sarong. Each skirt was a different pattern of colors and design. A plain long sleeved bouse finished the dress.

Each piece of fabric the women held out to us was colorful and soft to the touch. Precise patterns were repeated in each piece. Beth and I had to make difficult decisions. After touching the fabric and looking at the pieces offered to us, I chose a sarong-length piece of fuchsia and black. The mayor assisted us in making our purchases. He shook his head when I offered Bengali rupees, but grinned with delight when we produced American coins. We wondered, but didn't dare ask, where a resident from a communist island could spend American cash.

Our beautiful fabric wrapped in brown paper, we made our way back down the path to the awaiting motorboat. We glanced into huts lining the pathway and caught glimpses of small children peeking out from the darkness. Their big eyes staring timidly at the strangely dressed white people visiting their village.

Beth and I treasured our hand-woven purchases. The brightly colored fabric I purchased that day retained its dyes and shape forty years later. We returned back to the camp with our unique and beautiful purchases and rested. Another afternoon at the beach and we packed into the cars to return home to Dacca. I turned to look for the little musician boy as we drove away. He was there, standing by the cabin steps, balancing on one foot, and waving goodbye until we were out of sight.

NINETEEN
Trouble Again

Jim came home one evening with the news that the Pakistani government had detected unfriendly planes flying over East Pakistan. A blackout had been put in place until further notice. All outside lights were to be turned off. Windows were to be covered and all cars were prohibited on the roads after dark. I helped Abdul gather blankets and towels, anything we could find to keep light from escaping to the outside.

We stocked up on emergency supplies and settled in for evenings by candlelight. It was impossible to see well enough to knit or read a book, and we turned to playing board games and telling stories instead. The candlelight created a particular ambience that inspired the girls' imagination. Their stories took on a more somber flavor. They found this new turn of events to be rather exciting.

About a week later, the glamor of the situation began to wear thin. Jim and I turned to our friends, the Weavers, to arrange more frequent visits. We needed all the help we could get to make it through the long evenings looming ahead.

One evening we were at our friends' home, playing bridge, and sharing a lovely meal of chicken kebab and rice when the children asked for our attention. They had worked hard at preparing a dress-up production of their latest creation. We checked our watches and reminded them there was very little daylight left. They promised we wouldn't be long. We adults settled into comfy chairs in the living room with a small brandy and gave the children our full attention. The play was one of their best and we were having such a good time that we forgot the clock. Beth noticed and raised the alarm. "Quick. You are about to miss the curfew."

Jim and I jumped up, expressed our thanks for the evening and rushed the girls into the back seat of our car. We began to make our way through the dark empty streets toward home. There was no moon, no streetlights. No light whatsoever escaping from the houses along the way. Everyone in town seemed to be following the government directive.

It wasn't surprising, therefore, to find we were the only car on the road. Jim drove slowly, squinting his eyes to see the road ahead with only parking lights to show the way. Eager to get us home and off the streets as quickly as possible.

I was watching the road when Jim abruptly slammed on the brakes throwing me forward in my seat. Without thinking, I turned to check the backseat to see if the girls were ok. All three were still in place, sleepy eyed and quiet.

Melinda, the youngest, her red hair in a short bob, was snuggled between her older sisters. She was still wearing the pink tutu costume she had donned earlier that evening. Nyna's brunette hair was plastered to her head as she slumped against the door, a curry sauce stain on her blouse filled the cab of the car with an aroma reminiscent of our evening's dinner. Jenna's long blond hair, her pride and joy, was pulled back into a ponytail in an effort to keep her neck cool. A dried frangipani petal was stuck between the backseat and the arm rest next to her.

Jim rolled down the window when a figure appeared from nowhere and showed a light into the car. I covered my eyes to protect them from the glare. It was wintertime in the tropics and the man was wearing a thick brown shawl over his white shalwar. He mumbled something to Jim in Bengali as he trained his light onto the back seat.

There was no show of a badge nor credentials of any sort. Nothing to indicate that he was a person of authority. The man looked more closely and realized that Jim didn't understand what he had said. He asked the question again. This time in broken English. Didn't we know there was a curfew? Who were we? Where were we going? Jim apologized and began to explain. The man abruptly turned and walked a few yards to where a group of men were milling around, blocking the road.

All the men were dressed alike, except a few had long-barreled guns showing from under their shawls. One or two of the men looked in our direction. I strained to see through the dark, hoping for a pleasant, welcoming face. I saw nothing to give me a clue as to whom these men could be. Some had colored their faces with kohl. I couldn't help but think of the stories I'd heard about highway robbers. Could it be we were seeing remnants of Thuggees or Dacoity bands roaming the countryside again?

The acid and heat of my curry dinner made itself present again as my roiling tummy groaned in protest. A scent of damp magnolia blossoms wafted through the open window and clung to my skin. Sweat began to tickle down my armpits, darkening the sleeve of my blue blouse.

What had we done? Bringing our small children to a foreign place full of unknowns. Who could have thought we would be caught in the middle of an international dispute in a country of predominately rice paddies and water buffalo. I must be nuts. Be that as it may, there was no way I was going to let anyone touch my girls. Over my dead body.

Oh God. Don't let that happen! How could we be such a terrible parents to put our children in harm's way like this? Did I agree because I wanted an adventure? Because I had a romantic dream of changing the world? Just because I was bored with housework? What if this motley crew of men carried us away, leaving no trace of what had become of us? My father was going to kill me.

I held my breath and kept my eyes on the men gathered around the apparent leader. We sat in silence. Somehow the girls knew not to let out a peep nor did they stir an inch. We were all frozen in our places. The men stood around the leader, heads bowed and arms gesturing wildly in discussion. It seemed we had waited hours, but in reality it was only a minute, when the man appeared again at Jim's window. He issued a stern warning and before Jim could apologize, turned and walked back to join the group.

We rode in silence until the security gate to our compound clamped shut. Our guard, the chowkidar, stood silently watching us pile out of the car. If he gave us his usual welcoming smile, we didn't know. He was so bundled up against the cool evening that we could only see his eyes.

We rushed the girls into our candlelit living room where Lucy had been waiting anxiously for our return. Melinda ran into her arms and Jenna and Nyna began talking at once, asking questions. Who were those men? What did they want? Why did we have to be so quiet?

Jim and I looked at each other, unspoken questions reflected in our eyes. Shall we tell them we just had a close call? That the vigilantes had frightened us too? We were supposed to be grownups. We were not supposed to be scared. A few moments passed and the decision was made. The tension in the room cooled as Jim explained, as calmly as his racing heart would allow, that the men were Bengali security and wanted to make sure we were safe.

We hugged goodnight and Lucy corralled the children up the stairs to their beds. Any calm, confident demeanor I had been able to hold onto, crumbled. I hadn't wanted to frighten the girls. I gave up and collapsed into a lump onto the couch. I allowed the trembling in my gut to surface, covered my face with shaky hands, and sobbed.

~

We were entering our second monsoon season when Jim was asked to travel to Karachi in West Pakistan to liaison with USAID officers there. Jim's departure was uneventful, and the children and I went about our weekly routines.

Two days after Jim left, I received word from the AID office that Dacca was in the path of a hurricane coming in from the Bay of Bengal. I didn't know exactly what a hurricane would be like, but after speaking to friends, I prepared as best I could for what might come. I made a quick trip to the commissary and stocked up on candles and flashlight batteries, mac and cheese and cans of tuna. I relied on phone calls from the AID office to keep me informed about the situation.

There was no indication of bad weather when I put the children to bed that evening. I went to the roof of our house and looked out over the sleeping city. Our neighbor's porchlights were on as usual. The evening seemed calm and quiet. I lay in bed holding my breath, waiting for some indication that the storm was about to hit. Nothing was happening and I fell asleep.

Sometime during the night, I was awakened by a loud roaring sound. I knew the storm had arrived. My first thought was to get the girls to my room. I tried the electricity but no luck. I grabbed the flashlight next to my bed and made my way up the stairs to Jenna and Nyna's rooms. I roused the sleeping girls and we felt our way down the marble stairs. I stopped at Melinda's room and grabbed her from the crib.

The roar was increasing by the minute. I decided we would be safest in the master bathroom. I had always complained about the oversized tub. That night I was grateful for its width and length. I piled pillows, a blanket, and the girls into the tub and crawled in after them.

We snuggled with each other and listened to the roaring wind as it grew louder and louder until suddenly, it stopped. Stark silence. A frightening, eerie silence.

We strained to hear what was happening. Or for what was about to happen. The silence was more frightening than the roar. I hugged the girls as tightly as I could. Jenna had an apprehensive look on her face and Nyna's eyes were as big as saucers. Melinda looked confused, wondering what was going on. Minutes passed and we remained frozen in place. It was as if we were all holding our breaths in sync with the total silence.

I jumped! The roaring of the rain had suddenly started again. I was to understand later that the silence we heard was the eye of the storm passing over the house. We stayed put in the tub until the roar gradually gave way to a steady pattern of rain pounding on the windows. I moved us to my bed and exhaustion took over. The storm had passed. We slept.

The next morning, I told the children to stay in bed while I looked around. I crept cautiously to the bedroom door and opened it a crack. The floor in the living room was damp. I went searching for the source of the dampness and discovered a tiny stream of water running down the steps from the girls' upstairs rooms. I couldn't understand where the water might be coming from. I was certain that I had closed the windows in their rooms when I tucked them in the night before.

I held on to the railing and pulled myself up the stairs, water sloshing around my feet. I stopped at Nyna's door and stared into the room. The window above her bed had been broken open and rain was pouring through. Glass from the shattered window was sprinkled across on her pink quilt. The air conditioner that was installed above her window was hanging by an electric cord about a foot above her bed. Just short of where my precious little girl would have been sleeping. Acid rose into my throat, and I struggled not to turn and run. I went to check Jenna's room. The windows had held. I turned and walked gingerly down the stairs, trying not to slip.

I had reached the bottom of the stairs when a loud banging on the front door stopped me from going further. I hesitated. Wondering who could possibly be out in such wild weather? The banging continued and I heard Mark Weaver's voice call my name. Relieved, I waded to the door and struggled to pull it open. I was happy to see Mark's friendly face.

He entered and quickly shut the door behind him, but not before I caught a glimpse of a large slab of our neighbor's tin roof laying on our front lawn. I didn't want to think about what the world looked like outside.

Lucy and Abdul arrived and asked about the girls. Were we ok?

Why was the floor wet? I told them the rain was coming in through Nyna's broken window. Abdul rushed up the stairs, motioning for Mohommed to follow. He called down saying they would need to find something to cover the holes in the wall. Lucy asked, again, about the girls and I pointed toward my bedroom. She turned to join the children, but I stopped her to ask about her family. She said Abdul had sent runners to the servant's villages to assess the damage. She left to collect the girls and make them breakfast.

Mark reported on the situation at their house. Minor damage, he said. Tree branches were strewn across their yard and flowering shrubs had been uprooted from their beds. He likened the trip from their house to driving through a war zone. He had to weave and dodge flying objects and piles of litter scattered across the road. He cautioned me to keep the children inside until the wind calmed down. I shouldn't be driving until the storm cleanup was done, he said. I waved goodbye when he left for home. A warm feeling flooded through me. I was filled with gratitude, knowing that we were surrounded by kind and caring friends this far from home.

I tried not to think about the gaping hole over Nyna's bed upstairs. I didn't want to imagine what might have happened if she had been lying asleep in her bed and the air conditioner cord had not held.

That morning, more than ever, I wished Jim were home to give me a hug. The phone lines were down, and it was late in the day before I was able to speak with him. I assured him that we were ok, but for the second time in our overseas experience, Jim had endured hours of anxiety and worry. The stress was beginning to take a toll on both of us. I joked, about how he always managed, somehow, to be away in times of disaster. He would tease, "I'm just smart that way,"

KINDNESS

TWENTY
Excursions

The weather in Bengal was not a laughing matter. Monsoon, floods and hurricanes had an enormous impact on the food supply during the winter months. The paucity of food during certain months made life difficult for Bengali people. Every year they faced hunger and disease.

Jim and I reasoned that the weather was at least partly responsible for the solemn expressions on the faces of many Bengali people. We rarely saw children in Dacca laughing out loud or even smiling in public places..

This was particularly brought home to us when Jim and I were invited to visit Joe and Becky Toner in Nepal. They had taken the AID post there after they left Cyprus. Jim and I were thrilled to have a chance to visit that small mysterious country. Nepal was particularly mysterious at the time because the Chinese had kept the country isolated from the rest of the world for many years. Travel in and out of Nepal in the early 60's was difficult in the best of times.

Jim and I flew the short miles from Dacca to Nepal on a small propeller plane that carried two Japanese businessmen and chickens stacked in coops in back of the six-passenger plane. Jim and I were the only English speakers on board. Including the pilots.

The passageway through the Himalayan Mountains was so narrow it felt as if the wings of our small plane could touch the sides of the mountain as we flew through the pass. I was trying not to be afraid but making a lousy job at it. I was greatly relieved when our plane emerged into the valley. The astounding beauty before us erased all concerns. Mountains on the horizon were so brightly shining in the sunlight that they appeared to be lit from within. The mountain tops were frosted with snow and glistened so brightly it was hard to look at them for long.

I breathed a sigh of relief when we landed at the small Kathmandu airport safe and intact. An AID driver met us and drove us to

160

Toner's home. The short trip into town afforded us a glimpse of the fantastic countryside. The symmetry and lush beauty of the neatly terraced hills we could see from the windows of our car soon smoothed any remaining sharp edges of nerves.

We were greeted by the Toners and ensconced in their lovely home for the weekend. They were excited to show us around their new country.

The moment we stepped out of the car into the street we were serenaded by a small band of young boys. They looked to be around four or five years old. They were dressed in white shalwar chemise and several of the boys had black pillbox type hats on their heads. The two oldest strummed homemade stringed instruments made from gourds. The other three were singing and dancing with such joy and openness that Jim and I were taken aback at first. We couldn't help but think about the somber faces of the young Bengali children at home.

The contrast between cultures was apparent the moment we arrived in Nepal. The Napoli people appeared to be relaxed and happy. Adults as well as the children smiled easily and dressed themselves in bright colors. There were ornately decorated temples everywhere. Nepalis of all ages mingled with the monkey population at the shrines that peppered the environs. Monkeys and cows were sacred and roaming free in the streets and gardens of the houses. We were advised to give them plenty of space. It was taboo to harm them in any way, so they were at times brash and aggressive.

It was rare for Jim and me to take a trip without our children. We had always travelled with them at our sides. This time, we had no qualms about leaving them. We knew they were safe in the good hands of Lucy, Abdul, and our friends, the Weavers. It was a risky choice to make, and we debated long and hard before deciding it would be safe.

We thought we would enjoy some adult travel alone and then had to laugh when we discovered we had brought the girls with us after all. We thought of Jenna every time we encountered a Buddhist Temple covered with colorful flowers. We could just see Nyna dancing with the boy bands every time we were treated to a street serenade. We caught a glimpse of the 'Chosen Virgin' as she stood at her castle window looking down at the town square. We reminded ourselves to tell the children of the Nepali story of the Virgin when we reached home.

KINDNESS

We wished all three could see the garden full of monkeys frolicking in and out of the domed temple on the hill. The monkeys owned the place. They paid no attention at all to the humans laying flowers and bowls of food on the temple steps. I vowed to bring the children to visit Nepal someday.

~

Our next-door neighbor, Ruth Downing was a wealth of knowledge about the subcontinent. She had more to do with my growth and education than I realized at the time. The Downings were Americans from California. Ruth's husband was a contractor with an American engineering firm.

Ruth had lived in India for years and I was fascinated by stories of her many adventures. She had ridden an elephant with an Indian Raj and had explored villages deep in the Hill Country of Bengal where few were courageous enough to go. She had visited that same area to see the camps where the elephants were trained. I greatly admired her adventurous nature.

I was happy when she called one day and asked if I would like to go on a picnic with her and her Indian friend. Her friend had been an officer in the RAF during the war. He owned a small plane and would be flying us to a beach on the Bay of Bengal for lunch. I was excited to see another part of the country and jumped at the chance.

We packed a picnic lunch and put our bathing suits under our clothes and set off to the airport. I found it exciting to fly in such a small plane and asked the colonel a multitude of questions as we flew over scenes of rice paddies and groves of banana trees. I found it particularly exciting to see the forest and landscape so up-close. The low altitude made it possible to see exotic plants and birds among the trees and on the ground. I was delighted by the patchwork quilt of green and red when we passed over a clump of bright red flame trees in bloom below our plane.

I gripped the arms of my seat when the plane passed up the pristine white sandy beach and landed on the water. It was wasted energy. The landing was smooth and unexciting.

We wasted no time shedding our clothes and wading into the cool waves. I felt like a teenager again, spending a Saturday afternoon at the town pool. The day was sunny and warm and the ocean breezes were enough to dry our suits after our refreshing dip. No other humans in sight.

KINDNESS

The well-spoken and charming middle-aged man and Ruth had been friends for years. He was taller than most Bengalis and clean-shaven. He dressed and spoke like an Englishman. He had attended university in the UK.

We ate the picnic lunch Ruth and I had packed then we rested and made sandcastles. My tummy was full and the warm sun caught up with me. I dozed on my towel while Ruth and her friend talked about old times. It was the rarest of days. No responsibilities and no schedules, just time in the sun and sand with the quiet music of the waves. It was sheer joy.

As we prepared to leave, the colonel remarked on my interest in the plane and asked if I'd like to pilot the flight home. I laughed, thinking he must be kidding me. He assured me that he would be in the co-pilot's seat next to me and ready to take over the minute he was wanted or needed. I had to admit that I was yearning to fly the plane. There was no wind and no air traffic anywhere near the area. No clouds or hint of bad weather. The flight to the shore had been smooth as silk. My concern was about taking off in the water. He assured me that I would do ok and once again convinced me that he would take control the moment he was needed.

The plane glided along the waves until the colonel directed me to pull back slowly on the stick. I held my breath until the plane rose effortlessly into the cloudless sky. I took a deep breath and broke out in a series of nervous giggles.

What a rush it was! For a moment, a very brief moment, I felt a sudden twinge of guilt. Perhaps this was a reckless thing to be doing. Maybe I was giddy with the freedom and sea and air of the day. Who knows what came over me. I was the mother of three small children after all. I hastened to assure myself that the colonel was sitting right beside me, ready to take over the controls. We were safe. The colonel smiled when I admitted I loved flying the plane. I joked how I should have a plane of my own. Someday.

I had a 'lump-in-the-throat' moment as we approached the Dacca airport. I turned to the colonel and asked him to take over the controls. I had no idea how to land the plane on a runway and the strip of concrete below looked awfully small. The colonel wouldn't let me off so easily. He said he would talk me through the procedure. He convinced me that I could do it. After the wheels touched down on the runway I took a deep breath. We were home after an unbelievable day.

~

Ayah Lucy came to me one day with an invitation for our family to visit her village. She asked permission for Maudun to come with us to help carry a basket. She wanted our families to know each other. We agreed on a date and one day when the weather was not too hot, we travelled a few miles outside Dacca to visit her small village. A group of twenty bamboo houses stood facing a common area. A Christian cross adorned the largest grass hut. We assumed that was the church hall.

Lucy's house was located in the middle of the village. Her mother and daughter were standing on the porch to greet us when we arrived. Lucy introduced us to her family and motioned for us to sit at the small rattan table. A child's chair, fashioned from bamboo, was next to the table. Lucy picked Melinda up from her stroller, and sat her in the little chair, and handed her a cup of apple juice. Jenna and Nyna sat on stools next to us.

One of the young women, I'm not certain whether sister or daughter, brought glasses of sweet tea to Jim and me. Lucy reached into a basket and brought out a bottle of lemonade. She poured the lemonade into two small glasses and handed them to Jenna and Nyna.

Melinda smacked her lips when the cool apple juice reached her tongue. She emptied the cup without stopping to rest. She was obviously thirsty. Lucy wiped Melinda's sticky chin and moved her from the little chair into the arms of the oldest woman on the porch. She introduced Melinda to her elderly mother and Melinda smiled and burbled a whole long conversation to the brown, wrinkly faced woman. We had no idea what story Melinda was telling, which was probably the reason we all laughed. Melinda looked proud of herself.

Lucy's daughter left the porch and went inside the house. She returned with a six-month-old baby.

Lucy took her grandson and placed him into my arms. She beamed down at the baby as proud as only a grandmother could be. The tiny little brown baby looked at me with his big eyes and I was concerned my paleness would frighten him. I needn't have worried. The baby gave a big yawn and looked a tad baffled.

After we finished our drinks, we carried on a brief conversation with Lucy's family. Lucy acted as interpreter. They were shy, and pleasant hardworking farmers. It was evident that Lucy held a position of power and respect in her village. Her grandchildren, cousins, aunts and uncles and eventually the whole village crowded around so that Jim's movie camera could record the occasion.

Filming done, we said our goodbyes and Lucy led us around the village green back to our car. The residents came to stand outside their huts and greeted us as we passed. I looked back at Lucy's house to wave to her family and saw that every young person in the village was following us. The sight of a parade of villagers lined up behind us was baffling. I was never quite certain what a proper response should be on occasions such as that, but I was glad that everyone seemed to be having a good time. We waved goodbye, honored to have been invited to Lucy's Bengali home.

~

Spring break arrived at the girl's school and we took advantage of the free time to see more of India. We talked to the Weavers about our plans and they decided to join us. We decided on a trip to a tea plantation. We made arrangements to leave Melinda in the care of Lucy and Abdul. Travel in India at that time held too many risks for a toddler.

We purchased airline tickets to the Happy Valley Tea Estate in Darjeeling, India. There were no direct flights from Dacca to Darjeeling, which meant spending a night in Calcutta. I was both happy and apprehensive about staying overnight in the city. It had the reputation of having the most poverty and ill health in all India.

We arrived in the smoggy, sprawling city, tired and hungry. Our plan was to find a place to get a light supper, and hurry the children into their beds. We were piling out of the taxi to go into the hotel when poor Katie Weaver caught her finger in the taxi door. Mark and Beth took her to a first aid facility while Jim and I settled the other children into their beds. Even though they were upset by Kate's accident, exhaustion won the day, and they were asleep in no time.

The Weavers returned and agreed to stay with the children when Jim gave in to my nudging to see something of Calcutta. Jim and I walked to a nearby park. Calcutta was the largest city in northern India and people filled the large space as far as we could see. People were squatting around small fire pots in the park. Some were lying on the ground under trees. We assumed they were just napping. Shadowy figures with their heads covered, were hunched together. They didn't give us so much as a glance as we passed. Creating their own privacy. I supposed they had to form some sort of invisible wall with so many people packed close together.

Smoke from the fire pots mingled with the dampness in the air to create a dense, smoggy atmosphere. It appeared many of the people in the park were homeless. The city was poor and crowded and the park smelled of food and excrement and the burning coal. The scene in the park that evening reinforced what I had heard about Calcutta. I understood how Calcutta got its reputation as the Hell Hole of India.

The figures in white and brown flowing robes we encountered on our walk began to take on a slightly threatening vibe as the darkness began to settle in. There were few lights along the pathways, and Jim suggested we return to the hotel where we were staying. I begged for just a few minutes more. I wanted to see what the crowd would do when darkness came. Would they leave the park? Would they prepare to stay the night there?

I made the argument that Beth and Mark had put the children to bed. There was no rush. We still had a little time. Jim relented and we made our way through the throngs of people until we reached the Brahmaputra River. We stopped just off the path, our attention drawn to a group of people gathered at the water's edge. It looked as if a ritual of some sort was taking place.

We moved a few steps nearer to the gathering, being careful not to draw attention to ourselves. We watched a man, we assumed he was a religious sort, say words over what appeared to be a dead person lying in the bottom of a skiff. There were leis of frangipani around the dead man's neck and petals of cream-colored flowers sprinkled across his dark robes. A group of women appeared from out of the darkness. They escorted a middle-aged woman to the skiff. Her silk sari caught the light, and we could make out rows of jewels around her neck. The woman showed no emotion as she was lowered into the boat. She quietly settled herself next to the corpse.

We could hear the religious man saying more words. Prayers we suspected, then our innocent trespassing turned into a moment of horror The man tossed something flammable into the canoe.

We were stunned into disbelief. The man pushed the craft away from the shore and the crowd stood silently watching as the canoe floated down the Ganges. I felt sick at my stomach. We couldn't stand to see anymore. I pulled on Jim's hand and we fled the scene as quickly as possible. I took one last glance at the departing boat. The flames had risen higher and it seemed the craft was totally engulfed in fire.

I had read about this death ritual. This ritual was expected of wives in certain Indian cultures. Until death do us part was a literal commitment for some. We hurried back to our room and I tried to get the image of the burning boat out of my head.

We didn't speak of our experience the next morning but talked, instead, of the fun things we would see in the hills of Darjeeling. We hoped to shieled the children from an encounter with the poor maimed souls who gathered around public places to beg. We moved them through the airport crowds as quickly as possible and were relieved when the flight to Darjeeling was called.

Darjeeling is a district in the Northeast corner of India. Darjeeling was no Calcutta in 1965, nor Dacca either. We found the people there to be more prosperous, outgoing, and friendly.

The inn was a typical British facility with sturdy mahogany furniture and patterned fabrics on the beds and curtains. True to form, a full English tea was served in the dated comfortable living area every afternoon. Flower beds surrounding the hotel were filled with bright bougainvillea and frangipani bushes. Groupings of tables and chairs were placed along the shaded veranda. In my imagination it was like stepping onto a movie set. Beth and I sat on the wide veranda with a cup of tea and breathed in the cool mountain air. We were thrilled to have nothing to do but watch the children play on the large green lawn and smell the frangipani blossoms.

Jenna and Nyna were excited when, on the third day of our visit, we were fitted with horses and made ready for a ride through the plantation. We were guided along paths carved through acres of tea plants. The sun was bright and shown through the tender green tea leaves as we rode our horses through the well tended fields. The ride was beautiful, the air was very thin due to the high atmosphere, and I was happy we were on horseback rather than walking.

We enjoyed the outing even though young David was not very happy on a horse. I watched him closely to monitor his comfort. At one point I could see he was about to panic when his horse jumped at something, but Nyna coached him and encouraged him to relax and trust his horse. He was not the happiest of the children that day, but he managed to arrive back at the hotel without an incident.

Darjeeling was very civilized and sophisticated compared to Calcutta and Dacca. Everything was organized and life ran on a schedule as British as could be.

We took the children to a zoo not far from the hotel. The zoo was unique in that it was famous for its natural setting. There were no cages. The animals were separated from the visitors by post and wire fences. It was no wonder the animals looked to be so relaxed and happy. The zoo was barely different from their natural habitat.

A llama stood at the wire fence ready to spit at us. Two Bengal tigers lurked in the background. I was grateful for their lack of curiosity in us humans. Two young black bears played and wrestled each other to the ground, then chased after one another around the bushes. Being so upfront and personal and given the natural setting, it was easy to think of them as pets rather than caged zoo animals.

From our hotel rooms, we were able to see the Kanchenjunga Mountains. We had great expectations of seeing snow on top of the highest mountains in the world. Every morning we rose early with our hopes high and every morning we were disappointed. The mountain range never came into view because of the clouds that gathered along its base.

Our last morning before leaving Darjeeling, Jim and I and Mark rose early one more time, in hopes of catching a view of Mount Everest. That morning, our hopes were answered. The Kanchenjunga was in full view. What a sight it was!!! The sun peeked slowly above the horizon and the snow topped mountains took on a yellow glow. The glow took on a rose color, then morphed to a stunning gold. It was a magical moment. Watching the sunlight move across the mountain tops was akin to being in a prayer. The awe I felt that day is embedded in my skin. We stood entranced until clouds moved in to cut off the view.

A movement far below in a valley beneath our mountain perch drew our attention away from the clouds and down to earth. We watched as a village slowly appeared through the mist. In a short time we could make out the figures that began to move around the site. We could hear a bell ring from below and watched as the center of the compound was filled with scampering school children. Patches of blue and white formed into patterns as the children sorted themselves by classes. We were witness to a morning ritual: orphans attending a United Nations Refugee School as they began their day.

KINDNESS

TWENTY-ONE
Another Time in Limbo

We returned from spring break, eager to resume our normal activities. Monday morning the van picked the girls up for school as usual. Jim gave me a peck on the cheek and left for work. Melinda stood at the living room window waving goodbye to her Daddy as he backed out of the compound. I sat at the dining table with my notebook preparing a grocery list for Abdul. We were planning a dinner party for the coming weekend.

Half an hour later, I heard the front door open. I was surprised when Jim entered the room. He must have forgotten something, I thought. I saw his face and knew whatever it was, it was not good news. I fought down a feeling of dread. Best wait to see what his surprise appearance was about.

Jim motioned for me to join him in the living room. I poured us a cup of coffee and went to sit by him on the couch. I held my breath, afraid to ask what was going on. What if something had happened to the girls? Did he have bad news from Texas?

My fears were confirmed when I saw tears in his eyes. We cuddled our coffee cups and Jim gave me the news. There had been another international incident overnight. This time, a Chinese plane bound for India had accidently dropped a bomb on the outskirts of Dacca. The bomb had landed in a rice paddy. The bomb didn't detonate, but the State Department decided to be on the safe side in case there were further incidents. We were to be evacuated once again.

Women and children and all non-essential personnel were to be sent to the Philippines. I was even less thrilled to be evacuated from Dacca than I was from Cyprus. We had such a rich and loving community in Dacca. The children had made a large circle of friends and were doing great in school. Our household staff had become like family. Work at the AID mission was well established and flourishing. There was some talk in Dacca concerning independence from West Pakistan, but there was no outward sign of conflict. Evacuation didn't make sense to me.

It was no use to make a fuss. I turned my attention to packing our four suitcases. Jim had been declared essential personnel and would be remaining in Dacca.

Once again, our little family was faced with an uncertain future. I sensed an air of urgency in these evacuation orders that was lacking in the one we had received three years ago. And yet, like the first evacuation orders, we received no information as to what to expect once we reached our destination. We were, again, headed to parts unknown.

The morning of our departure, there were tears all around. Lucy cried as she helped pack Melinda's clothes. Our transport arrived and Melinda cried for Lucy when I took her from Lucy's arms. Jenna and Nyna were on the verge of tears, trying to be brave. They were happier when they learned their friends Kate and David were leaving for Manilla the same day.

Jim tried to smile and assured me he would join us as soon as possible. He admitted that he felt more at ease since the Weavers would be coming on the next plane. Nevertheless, this was a hard goodbye.

~

I couldn't believe my eyes when we were escorted from the airport terminal across the tarmac to a military plane. There were no stairs pulled up to the body of the plane. Instead, we were escorted to the rear of the plane. There was a gaping hole where the tail should have been. A maw of dark space appeared at the top of a wide ramp. A military man pushed Melinda in her stroller up the ramp while I helped Jenna and Nyna carry their little backpacks.

I stood, dumbfounded when we reached the top of the long ramp. There were no proper seats. Just rows of swings with mesh slings for seats. I took a deep breath and peered through the dim light to find three swings together. Jenna and Nyna looked at me.

"Are we supposed to sit in those things?" Jenna asked.

" Those things don't have backs," Nyna said. "Where are we supposed to put our color books?"

I had no answers. I was as confounded as they. I looked around at the other twenty-five or thirty passengers. It seemed none of them had answers to our dilemma either. I tried to reassure the children. "I'm sure we will arrive at the next stop before you know it." I was sure of no such thing, but it was the only answer I had at the time.

I settled Melinda onto my lap. She looked around the cabin and laughed at the sight of her sisters struggling to get comfortable in the unwieldy mesh seats.

A man in a blue uniform came to the front of the plane, gave a curt welcome and informed us we were flying in a C130. The plane was designed to transport parachuters and large equipment, he said. He apologized for the inconvenience and pointed to a curtain located at the back of the plane. The one and only toilet. He said the flight would be a short one and he left. A voice over the loudspeaker told us to buckle up and I showed the girls how to secure a strap over their skinny laps.

It was not easy to fit little bottoms comfortably in seats wide enough for men. I was concerned that one of them would slip out of the sling. I looked around the plane for an alternative. There was none. There was nothing to do but go through with it.

After the plane took off I tried to make things better by telling the girls, once again, that we only had a short way to go. The cabin lights dimmed and Nyna worked her body around until she could fit sideways in the swing. Her eyes closed for a nap. I believed Jenna found a way to dose off as well. The early morning and the stress of the moment was catching up with them. I sat upright cuddling Melinda.

I was trying to decide whether to be frightened or angry. Frightened that the danger was worse than we were told. It was obvious that we were asked to leave Dacca before proper planes were available. Angry because the children were having to go through this tiring, chaotic flight.

We were a few hours into the flight and the adrenalin was leaving my system. I had nodded off in spite of the uncomfortable situation. Nyna got out of the sling and announced that she needed to go to the toilet. I was thankful for Jenna's help as I settled Melinda into Jenna's lap. Melinda wanted to get down as well but there were no aisles on the plane. No place for her to walk. Jenna began a game of Patty Cake to distract her.

Nyna and I had returned, and Nyna was telling Jenna about the funny-looking toilet that was behind the curtain when a voice came over the loudspeaker. The pilot ordered us to strap up and to cease all conversation. I took Melinda and put my fingers across my lips, signaling the girls to stop talking. Jenna and Nyna immediately obeyed, their eyes as big as saucers. They had caught the urgency in my voice.

Without warning, the lights in the cabin shut off. We sat in pitch blackness. A darkness so thick I could no longer see Jenna and Nyna sitting next to me. The only sound left in the cabin was the roar of the plane engines. It was as if the universe was listening. I reached over and found Nyna's hand.

The eerie atmosphere was more than puzzling. It was frightening. There was no explanation as to what was happening to our plane. We were flying in a silent, black vacuum. Total silence and total darkness.

When the lights finally came back on, our fellow passengers uttered a loud sigh of relief. I asked Jenna and Nyna if they were ok and took Melinda's little fingers and began to play a game. Just a made-up game. I was relieved to feel the plane lose altitude and hoped it was an indication that we had reached our destination, wherever that was.

We landed and the military man stood again at the front of the plane to announce that we were in Bangkok, Thailand. We would regroup there and board a plane to our final destination. The airman thanked us for our cooperation during the flight. Someone in the row of swings behind me called to the airman. "What," the person wanted to know, "was the blackout all about?"

The airman replied "It was necessary to go dark because we were being trailed by a Vietnamese fighter plane. We followed procedure until the fighter plane pulled away without further action."

It took a moment for his message to sink in. Now I could be scared. Acid rose in my throat. I was having trouble grasping the fact that anyone might regard Americans as an enemy. Throughout the many political disputes in other countries, I had never heard of anyone threatening Americans in such a direct way. It was 1965 and the United States was not yet involved in the Vietnam war. At least not to the knowledge of the American public. I had to entertain the idea that I had been indulging in a fantasy. Ignorant of a more complicated world than I had imagined.

The back end of the aircraft opened, and everyone began to file out. Even before we stepped out of the plane, the girls began to complain about hunger. I promised it would be just a little while longer and we would have something to eat. They wanted to go to the bathroom and Melinda needed a diaper change.

After a visit to the ladies' room, we stepped out into the crowd of people rushing from one place then another. I assumed I would find signs pointing to a gathering place for Pakistani evacuees but saw nothing to indicate that anyone was aware of our arrival. The room sounded like the Tower of Babel. It was like we had arrived at a United Nations convention, and everyone was speaking their own language at once. I was tired and overwhelmed by the hustle and noise and confusion that met us at the door.

I found some people who were speaking English and got directions to the side of the room where women from the American Embassy in Thailand had set up a table with drinks and sandwiches. I guided my little ones to a seat close to the American group, settled Melinda into her stroller and asked Jenna to take over stroller duty. I made my way to the cue where people were waiting to get food and drink.

The line was long and consisted of American evacuees from all over the Middle East. I was tired and impatient, my mind filled with 'what ifs' as I edged to the front of the line. I chatted with another American standing in front of me. We exchanged news about the countries we left behind. Her group had arrived from Lebanon on a military plane that morning. She talked of meeting other evacuees from posts I'd never heard of. It seemed that Americans stationed in the whole of the Middle East were receiving evacuation orders. All routed through Bangkok to their destinations.

I finally reached the food table ready to order sandwiches and drinks. I spotted a sign above the table. The food was not free. Each item had a price next to it. American currency only. I had no American money. Pakistani policy banned possession of all currency, except Pakistani rubles.

I reached into my purse and pulled out all the rupees I had and held them out to the American woman behind the sandwich table. "This is the only currency we were allowed," I explained.

"I'm sorry, we cannot take rupees," the woman said. The American woman standing behind the table appeared tired and frazzled as if she, too, had gotten up too early.

"We just came from East Pakistan and my children are crying for something to eat," I said.

The poor woman shook her head. "Sorry," she repeated. "We can only take American money."

She didn't look very sorry to me, but I was not feeling very understanding at that moment. I was angry and tired and when I looked over at my brave girls it was all I could do to keep from crying. My emotions echoed the atmosphere created by the mob of people struggling to find a way out of Thailand.

I made my way back through the crowd and pulled the girls in for a hug. I hated giving them the bad news. We sat. Hungry, and disappointed. There was nothing to do but wait for directions as to what was to happen next. I did the best I could to explain to the children why I couldn't get them food. They looked at me with disappointment on their faces and protests in their voices.

I had run out of ways to explain the situation to the girls when a man, a stranger, walked over to me and introduced himself. He said he had come from the American Embassy in Karachi. He claimed to know who I was and asked about how I was doing. I looked like a wreck. I could hardly keep my voice from trembling as I explained the money situation to him.

"No problem," he said. "Relax. I'll see what I can do." We waited impatiently until he returned with sandwiches and drinks.

I was in such a daze I didn't remember his name. I barely managed to thank him before he disappeared into the mass of humanity. He was the archetypal Good Samaritan appearing suddenly in the midst of an anxiety filled, foreign airport. I silently thanked all guardian angels everywhere who came to our rescue that day. Names may be forgotten, but kindness lives forever.

The hours spent in the airport terminal that day seemed to last forever. I fumed and seethed, angry at the American embassies in Pakistan and Bangkok for being so ill prepared for our evacuation. I couldn't believe being asked to pay money for the meager lunches and particularly that American money was required.

At the same time, I could see the American Embassy women were being stretched to breaking due to the hoard of American evacuees pouring through the Bangkok airport. The anger was only wasted energy since I could do nothing now but complain to myself. I reminded myself to be thankful for the Good Samaritan providing the light lunch. The sandwich and juice helped the girls make it through the long wait.

I longed for a strong Scotch and soda and strained to hear if a plane to Manilla was announced. It was not easy to make out the words over the loudspeaker. The constant din of the waiting room didn't help. I perked up when a boarding time for an American Airlines plane bound for Manilla in the Philippines was finally announced. I gathered my dear, tired, little ones for what I hoped and prayed would be the final lag of our journey. Jenna and Nyna were as happy to get onto a plane and out of the chaos of the terminal as I.

I felt a sigh of relief when we were settled into comfortable seats on the American Airlines commercial plane. I leaned back into the padded seat and only then did I realize I'd been breathing in shallow gulps since being told how close our military plane had come to being attacked. I took several deep breaths and sank into the soft seat, pulled Melinda closer to my chest and fell asleep.

~

Americans arriving in Manilla from East Pakistan were housed in a small hotel close to the middle of the city. The Cyprus evacuation taught me that I could make our lives more normal if I moved quickly from the hotel into an apartment. I called the American Embassy the day after we arrived in the Philippines and began the process of finding a proper place for us.

Beth Weaver was in the same hotel and I urged her to bring her children and move into an apartment with us. She hesitated, unsure it was the right thing to do. Rumors were circulating through the American evacuee community daily. Some said we would be back in Dacca in a few weeks. Others were reporting that we would all be sent back to the United States before the week was out. The American Embassy in Manilla had no orders as to our final destinations. Rumors and confusion as to how long we would be staying in Manilla continued to run rampant. Experience told me that we would not be leaving Manilla anytime soon.

I found a lovely, clean, furnished apartment within the week and moved to get us settled. A few days later the Weavers moved into an apartment down the hall from us. Mark was released from duty in Dacca and followed us to Manilla. The apartments were plain but comfortable and met the needs of our families. Each apartment had two bedrooms, dining, kitchen, baths etc. Three days after we landed in Manilla, Beth and I enrolled the children in the American school at Clark Airforce Base.

There was a large American military presence in Manilla. A military bus picked our children up every morning and brought them home in the afternoon. Jenna and Nyna felt like normal American students. Neither gave much detail about their school life. Both were doing ok in their studies. Five-year-old Nyna's eyes lit up when she discovered a small school kiosk that sold paper, pencils, crayons, paints, and school supplies. It was her joy to use her allowance and buy a new pencil or some little sweet every week.

Life outside of school was fantastic! Evacuated personnel were issued passes to the American Air Force Club. Every weekend Beth, Mark and I packed the children into a taxi and took them to the Officer's Club. The weather never changed. The temperature was warm to hot and dry. There was a place for hamburgers and fries and, oh happy day, ice cream. We were able to buy real milk, a true luxury after the dreaded powdered milk available in East Pakistan.

Manilla was a thriving city. A large segment of the population was fluent in English. It was a pleasure to become acquainted with the native crafts. I was as enthralled with the beautiful shops as Nyna was with the school kiosk. I particularly liked items made from the acacia wood grown there. I bought wooden plates, trays and small bowls to send back to the States.

Melinda missed Lucy but she seemed happy when I settled her into the stroller for a trip to town. Her big eyes were wide with interest in all the new sights and sounds around her. She continued to learn more words and became quite good at running. She enjoyed the club pool as much as Jenna and Nyna. We purchased a floaty tube so she could paddle around in the water. Jenna and Nyna had as much fun pushing Melinda around the pool as Melinda had being pushed. I learned the hard way that she was extremely prone to sunburn.

October 25th, Melinda's third birthday, we had a party with balloons and cake. The Weavers came bringing small gifts and she made us all laugh when she took one look at her pink cupcake and dipped her fingers into the icing. She put the finger into her mouth and beamed out at us after she tasted the sweetness of it.

Jim was able to get away from his work guarding the American Embassy for a brief vacation to Manilla. The reunion created much excitement. Jenna and Nyna had so much to tell him about school and about riding the bus out to the base every day. They could hardly wait for the weekend. Joy was rampant when they were back in the water with their Dad again.

No one was happier than Jim. He frolicked with the girls, holding them high above his head then throwing them into the water making a huge splash. He encouraged Nyna to practice her floating skills and applauded Jenna's swimming progress. He wrapped Melinda in an oversized pool towel and snuggled her in his lap until she fell asleep. We stayed at the officers' club and relaxed around the pool until sun and water tired us out.

We had dinner with the Weavers in the evening and listened as Jim filled us in with news from Dacca. We wanted word of Lucy, Abdul and the others in our household. We wanted to know how they were taking care of him. Were they feeding him well? We were curious as to which families had remained in the Philippines and which ones had returned to the states.

That first night, Jim opened up to us about things that had occurred after we had left. He told us about the night a bomb had gone off outside the Consulate. He was the lone officer on duty. Two Marines stood guard outside the door of the building. Jim was sitting in his office scanning computers for news when the lights suddenly went out. He sat for some very tense minutes straining to hear what was happening. Every ounce of him alert for sounds of footsteps indicating someone might be inside the building. I couldn't hold back the tears when I thought of him there alone and in danger. I gripped his hand.

Jim talked about the lonely nights standing watch at the Embassy. He surprised us with some personal news. He had ordered a banjo from Hong Kong and spent the lonely hours on watch teaching himself to play the instrument. He was hoping to play along with Mark when we were together again. Our families loved sitting around after dinner singing folk songs.

The highlight of Jim's visit was taking the children to a real movie theater to see their first technicolor movie, *My Fair Lady*. They loved every minute. They talked about their favorite parts for what seemed to be forever. Before we left Manilla we were able to take them to see *The Sound of Music*. Movies, books, and theater were their constant companions and formed the walls within which they built their lives.

His story was much more upsetting to me than my own, even when I thought about the hellish flight to Bangkok. I hadn't planned to tell him about the scary close call with the enemy plane, but I relented and admitted how frightened I'd been. I couldn't help but sound off about how angry I was to be unable to feed my hungry girls. Jim shared my anger and promised to pass it along to higher-ups at the Embassy.

Mark and Beth recounted the story of their own chaotic evacuation journey to the Philippines. We all agreed the experience was one we never wanted to repeat. We felt blessed to be sitting safe and happy to be together again.

On Jim's last evening in Manila, he began to pack for his return to Dacca. I was sad, reluctant to let him go. He pulled me into a hug. "I have something to tell you," he whispered. "But you have to promise to keep what I'm about to tell you a secret."

I looked up at him and his face was serious. "I promise," I said.

He continued, "I have information from a reliable source that you and the girls will be back in Dacca for Christmas." I threw myself at him and we fell into a heap on the bed. Both trying to laugh quietly, not to wake the children in the next room. My inner clock started at that moment, and I began to count the days and hours until that promise became reality.

The next morning, amid tearful goodbyes and hugs for the girls, Jim left for East Pakistan. Two weeks later we received word that we were to return to Dacca in time for Christmas. Oh Joy!

I hurried to mail some Christmas packages back to our parents in the States. There were beautiful wooden table settings made from Acacia trees, unique jewelry fashioned with pearls and semi-precious stones, and antique carved religious figures, their finery brushed with faded paint. I packed a few items for Lucy and Abdul and a few keepsakes for us. I hardly had room for our clothes.

Jenna was making plans for reuniting with her friends in Dacca and Nyna chatted with excitement about the box lunch the airline would be issuing for our trip. I was thinking what fun it would be to have our familiar Christmas ornaments again. I couldn't keep my mind from going to the one big question. What would we do for a Christmas tree in the tropics this year?

The Weavers were able to book on the same flight as ours and we chatted among ourselves. Wondering out loud if we would notice many changes in our homes when we arrived. We wondered together if the Bengali people would be as welcoming as before. I wondered how many of my American Welcome Committee friends would still be around.

~

On the home front, very little had changed. The servants had kept to the routine and taken good care of Jim while we were gone. We jumped right back into our usual activities. Lucy and Melinda were reunited, and the servants clapped their hands to see Melinda running joyfully around the house.

There was so little time left before Christmas. I depended on my 'To Do' lists once again. We dragged boxes of Christmas decorations from the storage room. I began pouring through catalogs and hunting the PX for something that would resemble the items listed in the Dear Santa letters the girls had composed on the plane back.

No matter where I looked, I had no luck finding a plant in this tropical landscape that could possibly resemble a Christmas fir. At the last minute I found a bush that had green feathery-looking leaves and decided it would have to do. I asked Abdul to fill a bucket with sand and together we tied the branches of the bush together to make a tree. Sort of. We placed our favorite ornaments into the branches of the bush. Jim worked his magic with the twinkly lights as best he could. Jenna was still not convinced and asked for the tinsel tree and colored light machine to be added to the room.

The makeshift decorations only added to our Christmas spirit. We were together for Christmas and that was what mattered. We gave ourselves and our families back home the gift of short telephone greetings. Our parents were relieved to hear our voices and anxious to receive the movies of our recent activities.

We were planning a New Year's party with our friends when our happy celebrations came to an abrupt halt. Jim got a call from Director Johnson that he was to be transferred to West Pakistan by the first of the year.

Jim was not happy to tell us the news. He was aware the children were overjoyed to be united with friends in Dacca. We were all happy to be with Lucy, Abdul and Mohammed again. It was a safe and comfortable. Like being home. We had begun to make plans for dinner parties and arranged play dates with the girls' friends. I was sad to think the girls would not have another chance to learn more about Bengali culture.

Well laid plans and all that. I turned my mind to packing. Once again. This new assignment involved more than packing a suitcase for each of us. This move required packing to leave the country. We would be packing up the household to move into a new home in Rawalpindi.

Everything was turned upside down. Dacca was moist and green. The tropics. West Pakistan was mainly a hot, dry desert. East Pakistani's were farmers and fisher people living close to the land. West Pakistani people were made up of tribal people, many of whom were historically nomads. The two sides of the country were very different cultures, held together by their religion.

The idea of house hunting again, gathering staff, and making community again was daunting. The Welcome Committee in Dacca had spoiled us. There was no such committee set up in the West as yet. We were on our own.

Jim and I sat with the news of the transfer for a day or so, trying to think through the logistics of such a drastic move. We knew we had to break the news to the children. And to Abdul, Lucy, and the rest of the servants. We came up with a partial solution. We asked Lucy and Abdul to come to West Pakistan with us.

Much to my relief, Abdul agreed. I was able to give some of the burden of household packing to him. Unfortunately, Lucy could not bring herself to leave her grandchild and declined the offer. We were disappointed, but totally understood and respected her decision.

We had a better idea of what was required of us after Jim took a quick trip to the West to visit the site and become briefed on his duties there. The Pakistani government was moving their capital from Karachi to a new city named Islamabad. Jim's mission was to prepare for a USAID presence in the new capital. In time, the AID mission in Karachi would be moved to the new capital city.

We knew that breaking the news about the move to the girls would be hard. Eleven-year-old Jenna would be affected the most. She had made good friends and was at an age when social life was very important. We called Jenna and Nyna into the living room one evening and told them we had some hard news. Jenna knew we had something serious to say as soon as she saw our faces. I put my arm around her and struggled to hold my emotions inside.

Jim explained the situation and Jenna struggled with her own tears. Nyna had questions. Was there a school there? Could the Weavers still come to our New Years party? Were we coming back to Dacca?

Jim and I tried to paint a picture of West Pakistan in the best light possible. We promised the girls a weekend in a fancy hotel in Karachi.

The hotel served real ice cream and had a swimming pool.

As word of our transfer became known, our lives were filled with parties. Friends and colleagues gathered to wish us goodbye. We were feted to an office party at the AID director's house. We hosted a round of dinner parties to express our gratitude and said goodbye to the group of young couples who had worked so closely with Jim in his department. The children were given goodbye parties by their friends.

For a week or so we were too busy to be sad about the move. And then the day arrived for us to leave. The Weavers were there to see us off. They had become our extended family and we all knew the relationships would leave a huge gap in our lives. All the servants stood in the driveway with sober expressions on their faces.

Lucy had been wiping her eyes all morning as we made last-minute preparations for the trip. She finally placed Melinda into my arms and stepped away from the car. The girls, Melinda and I were packed into the back seat. The car began to drive away and Melinda stood up in the seat, looked out the rear window and began holding her arms out. She screamed for Lucy. Tears were running down her chubby cheeks. I looked back. Lucy was running after us, her empty arms reaching for Melinda. I cried with them.

TWENTY-TWO
West Pakistan

This was our sixth move overseas. We had developed a ritual of arrival. We entered the property surrounding our new home in Rawalpindi and walked around the compound. Rows of sweet peas grew on a fence the entire length of the white stucco house. No blossoms yet. It was January, winter in West Pakistan. A rude contrast after being surrounded by the tropical green of the East. We walked through the house, pleased that all the rooms were on one floor. The bedrooms were arranged so that there was a small room for Melinda adjacent to the master.

Abdul had arrived a few days earlier and had hired an ayah named Maria to care for Melinda. He was still in the process of interviewing workers for his staff. We found it interesting that he decided to run the household with only one sweeper and the ayah. By the time we were unpacked and the children were enrolled in the American school, Abdul had the household running smoothly.

Jenna and Nyna entered school mid-semester. Once again they went about making new friends and adjusting to an entirely new routine. The most exciting aspect of the new school was the teachers. The principal of the school was an American, Mr. Petrie. He was a particular favorite of our children because he had a creative way of teaching dull subjects. Jenna memorized and constantly sang the version of the Declaration of Independence that Mr. Petrie wrote. A fun way to remember the Declaration.

Having Abdul move with us was the best gift possible. He was indeed amazing in so many ways. He was not only intelligent and wise, but he was also a good Muslim. We trusted him with our children and with our own lives. I totally relied on him. When the snake charmer came to our gates, I called Abdul to ask if it would be safe for the girls to watch the performance. When the monkey man came to the gates I asked Abdul to stand with the girls as they watched the scrawny little monkey dance to the owner's drum. He cared for us with wisdom and kindness.

Abdul ran our household with order, and precision. He had been trained from childhood for the role he was playing in our lives. His parents had sent him to Calcutta as a boy to be trained in the art of running a household, British style. He had worked his way from sweeper to head bearer over the years and had learned several languages on the way. He learned to read English and it was a joy for me to simply hand Abdul a recipe book from which to prepare our meals.

With Abdul's help our household was soon settled and running smoothly, just in time for Jim's first assignment in his new role. As USAID representative in the new capitol, Jim was asked to entertain an American Congressman and his wife who were touring the area. It was Jim's job to educate the Congressman about the plans to move the AID offices to Islamabad.

Abdul and I worked on a Western style dinner knowing that the couple would have many opportunities to sample Indian food while in town. Abdul was improving in the culinary department, and we wanted to try new dessert. It was risky, but we decided to make a Grand Marnier souffle. I was in and out of the kitchen that day watching as the different dishes were coming together. The meal was perfect. We had set the table with china dishes and I fashioned a centerpiece of candles and greens. I wished for a bowl of the anemones from Cyprus that evening. It would have been a great addition to the elegant table setting..

Soon after our guests arrived it became clear that the wife was not happy to be in Pakistan. She began the conversation by asking how I could stand the heat and the dust. She was appalled at the poverty and squalor she had seen on the fringes of town. She didn't like the food. Just the smell of curry made her want to throw up. The hot spices gave her a stomachache. She wasn't impressed with the bazaar or interested in the jewelry or carpets sold there. In short, there was nothing she had experienced on the trip to the Middle East that appealed to her.

Jim spoke of the history of Pakistan and the political position the country held in the Middle East. I mentioned my fascination with their music and artistic designs. Jim turned the conversation to a discussion of financial issues facing AID. The wife sat with a frown on her face and I was searching for something to say to make her feel better when she asked, again, how I could stand anything about the place. I realized there was nothing I could say that would make her feel better. The evening definitely was not going well.

Jim and I couldn't help but throw a few disgusted glances at each other. I was concerned the couple would notice but hoped a good cocktail and delicious food would help Mrs. Congressman to loosen up.

My wishful fantasy evaporated after a short time and it was clear I was entertaining an 'Ugly American.' That type of visitor was incomprehensible to me. I neither understood nor had patience for her and I could hardly wait for the evening to be over. It didn't make me feel better knowing I'd had never had such a miserable failure of a dinner party before that evening.

Dinner was served and I was happy with the choices Abdul and I had made. The roast chicken was crusty brown on the outside and juicy inside. Chunks of tender potatoes were smothered in a sour cream sauce, and the Turkish green beans were perfectly seasoned. An all-American menu. Mrs. Congressman gave a backdoor compliment, saying she was surprised I had found a chicken with enough meat on the bone to feed the four of us. I tried to ignore the unhappy guest and hugged myself in anticipation of Abdul's special surprise dessert.

Dinner plates were removed from the table. Abdul returned with the flaming masterpiece and ceremoniously placed the delicate concoction in front of Jim to be served. I clapped my hands and Jim congratulated Abdul on the beautiful presentation. He picked up the serving spoon and asked the guest to present her small plate. Halfway to the plate, the souffle slipped off the spoon and plopped onto the dining room table. Jim didn't bat an eyelash. He proceeded to scoop the souffle off the table and place it onto the woman's plate. He acted as if nothing untoward had happened.

I glanced at Abdul, who had been standing behind Jim to watch the presentation. I was having trouble keeping a smile off my face. What I really wanted to do at that moment was stand and wave my arms in celebration. Abdul was lucky. He only had to turn and leave the room. Which was a good thing because I would not have been able to keep a straight face had Abdul's mouth made even a twitch. I looked down at my own plate to hide my expression as Jim continued to serve the dessert to the Congressman and me.

Congressman's wife looked startled and hesitated before setting her plate before her. She had a disgusted look on her face but took a small bite, then, she wiped her mouth with a napkin and crossed her hands in her lap. I'm sure it was a relief to our guests as well as to Jim and me when they departed soon after the meal. I was never prouder of Jim as I was that evening.

~

One morning I went to Melinda's room to get her from her crib. She was not there! My heart clutched. It was obvious she had learned to climb out of her crib by herself. I went to the girl's room assuming I'd find her there. Jenna and Nyna were fast asleep. No Melinda.

The feeling of dread that had gripped me was beginning to become a full-blown panic. I rushed into the kitchen to ask if Abdul had seen her. Abdul wasn't in the kitchen and I realized he would be at prayer. I looked out the kitchen window and just as I'd thought, Abdul was on the lawn facing East and saying morning prayers. And right by his side was three-year-old Melinda, bending her forehead to the ground in sync with Abdul's.

I stood taking in the image of the two of them, praying toward the sun as the sun rose to greet them in return. Relief flooded my body. I took several deep breaths, turned, poured a cup of coffee, and returned to my bedroom. I had no doubt that the God we all pray to is the same loving and living God that Abdul and Melinda were praising that morning.

I needed Abdul to educate me about the ways of western Pakistan. There were obvious differences between East and West Pakistani cultures. Tribal men were larger in structure and some more aggressive than their smaller and quieter Bengali countrymen. Some Pakistani's wore tall starched turbans while others wore pillbox headgear woven with different designs and colors. Headwear in West Pakistan seemed to be source of identity and pride among the men. Commerce in both provinces were similar but Abdul taught me that doing business in the west was slightly different. As a result, I had very little to do with shopping in Rawalpindi. Abdul was happy to handle the necessary purchases.

One Friday Abdul came to the dining room where I was planning menus. He said that some Pushti men had arrived at our gate. They were selling wood for the fireplace. Evenings in a desert climate were chilly and we enjoyed having a small fire to take the chill off. I told Abdul I would like to buy the wood. He was not a particularly expressive man. He usually kept a calm non-judgmental expression, but today I detected a sly smile on his face. I was intrigued. I hunched there was something for Abdul to enjoy in this interaction. And I was right.

Abdul suggested that it would be best if he could go with me to translate. He said we needed a plan. These merchants were not to be trusted, he added. Abdul said he would converse with the men in Urdu. Urdu was the universal language spoken in India before Independence. He said the men would assume that he didn't understand the Pashto language. Abdul did know Pashto. It was clear to him that the men did not speak English. He said that they would try to trick me by doing something to make the wood on the scale weigh heavier than it really was. He asked me not to agree to buy wood until he gave me a sign.

Abdul and I went to the back yard to greet the three tall men who were selling wood. A young boy was standing next to a small cart stacked with two feet long pieces. A man dressed in a beige gown was holding a thick piece of wood with a shallow metal bowl at the end. Abdul spoke to them in Urdu and told them I would like to buy a bundle of wood. Two of the men wore turbans made of starched white fabric with one end standing above the crown. The dress indicated the men were from the Punjab region.

One man stepped toward me and bowed. He nodded to the boy who began piling sticks of wood onto the scale. Abdul and I watched as the wood grew to be a proper bundle. Abdul asked, again in Urdu, how much the men wanted for the wood. Abdul told me they were asking far more for the wood than a Pakistani household would have to pay.

"Memsab," he added, "pretend I'm talking about the price of the wood and don't look surprised, but watch the man putting his leg against the scale."

I looked more closely at the scale. As Abdul had predicted, the man had his leg resting next to the scale. The subtle gesture added ounces to the scale. Abdul told me that I should offer a certain price and if the men didn't accept, I should turn and walk away. I had a hard time keeping a straight face and though I wanted the wood, I followed Abdul's advice. Abdul told the men how much I would pay for the wood they had placed on the scale. It was a good full bundle. Enough for several evenings around the fireplace.

The main man began to argue. "Memsaab, Memsaab..." The merchant looked offended. Abdul stepped in at that moment and spoke to them in their own language, telling them, I assumed, that he knew what had taken place. He spoke to the men in Pashto saying it might be best if they gave me the wood at my price. I could see by the expression on their faces that the men were genuinely shocked to hear Abdul speak to them in Pashto in their own language.

I looked at Abdul. His face glowed with satisfaction. The men had assumed that this 'foreign' servant was too unsophisticated to know their language. They could see by the look on Abdul's face that this 'servant' had not only understood their plans to ask an outrageous price for the wood, but had caught them in the act of cheating. They wasted no more time. They nodded and took the rupees I handed them. The young boy unloaded the wood next to the house while the men packed their scales onto the cart. They departed without another word. Abdul and I pumped hands behind their backs. We had pulled off a delicious coup that day.

~

Like all of India, Rawalpindi had a history of British rule and as usual an amateur theater was the primary entertainment for English speaking folk. Shortly after arriving I was approached to play the part of Marilyn Monroe in *Bus Stop*. Jim was asked to play the part of a sheriff. We were happy to become members of a theater company again.

The director of the Rawapini theater group was Principal of the American school in the daytime. The principal and one of his teachers, a young Canadian man who Jenna and Nyna nicknamed 'Handsome,' became our friends. The girls loved the fact that their school principal was directing the play. We missed our community in Dacca and as USAID personnel had yet to be relocated to the new AID office, we welcomed the opportunity to join the theater community.

We had completed three successful productions of *Bus Stop* when Mr. Petrie approached us with an unusual proposition. He had received a request to bring the *Bus Stop* production to an American Air Force base some miles away in the city of Peshawar.

The very existence of the Air Forse base in Peshawar was unknown to the American public. Its presence had been kept under an umbrella of strict secrecy. For years, stealth planes from the base had been successfully carrying on covert information gathering. Until a pilot named Powers had crashed his plane and been captured in Russian territory. Jim and I talked it over and agreed to the trip but only if it were possible to bring our children.

One very, very hot weekend, Jim, the children and I boarded a bus taking us to Peshawar about an hour away. The cast played with the girls as our bus rushed through the dry desert leaving a trail of dust behind us. We were in good spirits until the air conditioning on the bus blew a fuse. There was no way to open windows to get a cool breeze as the temp outside the bus was over one hundred. We fanned ourselves and each other and shared water, doing everything possible to stave off the heat.

It seemed as if we had been on the stuffy, sultry bus for days when at last we staggered into the air-conditioned guest rooms at the Air Force base. We took time to cool down and refresh our appearances. I gave the girls a snack and reminded them they would be staying in the cool room with their friend, the costume lady. We had brought books and crayons. They didn't object. They were happy to be out of the heat.

I prepared to go on stage. I put on makeup and slipped into the purple satin close fitting dress a Rawalpindi seamstress had made for the role. I donned a blond wig and the transformation was complete.

We walked quickly through the hot sun to the air-conditioned auditorium. Jim, decked out in his boots, cowboy hat, and tin star, walked with me to our place backstage. I had begun to 'glow' even before I arrived. I peeked through the curtain and was surprised to see such a large auditorium. The seats were beginning to fill. I was relieved when the air from the hall cooled my face. The relief was brief.

Let's face it. I was nervous and the oppressive heat made it worse. Our little group had never performed in front of such a large audience. Or an audience of only men. The hall was packed with men. Men of all sizes and ranks. I tried to calm myself and stepped onto the stage. Heat from the stage lights hit me. The temperature climbed to over 100 degrees before the curtain was raised. I took my place at a counter, center stage. Jim was sitting at a table downstage.

The curtain opened and a collective "Ah" rose from the audience. I was dumbstruck. What could be going on? I wondered if something was wrong with my costume. Or on stage?

I looked to the director standing in the wings for answers. The director gave two thumbs up and the dialogue began. I didn't understand until later that the collective sigh from the audience was a response of young men catching sight of an American woman after living months and years in the Middle East surrounded by women who were covered head to toe in burkas.

The play went on and the floodlights on stage raised the temperature by degrees. I could feel rivulets of perspiration creeping from my armpits making dark circles of purple on the satin costume. I was thankful that wigs didn't sweat.

The cast dripped and sweltered under the intense heat on set but the outpouring of delight and appreciation from the airmen made us ignore the discomfort. We got into our roles, the heat forgotten. Three curtain calls and the cast rushed back to our air-conditioned guest rooms to get cool.

We had a light supper and fell into bed, exhausted. The air-conditioner on the bus was repaired and we were up early the next morning, eager to return to Rawalpindi before the heat became unbearable again.

I dressed the girls, took their hands, and struck out for the waiting bus. I wore jeans and a rumpled camise-type blouse. I had not taken time to put any makeup. I was still tired and already feeling the heat. I had sweated so much under the wig the night before my auburn hair was plastered to my head.

Nyna and Melinda were not happy to be facing another long bus ride and both were whining a bit, asking for breakfast. I was holding a sluggish girl in each hand. Pulling them along. Our clothes were rumpled and looked like we had slept in them. We walked past a couple of young men who had obviously been to the performance the night before. They stopped, turned and stared at us as we passed. I believe I nodded good morning and continued to walk steadily toward the waiting bus. I heard one of the men say, "That's her! That's her!"

The second man turned, took a long look at us and shook his head. "Naw. Naw. That couldn't be her." I didn't have the heart to stop and correct the young man. I thought it was best he keep his dream of the sexy blond onstage the night before. What a tickle I had reporting the conversation to my fellow thespians.

Jim and I visited Peshawar several times during our tour of duty in West Pakistan. Jim had business in the city, and I welcomed a chance to explore the culture. I had been told of craftsmen who fashioned beautiful patterns of brass into wood.

Jim was given a driver for the trip. The young man spoke English well and was enthusiastic about introducing us to the local artists. He drove to the edge of the city until we reached a large warehouse. We stepped inside a long, shady hall. The sight before us was stunning. Rows of men dressed in loose clothing were squatting on mats. The rows looked to be about twenty men long. There must have been no more than three feet between each workstation.

A tall dignified foreman led us to stand behind the first artist in the line. The artist held a roll of thin brass the size of embroidery thread in one hand wielded a small hammer in the other. He was following a pattern drawn into a piece of wood lying across his lap. The intricate patterns of brass shined through the dark wood catching every ray of light available. The ease with which the men formed the patterns made the process seem magical. Examples of the crafts were scattered around the periphery of the long hall. Tables, chests and chairs. All manner of furniture.

The foreman introduced us to the artist. He didn't look up but continued to tap a thin thread of brass onto a piece of wood. Jim and I greeted him and admired his artistry. He looked up at us, a slight smile on his face, tipped his head, and resumed his work.

With Jim's consent I ordered two chests. I gave the foreman the size and configuration of the chests I desired. I pointed to the artist we had met and told the foreman I'd like that very pattern. We made a leap of faith and Jim gave money to the man. We crossed our fingers, hoping we would see the chests reach our home in Rawalpindi some day.

We made several trips to Peshawar. One trip included the girls. We took them to see the famous Khyber Pass. Jenna was very impressed that she could stand with one foot in Afghanistan and one foot in Pakistan. The pass was a border crossing between Pakistan and Afghanistan.

Our first trip to the pass was memorable. Jim and I were driven out of the city along a flat desert road until a range of mountains came into view. We drove up the rocky cliffs and our driver stopped. He called our attention to the side of the mountain. Brass plaques engraved with the names and dates of soldiers and fighters covered the rocky hillside.

Jim and I got out of the car and stood reading the names on the brass memorial plaques honoring the famous British and Indian soldiers who had died in the battle of Khyber Pass. The year of 1842, a battle was waged to get control of the narrow road between Kabul and Peshawar. The pass was a crucial military and trade route between Afghanistan and India. Thousands of British and Indians lost their lives.

We were interrupted by the arrival of a scruffy-looking soldier carrying a large rifle and bands of bullets across his chest. He marched up to our driver.

The soldier was dressed in an ill-fitting khaki uniform and a pakol, a flat pancake shaped hat. He made an exaggerated salute and appeared to be demanding our driver identify himself. And us. An animated discussion between the soldier and our driver ensued as Jim and I paid close attention to the body language between the two men. We didn't understand the conversation which we assumed was Urdu. The driver finally turned to us and explained that the guard would not let us come into the area because he thought we were government personnel. The driver and a few rupees finally convinced the man that we were only tourists.

It seemed it was ok for tourists to enter the area. The sentry, who looked to be around thirty years old, twisted his full lip mustache and nodded his permission. He looked a little comical when he shifted the rifle across his baggy clothes. He adjusted the bands of bullets across his chest and stepped aside so that we could come closer to the plaques embedded into the rock. Some of the names on the plaques were legendary figures and I wished I'd had a better grasp of world history.

The sentry became alert when Jim took out his Brownie movie camera to record some of the names on the plaques. He wasn't sure what Jim had pulled out of his jacket, but on discovering it was a camera, he forgot his threatening military attitude. He began another animated discussion with our driver. It seems the sentry thought our camera was a polaroid. He wanted his photo taken. Our driver explained Jim was holding a movie camera.

Jim and I asked if the sentry was Pakistani. Our driver guide told us the story of Khyber Pass. He said the border guards were neither Pakistani nor Afghans but were a tribe of their own. The tribe held no allegiance to either the Pakistan or the Afghanistan governments. They lived by their own laws and rules. They were supposedly in place to regulate traffic between the two countries. They charged a fee for goods being transported between the two countries.

The soldier pointed at the camera and Jim turned the camera from side to side so the man could get a better look. The soldier examined it, grinned a wide smile showing some missing front teeth and asked Jim to take a photo of him. We asked the driver to explain one more time that the camera was not a polaroid but a movie camera. The soldier gestured. He wanted to be in a movie with me. He moved to my side and stood at attention. Just as Jim punched the camera button, the man slipped an arm around my waist. I was startled and jumped away. The young man grinned.

He seemed pleased with himself for having sneaked an arm into the photo but acted as if it was nothing. I dared not say anything. After all, he did have a munition belt across his chest and a rifle hanging from one shoulder. He spoke to our driver and motioned for us to follow him.

Our driver said we had been invited to see the camp at the base of the mountain. Jim agreed and took my hand as we followed the soldier down a well-worn dirt path. The path was partially hidden and we would never have known it was there had the sentry not shown us. To our surprise, the end of the path revealed a vibrant, bustling village. As far as we could see, stalls had been erected to house merchandise from all over the world.

The latest style of stoves, refrigerators, washing machines, coffee makers, large and small appliances of all kinds were on display. Down the line I could see clothing, jewelry and kitchenware. A whole stall displaying French perfumes was close by. Any and all brands of merchandise from the US or Europe could be had in that smuggler's den. We gaped at the riches. I wanted to see every one of the stalls but we were whisked away before we had time to explore too deeply. I'm certain there were firearms and ammunition to be bought. We could see a small tank parked in the back lots.

The stern look of some of the men who had begun to surround us made me uncomfortable and I asked for our car. I was sensing danger and eager to get back to the city. We hesitated a moment as we reached the top of the path. Our driver kept his voice low and didn't look away from the path but in a low voice, he told us to glance back at the valley opposite the village. We looked back and saw three men walking along a ragged path that stretched for miles into the distance. The path was an illegal smugglers route between Afghanistan and Pakistan, our driver said. The robed figures were guiding donkeys laden so high with contraband that I felt sorry for the poor animals. The keepers of the pass were ignoring the smuggling, as usual. This illegal activity had been taking place for centuries.

~

We kept our promise to the girls and one weekend we boarded a plane to Karachi and booked our family into the Intercontinental Hotel.

KINDNESS

Jenna and Nyna had hardly gotten settled into our room before they ordered ice cream. Not many choices but chocolate and vanilla, but there
was no fuss. Ice cream was the treat of the day. They were eager to get
into the pool for a swim but Nyna lingered in the small kitchenette that
was part of the suite. Little did we know that was the beginning of her
love affair with hotel amenities.

Our six months in Rawalpindi were filled with business and
pleasure. Jim was called back to Dacca to finish up some AID business.
The girls and I went along for one more visit with friends. The Johnsons
feted us with a welcome home/goodbye party.

It was so great to be back. We had missed the lush green gardens.
The children played on the lawn and Jim and I sat under the veranda with
friends having fun remembering some of our best moments together. We
were given the news that Weaver's tour contract with the University had
come to an end. They were headed back to the States. We invited them
to stop in Rawalpindi for a visit on their way home.

Change was happening everywhere. Our USAID mission was
well established and thriving in Bengal. Some of Jim's young assistants
were being assigned to new posts around the world. Lucy and the rest of
our servants were already working in another family home. We gave
hugs, a final goodbye to our Bengali home for the last time.

Springtime in Rawalpindi was hot and dry. We were having a
spate of unusually hot weather and were wishing to get away from the
city heat. Jim was told about a small resort town in the mountains nearby.

Murree was the perfect weekend retreat. Jim was able to find a
small cabin up in the cool mountain air. The house only had three bedrooms and limited our capacity for guests but the view from the cottage
was spectacular. The balcony at the back of the house overlooked the
mountains of Kashmir. Snow covered mountain peaks and green valleys
spread out before us.

Travel into the province of Kashmir was heavily guarded. We
were overlooking a contested part of Pakistan located north of Islamabad. There was continuous tension between the Pakistani government,
India, and the people of Kashmir. The view from our house was enchant-
ing. The people were famous for producing cashmere goods sold all over
the world. It was very frustrating that we were not allowed to cross into
that country when we could see the lush snow-capped mountains from
our backyard.

We made the Murree cottage our weekend destination. We invited our new friends to join us for the weekend. We enjoyed the company of Jim's secretary, Sadie, a single woman who had long served the State Department. Sadie was a huge help to Jim in his job. The principal of the girl's school, Mr. Petrie, and his friend were also our frequent weekend visitors.

We were excited when the Weavers stopped by on their way back to the States. We were eager to share the beauty and cool mountain air of Murree cottage with our friends.

The reunion was bittersweet. We put wood into the fireplace and sat around with Mark and Jim singing while they played the banjo and guitar. The children wrote another play and we adults talked about how much more sophisticated and grown up their play writing had become. Beth and I talked about how good it would feel to be back in the US and about the things we would miss about Bengal.

We rented horses and took the trail along the mountain paths to see the views. Time had not improved little David's appreciation of horses. The horse we chose for him had the reputation of being the tamest horse in the group. At least according to the owner. David wanted to believe the man, but he was not comfortable on his horse. He was trying his best to be brave.

Unfortunately, the poor boy had bad luck again. His 'tame' horse began to run ahead of us and the horse owner had to run after them. The horse threw David to the ground. The old bag looked like it wouldn't have the strength to throw a fly. The horse handler was beside David and in a swift move scooped the boy up and brushed him off. We rushed to check his little limbs. He was unharmed but too frightened to get back onto the horse and we turned back down the trail to the house for some hot chocolate. Things were right in the world again.

Until we decided to go to the movies.

We discovered a theater down in the village of Murree that was showing a movie with English subtitles. We dressed in clean clothes and walked down the hill to the village hoping to see the film. Villagers stared at us. Staring at people was not impolite in that part of the world.

Beth and I commented on the people on the street appearing to be a grumpy lot. We were not comfortable with their stares. We kept our eyes straight ahead and tried not to stare back. We stood outside in a small circle while the men went to buy movie tickets. Sadly, the movie space was small and there were no more tickets by the time we arrived. I must admit we were a bit late.

We were disappointed but chose to stroll about the small-town square until we felt rain approaching. The sprinkles became a downpour and the children were squealing and we were all trying to cover our heads with whatever we could find. Jim and Mark hailed a rickshaw and Beth and I pulled the children in close under the canopy to stay as dry as possible. The two men sat on a narrow bench in the front of the carriage.

The bicycle driver took the path up the hill toward our house but we suddenly stopped. The carriage had become bogged down in mud. The men got down from the bench and tried to help the bicycle driver pull the rickshaw out of the muddy ruts and up the hill. Jim and Mark stepped into the mud and were soon splattered with sticky, red clay from pushing and pulling the rickshaw up the hill. They were not making much progress and, finally, Beth and I got down from the rickshaw to help the men.

It was no use. We told the children to get out of the rickshaw and run to the house. Jim picked up Melinda and we all ran. Inside, we looked at ourselves. We were soaked and muddy, our hair dripping and our shoes covered in mud. We broke into a giggling spree. Not a pretty sight.

~

Our tour in West Pakistan was rich and full. Jim was great in the theater production of *The Fantasticks*. Jim was cast as the father of the daughter in the play. We were impressed that a diplomat's wife had brought a full-sized harp with her when they came abroad. Jim sang and danced and was universally praised for his performance. The entire production was a huge success and Jim enjoyed a short spate of celebrity around the community. The girls and I loved to watch him at the rehearsals and we memorized the words to his songs and dialogue. A line from his character came in handy at times. "You are stepping in my cumquats" was adopted as a quick retort when one of us was interfering with another's space.

The waning days of our tour became complicated. We were trying to stay focused on our Pakistani activities but also aware that we were due for home leave. Both Jim and I were working to leave everything in the office and home in order. The stress was wearing on us all and I asked Abdul if he knew of a place we could take a break. Maybe have a picnic.

Abdul found a place close to town near a small stream. The

stream emptied into a pond deep enough for swimming. The girls had their swimming suits on under their clothes and couldn't wait to put their toes into the water. They were having a great time splashing and playing. Jim joined in the fun until we spotted a couple of young Pakistani boys peering at them from behind a rock above. They squealed and the boys ran away only to return and have Abdul chase them away again. After the cooling swim, we sat on pallets under the bridge and relished lamb kabob hot off Abdul's hibachi.

We were treated with a more elegant picnic in the country when, a few weeks later, a prominent Pakistani businessman invited us to his estate. The dignified elderly man invited Jim to bring the girls to his place for a swim. We could hardly believe our eyes when the dusty road turned into a lush compound with a tropical-like lagoon surrounded by beautiful shrubs and trees. Cream colored flowers with heads the size of saucers peeked through the greenery. Large shade trees towered above rock benches and provided a cool oasis atmosphere. A surprising tropical oasis in the midst of miles of dry desert.

The owner of the estate was a grandfatherly man, very distinguished with gray hair and beard and dressed in a black Pakistani suit of long coat with a band for a collar. The girls changed into their bathing suits as did Jim. They squealed as their toes touched the cold spring fed water. They became acclimated to the water and then splashed joyously among islands of water lilies. Jim joined the girls in the pool and stayed close by for safety. The children couldn't touch the bottom.

Our host and I sat on the lawn with glasses of sweet tea. Jenna floated happily along the pond singing "I'd love to swim in a clear blue stream," a song from *The Fantasticks*. The place, the lush garden, the cool respite from the desert heat, the day was like a dream.

Easter came early that year and we hosted an Easter egg hunt in our backyard. It was fun to watch a yard full of children flitting back and forth across the dry lawn. Melinda had a little basket and toddled around not quite certain what she was supposed to do. One at a time, a sister would take time out from their own hunt to steer her toward a dyed egg close to the ground. The long row of sweet peas were flourishing and their perfume filled the air between the children's shouts when they discovered a candy egg.

I regret that I don't remember the Embassy women I met there. There was no excuse for it but it seems I was always organizing and preparing a new home. And packing. I had little time or focus when it came to following up with new people.

I am particularly unhappy that I cannot recall the name of our neighbors across the street in Rawalpindi. The family was a mixed-race family. Mixed marriages were unique during our stay overseas. The wife was a jovial, heavy-set American woman married to a distinguished mustached Pakistani military man. Both children were beautiful with the typical satiny brown skin, black hair and dark brown eyes.

The day we moved into our Rawalpindi house, the family brought flowers to greet us to the neighborhood. The couple had met at a training camp when the husband had visited the states. The woman was happy to have someone to speak English with and her children loved coming to visit and play. Nyna liked playing with the little sister. It was like playing with a live doll. From the beginning of their visits it was evident that the little boy was very taken with Nyna. They played with balls in the front yard and couldn't wait for the treats I always provided. Cookies and juice at a table in the backyard. They never stayed long but it was evident that a visit to our house was a special treat.

Two weeks before we were to leave, I received a call from the mother asking if the children could come for a visit. Something in her voice intrigued me. It was unusual for her to make a formal playdate. It was a weekend and I happily agreed.

An hour later the doorbell rang and I answered the door and stared, gob smacked. The sight before me caught me unaware. The three neighbors standing before me were dressed in their formal clothes. The little girl and her mother were dressed in pink silk shalwar's with scarves laced with gold braid and semi-precious jewels. The boy was a sight to behold as well. He was dressed in a black tunic that came to his knees. His black hat was topped with a starched white scarf. The six-year-old boy had a small bouquet of flowers in his hand.

I stood for a moment wondering if I had missed a national holiday or something important. Perhaps a birthday? I gained my composure and invited them inside. I was unsure what to do next. I began by commenting on their beautiful attire. I wondered out loud if there was a National celebration of some kind that I was supposed to be aware of.

The Mother assured me that was not the case. She smiled at the suggestion then asked if I would call Nyna into the room. I called and Nyna came bouncing in with her usual smile and joy of being. I could see the boy's eyes light up as the mother began to speak. It seems the young lad had fallen in love with Nyna. He had begged his mother to ask that Nyna become his bride when they came of age. Ever since the boy heard the news of our departure to the States, he hadn't left his mother alone. He wanted Nyna to be his bride and the family had agreed to his wishes.

I was uncertain for a moment as to what I was being asked to do. I couldn't quite take it in. It seemed the mother was asking for us to commit to some kind of agreement of marriage. The beautifully and formally dressed youngsters, the flowers in the boy's hands, and the way that he looked at Nyna when she entered the room. There was no doubt what was happening. I was tempted to make a joke of it. Like, 'you've got to be kidding,' but I looked at the boy's face and realized this was no joke to him. He was truly smitten and hoped he would hear a consent.

I reminded myself that an arranged marriage would not seem to be an unusual request to the young man. I wondered if his mother warned him that our American ways were different. I wanted to be kind and yet, there was no way I was going to commit my little girl to an arranged marriage. I smiled and put my hands together and bowed to the little boy.

I turned to the mother and, trying to keep my voice kind and respectful, I explained that we were very, very honored and proud that the boy would consider taking Nyna for his bride. I reminded her that unlike their culture, we did not make promises for our children. Nyna would have to make her own choice of husband after she finished her education.

The mother nodded, obviously hesitant to break the news to her son. The boy had been watching the expression on our faces as his mother and I talked. Perhaps he understood some English. He stood with his head bowed, looking at the floor as his mother translated my response in a quiet solemn voice. Nyna looked at me, not certain what was happening.

I shook my head slightly and we both watched to see what would happen next. All was silent in the room until the young boy raised his eyes to his mother and nodded. We could see that he was doing his best not to cry. He gathered himself and walked bravely over to Nyna and presented her with the flowers. He bowed slightly as he had evidently been taught to do. Nyna didn't know what was happening but said thank you to the boy and looked to me for advice. I nodded that she had done the right thing.

The children's mother turned to me and asked if we could take pictures of the two of them together. We went into the yard for photos before they said their goodbyes.

~

We were eager to go on home leave and I happily packed swimsuits and comfortable warm weather tops. We were headed to the Italian Riviera.

We left Abdul in charge with instructions to take care of the dog, Misty. We had inherited the little dachshund from a British couple. Britain was not allowing dogs into the country from foreign places until they had quarantined for months. We expected to be back by the time school opened in September. We had several 'so-long' dinner parties with our friends and promised to bring special goodies back from the States.

We wanted to introduce the children to the glories of ancient Greece. Tourist season was in full swing and crowds of people filled the main square. We had only two days in Athens and our accommodations were not ideal. We had a very small hotel room overlooking the town plaza. We had two regular-sized beds and no space for a crib. Melinda was still small enough to sleep in a large chest of drawers.

The July heat was unbearable and we tried to keep the girls occupied until the fierce sun went down. The day began to drag until finally it was cool enough to venture out. We walked a few blocks from the square to the Acropolis. I was thankful the well-travelled stroller still held together. The girls climbed up the steps of the Parthenon and wandered between the columns. The crowd began to thin out. We rushed to find space to sit on a grassy knoll overlooking the shining artifact. We watched the sun sink slowly into the horizon and turn the columns a rosy pink. It had been a long and tiring day.

The next morning before the sun was too hot we took a tour bus to a site outside Athens so that the girls could see a real, ancient amphitheater. The tour guide gave a talk about how the actors made their entrances and exits. It didn't take long for the girls to imagine the audiences sitting on the stone steps, watching the drama below. We had lunch under an umbrella in the busy downtown square then rushed back to our tiny sweltering room.

We were greeted with some shocking news. Intercontinental Airline personnel had gone on strike. Our flight out of Athens had been cancelled. Tourists throughout the city were scrambling to book flights on any available airlines. The city was swarming with hot, unhappy tourists. I tried to keep the girls occupied and wandered around the square until the heat was too much. Jim went to the ticket agent to try and make a connection somewhere. Anywhere out of the sweltering heat. He stood in line for hours only to return with the news that we could not get out that day as planned. There was no air conditioner in the small hotel room and I tried to keep the children cool with a small fan and damp wash-cloths to their skin.

The heat, the dusty square and the crowds of grumpy people were getting to us all and the next day didn't promise anything different. Jim spent another morning standing in a line with other sweaty travelers struggling to find a way out of Greece. There were no flights going any-where close to Italy. I was becoming as cranky as the children when I realized I had to give up the idea of our vacation on the Italian Riviera.

Around mid-afternoon Jim arrived with good news. He was able to get a flight out of the country. By evening we were on our way to Zurich, Switzerland.

We arrived in Zurich with swimsuits and shorts and little cool tops and found the weather incompatible. The girls were disappointed we were not at the seaside. They wondered where in the world we were. They wanted to know about Zurich and what there was to see in Zurich. They wanted to know if we could get a plane to the seaside now that we had left Athens. Nothing we had to say made up for the disappointment of a spoiled beach vacation.

They climbed into bed that evening tired and close to tears. They had delighted, surprised looks on their faces when they sank into a cloud of soft fluffy goose feather duvets. They giggled and began to wave their arms and legs, making snow angels in the soft covers. Maybe Switzer-land wasn't all that bad.

We were stunned the next morning when we were greeted with sixty-degree weather. Jumping overnight from the hot, humid, dusty de-sert to cool, neat, organized Switzerland was a huge culture shock. The children sat down for breakfast with cold milk and a croissant on their plates. Sausages and berry jam and an unexpected treat, real butter, si-lenced any lingering complaints about a beach. Curiosity had replaced grumpy faces. Jim and I hugged them and told them how proud they made us.

The hotel guidebook had given us the information we needed to treat the children to the joys of Switzerland. The first order of business was to find proper clothing to fit the cold Swiss weather. It was obvious the little shorts and sleeveless tops would not do. We packed into a cab and made our way to a famous Swiss department store. After spending months in Pakistan the immaculate rows of merchandise were dazzling to behold. I hadn't thought about how different it would be for the girls. They hadn't been in real department stores since the Philippines.

The department store seemed to have everything under one roof. It even provided a fenced in kindergarten area where Melinda could play with toys under a nurse's observation. The Western version of having an ayah.

I allowed myself a few minutes to roam around taking in the merchandise. I couldn't believe how expensive everything seemed to be. I got down to business and found little striped sweater jackets and navy pleated skirts for the older girls. A light pink sweater for Melinda was just the color to highlight her light red shock of hair. We informed the store person of our clothing dilemma and soon left the store, dressed in warm, cozy togs. Our shopping bags held the shorts and tops. Socks and warm pjs were necessary additions to our treasurers. The joy of seeing the girls in new clothes was catching. Jim and I couldn't help but glow with pride.

We never stopped being amazed with the cleanliness and order of everything Swiss. We headed from the store to the famous Zurich zoo. We took the children on a bus tour of the city. They were fascinated by the beautiful bridges and tall buildings. We took Jenna with us on a train ride to Lucerne. Nyna chose to stay and play in the hotel suite with Melinda and a sitter. The scenery, the order, and everything about Switzerland was thrilling.

We ran into a small glitch in the fairy land. We were in the train station preparing to make our way back to Zurich and asked Jenna to choose chocolate bars to take back to Nyna and Melinda. Jim and I stood in front of an immaculate array of various chocolates. Jenna made a decision and put out her hand for the chocolate bar. The woman behind the counter squawked. Jenna, Jim and I were startled. What had gone wrong? The shopkeeper scowled down at Jenna and said in broken English, "No touch!" Jim and I recovered from our fright and Jim spoke to us in a low voice, "It seems it's more important to keep the display straight than it is to sell the chocolate."

I scowled back at the woman and told Jenna we would get chocolate at another counter. Which we did.

Jim and I made the decision to cut our vacation in Zurich short as we were eager to return to the States. Two days later we were in the airport. Our flight was called. We checked the seats and gathered the coloring books and sweaters and handed Jenna and Nyna their backpacks. I looked around to put Melinda into her stroller and couldn't find her. We told the girls to stay put and set out to look for her. She was nowhere to be seen.

I thought she might have gone back to play with the children at the airport kindergarten. No Melinda. The kindergarten lady put out an SOS on the airport intercom asking anyone catching a glimpse of a three-year-old child who was without parents to bring the child to the service desk.

I knew Melinda was not afraid of strangers. We had not been called upon to teach her to be cautious. She was simply interested in everything around her. This place was new to her, full of strange people and interesting things to see. Jim and I went in opposite directions and to my relief I spotted her red hair a short distance ahead of me. I stopped and held my breath. Melinda was standing at the top of an escalator.

My heart skipped a beat and I called her name just before she stepped forward. A well-dressed Swiss man was standing just behind Melinda and he reached out and took her by the hand. Melinda looked at the stranger. I had a moment of panic that she would pull her hand away and step out onto the moving steps. She looked back at me when she heard me call her name. I reached for her and pulled her into my arms. I was flooded with relief.

We stepped aside and I thanked the man over and over again for his saving Melinda from a tumble down the escalator. We were both shaken by the close call. The kind man was gracious, tipped his hat at me and we went our separate ways to board our planes.

TWENTY-THREE
HOME

Mom and Dad wanted to hear about our adventures, and we wanted to catch up about the rest of the family. True to family ritual, Dad was eager to take the girls to go horseback riding. He couldn't wait to get Melinda on a horse. Jenna went first. She was a pro, trotting around the paddock with ease. Nyna followed and surprised my dad with her expertise. I told him about their horse-riding experiences overseas. Nyna begged for one more time around, but I pulled her over the fence assuring her there would be another chance to ride. It was Melinda's turn.

Melinda had a concerned expression on her face when Dad lifted her up into the saddle. The horse began to walk and Dad walked beside her, keeping his arm securely around Melinda's back. I watched, ready to take her in my arms at the first sign that she was scared. The horse tossed her mane and the serious look on Melinda's face morphed into a smile. I could feel Dad's relief and his joy echoed Melinda's. My father was never happier than when he was with his grandchildren in the horse paddock.

Jenna and Nyna remembered their favorite things about previous visits to the Grands' home and lost no time asking for a trip to the soft ice cream shop. I put in a request for dinner at my favorite Lubbock BBQ restaurant. My mouth watered just thinking about the brisket. We were sitting at the table, Melinda at the head in a highchair next to my Dad. She spotted a bowl of jalapeño peppers in the middle of the table and asked for one. Dad told her no, they were too hot. Melinda insisted and I told him it was ok. If she tasted it and didn't like it we could give her water. He hesitated but handed her the smallest jalapeno pepper in the bowl.

All eyes were on Melinda as she took a bite of the pickled pepper. We watched while Melinda chewed. She swallowed. We waited. Melinda reached out her hand to the bowl and said, "More." My father laughed so hard his eyes began to water. He doubled over shaking with laughter. I thought he might fall out of his chair. I explained to him that we had found Melinda having hot curry with the servants and obviously the spicy heat of the jalapeno did not phase her.

Mom, Jim and I were sitting around the table in Mom's kitchen, having a second cup of coffee. The girls were becoming acquainted with Mr. Rogers in the TV room. The phone rang. I answered and listened as a deep male voice asked to speak to James McGraw. I handed the phone to Jim and watched his face. The man on the phone was doing all the talking. I could tell from the expression on Jim's face that this was a business call but I had no clue if the call was making him happy or disappointed. I suspected he was receiving orders for our new foreign service post.

I couldn't keep from fantasizing about where it could be! There were so many interesting third world countries that I would like to see.

One quick glance at my Mom and I could see that she was concerned. Our parents hadn't said anything out loud, but they had been through some rough moments as well. They tried not to show it, but they would have preferred we live in the US. I motioned for Mom to follow me into the living room. Best to wait for Jim there and delay any talk of concerns until we knew the real situation. I was holding my breath trying to catch the tone of Jim's voice.

Jim was on the phone for what seemed a very long time. When, at last, he joined my Mother and me, there was no doubt that he had received news of some import.

"Are you ok?" I asked. "Yes," he answered and took a deep breath. "How would you feel if we did not go back to Pakistan?" I thought for a moment, unsure what he was asking.

"Are we being sent to a new country? Did they offer you a new post?" What was he thinking? Were we just supposed to walk away and leave all our possessions behind? All of our worldly goods remained in Rawalpindi. I had a fleeting image of the elderly couple in Nicosia, concerned for the safety of their goods. I caught the irony of the situation straight away.

"What about our little dog Mitsie? Abdul is expecting us to return to Rawalpindi." I was anxious to know what had been offered and afraid to ask at the same time. I didn't trust my voice to remain steady so I said nothing.

He went on. "I've been offered a job in New York City working for a corporation in the treasurer's department." One of his former bosses in the government had become an officer for ITT and was offering Jim a door into the corporate world. Jim taking the New York job would mean a radical change in our lives.

I was stunned. I didn't know what to say. My emotions were mixed. Another foreign post or back to the United States.

Jim and Mom waited for my reaction. Yay or nay. At that moment, I didn't know myself. Yet, before a minute had passed I reasoned that staying in the States was a good idea. After all, the girls were Middle School age now and would benefit from everything the US had to offer.

I didn't have to ask Mom and Jim what they were thinking. Jim didn't even try to keep a grin off his face, and Mom swiped at her eyes. I was sure she was shedding a tear of relief. Trying not to let me see her cry.

I sat for a moment, letting this new turn of events sink in. My thoughts went to New York City and the tall buildings and hordes of people hurrying to and from work. We'd be trading dusty desert roads for concrete. While it would be exciting to introduce our children to their homeland, I would truly miss my foreign service community (not to mention having help with the daily chores). My mind went back and forth, pro and con. It didn't matter. I knew it was time to come home. The decision was made, and a new adventure began.

Acknowledgements

I am grateful for all who encouraged me to recall these stories. The journey into the past brought many rich memories of friends and family woven into the tapestry of our lives. I am grateful for the extended families here and abroad who shared our lives and created supportive communities for our children to grow up in.

Thank you, Melinda, for introducing me to Jack Grape's teachings and nagging me until I actually wrote the words. Thank you my Kimball Farms round table group: Suzanne, Dorothea, Sheila, Nancy, and Molly, all of whom kept me laughing when I was bogged down in difficult memories. Many thanks to Emi, my new granddaughter-in-law, for her beautiful cover design. And thank you, Carl Vigeland, my publisher, for encouraging me to tell the story in my own words.

Made in the USA
Columbia, SC
24 November 2024